LAN Primer

3RD EDITION

by Greg Nunemacher

M&T BOOKS

M&T Books
A Division of MIS:Press, Inc.
A Subsidiary of Henry Holt and Company, Inc.
115 West 18th Street
New York, New York 10011

Library of Congress Cataloging-in-Publication Data

Nunemacher, Greg
   LAN primer / Greg Nunemacher. —3rd ed.
      p.   cm.
   ISBN 1-55851-441-4
      1. Local area networks (Computer networks)   I. Title.
TK5105.7.N86   1995
004.6'8—dc20   95-326
                                                                   CIP

10 9 8 7 6 5 4 3

Associate Publisher: *Paul Farrell*

Managing Editor: *Cary Sullivan*	**Production Editor:** *Anne Alessi*
Development Editor: *Jono Hardjowirogo*	**Technical Editor:** *Steve Ohr*
Copy Edit Manager: *Shari Chappell*	**Copy Editor:** *Brian Oxman*

Table of Contents

SECTION II: NETWORK OPERATING SYSTEMS, SERVERS, AND SOFTWARE

SECTION III: MANAGING AND TROUBLESHOOTING LANS

SECTION IV:
LAN STANDARDS, ARCHITECTURES, ACCESS METHODS, AND PROTOCOLS

SECTION VII: CASE STUDIES

WHY THIS BOOK IS FOR YOU

LAN Primer explains local area networking in terminology and concepts that you, as a LAN novice, can understand. The text provides explanations and insights into the terminology and principles that are often heard—and often misunderstood.

In addition to understanding LANs, four chapters are devoted to the systems analysis that is needed for a LAN implementation, and case studies are provided. *LAN Primer* will assist in the decision-making process you may encounter when contemplating the setup of a local area network.

Local area networks can be complicated and technical. While one book can't possibly detail the entire scope of local area networks, *LAN Primer* covers the most important aspects of LANs and provides you with a solid foundation of the concepts on which you can build an understanding of a LAN.

SECTION I

LAN Basics

CHAPTER 1

AN OVERVIEW OF NETWORKING

The generally accepted definition of a *Local Area Network* (LAN) is two or more connected microcomputers that communicate with one another through some physical medium, such as twisted-pair or coaxial cables. These microcomputers share data and peripheral devices and usually have transfer speeds of at least 1 Mbps (millions of bits per second). They also are usually located in the same (limited) area, such as on one floor of a building.

This definition is admittedly simplified. Some LANs are wireless and others have additional hardware and software, but for now it will serve as a basis for understanding networking.

Components of a LAN

The basic components required to operate a LAN can be divided into two categories: hardware and software.

A LAN requires the following hardware components:

- File server
- Workstation
- Cabling
- Network interface cards (NICs)
- Hub, concentrator, or wiring center (optional)

The software necessary to operate a LAN consists of:

- The network operating system
- The operating system for the workstation
- The workstation network shell, requester, or redirector

While each item is defined in this chapter, they will also be discussed in more detail later.

Hardware

The *File server* is a high-speed or high-capacity PC that serves the same role as the host computer in a mainframe environment. It functions as the central repository of data and/or application programs for the network. It also performs network traffic management functions and provides security for the data. The file server only performs information retrieval; it can't do computations (number crunching) or specific record searches within a database. A large-capacity storage device is also usually attached to the file server.

Workstations are IBM computers or compatibles, Apple Macintosh computers, or engineering workstations from such vendors as Sun Microsystems and Apollo Computer Systems. All the number crunching, computations, calculations, and actual execution of application programs takes place at the workstation, which receives data from the file server.

Cabling connects the file server and workstations. Cabling is also called a *transmission medium*. Transmission media can take various forms, including coaxial, twisted-pair (both shielded and unshielded), and fiber-optic cable. More information on transmission media can be found in Chapter 2.

Network interface cards (NICs) are located in every workstation on the LAN and in the file server. This board plugs into one of the expansion slots on the motherboard of the workstation and the file server, providing a connector that can be hooked to the transmission medium.

Every workstation on the LAN must be connected to the file server via some sort of transmission medium. However, it is virtually impossible to attach every workstation on the LAN to the file server because the file server usually has only one NIC. To accommodate multiple workstations, the LAN may use a *hub* or *central data-collection area* (although certain network architectures, such as linear bus structures, don't use hubs or concentrators). On certain networks, a hub also allows for multiple connections or splitting of the network cabling. This technique is discussed in greater detail in a later chapter.

Software

The *network operating system* is the software on the file server. It controls virtually all the activity on the network. It also manages the data on the file server's hard disk and handles data security for the file server's storage devices. The network operating system provides true multiuser capabilities and is probably the most important part of the network.

The operating system software for each workstation is loaded at the workstation. On an IBM-compatible computer, for example, this software may be MS-DOS. This component is essential for operation of the workstation, even if that workstation is not part of a LAN.

The *network shell*, (also known as a *requester*, or *redirector*) is created by the network operating system but is loaded on the workstation. Each network operating system may have a slightly different name for this shell, but whether it's called a shell, a requester, or a redirector, it performs basically the same function: It determines whether the requests made by the workstations are for local processing or network processing. Shell software determines the status of the request at the workstation. If it's one that MS-DOS should handle, the request is serviced by MS-DOS; if it's something the network operating system should handle, it's passed on accordingly.

Naturally, the shell and the workstation operating system have to work together since the operations of various hardware and software are closely interrelated. Combining these components is the heart of the theory on which networking is based. This mode of operation is known as *distributed processing*.

Distributed Processing

The creation of local area networks has forced a need for new terminology and redefining existing terminology. Because of this need there is currently a debate over the names to be applied to certain network functions. One such term is *distributed processing*. Some vendors suggest that a more accurate term is localized processing or decentralized processing. They recommend that distributed processing be reserved for a type of software application that executes on multiple workstations concurrently, so all the workstations involved with that program can communicate. (This is also called *cooperative processing*.) However, this concept is well beyond the scope of this book.

For our purposes, the term *distributed processing* means local, rather than central, processing. The difference is in the way data processing occurs: In a mainframe computer, data is processed centrally; in a LAN, data is processed locally.

Distributed processing occurs when each network workstation executes its own application. To the user, his or her workstation appears to be the only one on the network. The concept behind distributed processing is to divide or distribute the computational workload among the workstations. For example, a user asks a certain application program to execute by loading the application into the workstation from the file server. The application is now in the workstation's memory. Whenever the application needs data, a request is issued and the shell sends the request to the file server. The file server answers the request by transmitting the appropriate data to the workstation. The workstation receives the data, determines which records are required, and processes those records. The updated records are then sent from the workstation back to the file server and replaced in the file in which they originated.

Essentially, this is a perpetual four-step process (see Figure 1.1):

- Set an application running on a workstation.

- Retrieve information from the file server as data for that application.

- Process the data at the workstation.

- Return the new or edited data to the file server.

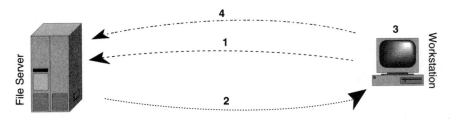

1. Request for application from file server
2. Request answered and data sent to workstation
3. Processing done at workstation
4. Updated record transmitted back to file server from station

FIGURE 1.1 **Requesting an application over a network.** It should be noted that, outside of input and output, the file server does no actual processing.

All workstations on a LAN function in the same manner, doing their own processing and constantly sending and receiving data from the file server. Therefore, all the processing is distributed among the microprocessors of the workstations and the file server, increasing the speed and efficiency of the computer system.

A mainframe or minicomputer operates quite differently. In a mainframe environment, all the processing is done by a central processor at the mainframe. As remote workstations—terminals, in mainframe parlance—are added to this environment, the mainframe's central processor must do more and more work. Eventually, the central processor can no longer efficiently service all the terminal requests. At this point, it's time for a costly upgrade.

The Evolution of Networking

The sophistication of the LANs that exist today was not an overnight development. LAN technology has undergone significant growth and maturation since 1983, when LAN concepts involving file servers essentially began.

ABC Switch Boxes

The ABC switch box was an early attempt to share peripheral devices, such as printers, among a number of PCs. This box, commonly called a *resource-sharing device*, has a knob that allows the user to select channel A, B, or C; those channels can be connected to three computers that share the printer. While this is an excellent way to share resources when cost is a factor, there are drawbacks to such a system: It is cumbersome; each user must dial the switch box to his or her respective channel in order to print; it supports a limited number of computers and printers; and it forces a user to wait until the current user is finished printing.

Resource-sharing devices that accommodate more than three PCs are now available. In fact, it's not uncommon for 16 PCs to share one printer. It's also possible to share devices other than printers—modems, for example, are often shared by switch boxes.

Switch-box systems can also be reversed, making three printers available to all the users. Each user can direct a print job to the appropriate printer simply by dialing channel A, B, or C. The job is sent to the printer attached to that channel; for example, channel A may direct the print job to a plotter, channel

B to a high-speed dot-matrix printer, and channel C to a laser printer. Again, the drawback of this system is obvious: Only one printer is on-line at any given time; when the switch box is dialed to channel C, all the users' output goes to channel C. Flexibility is sacrificed in exchange for low cost.

To improve flexibility the switch box has developed into a multiport spooler, a resource-sharing device that allows multiple PCs to send jobs to various printers. No longer is only one printer or one PC active. Once software accompanying the spooler is installed, the PC user simply needs to activate the spooler program and chooses a printer.

Disk Servers

Before the advent of file servers in 1983, PC networks were considered disk-server systems. In a disk-server network, the local workstation was fooled into believing it was accessing a local disk, when in fact it was making direct calls to an external shared disk. This mode of operation was satisfactory for single-user applications, but no real shared-file management was provided. And with multiple users accessing the same information, data integrity was hard to maintain.

RS-232

RS-232 is a network of PCs that are connected via the workstation's serial port (RS-232). These PCs are usually connected to one central PC, with no other network cards needed. Thus, this system works like a disk server. It's an inexpensive way to share files without the cost of a LAN.

File-Server System

The file-server system—or LAN, as we know it today—emerged in 1983 and 1984, when Microsoft released Microsoft Networks (MS-NET) and IBM announced its PC Local Area Network Program. These products were based on MS-DOS and, as a result, inherited all of DOS's limitations.

At the same time, Novell, Inc., an independent software development firm based in Utah, was developing LAN software that wasn't based on MS-DOS. This was the beginning of Novell's disputed "proprietary network." Other companies, including 3Com Corp., Ungerman-Bass Inc., AT&T, and IBM, all licensed MS-NET and produced their own implementations.

These network operating systems, along with the release of MS-DOS 3.1, brought on the file-server era with centralized file system management. The network operating system running on the file server could now manage access to the shared disk and shared data. These operating systems were designed specifically to handle file sharing in a true multiuser environment.

By 1986, more data-processing professionals were taking a serious look at LANs. By then, LANs had evolved into small networks of eight to ten users and were primarily for office automation. They initially were established only in smaller companies and corporations, but the LAN was beginning to give the minicomputer some competition.

One year later, many industry forecasters were saying that the year of the LAN had arrived. This would mean LAN proliferation in both large and small Management Information Systems departments throughout the country. Value-added resellers were anticipating increased network sales; however, sales did not live up to expectations.

Industry forecasters then declared that 1988 would be the year of the LAN. That year saw more LAN installations, but still fell short of the sales that had been predicted. By this time, internetworking was developing and gateways were providing access to minicomputers and mainframes and links into wide-area networks. However, while the Fortune 500 companies were just beginning to take PCs seriously, they still were not taking LANs seriously. Mainframes were still the answer to their data-processing needs, and the minicomputer could handle their departmental needs just fine.

By the 1990s, LANs were finally creating quite an uproar in large and small corporations. The power and flexibility was finally taken seriously. The LAN industry grew at unbelievable rates as third parties were developing software and hardware to complement and extend the capabilities of the LAN. Downsizing (discussed later in this chapter) became a data-processing trend, and the LAN administrator was acknowledged as a skilled professional.

The Role of the LAN in Today's Computing Environment

The computing environment has traditionally been categorized by the computer system being used. The three initial environments were mainframe, minicomputer, and microcomputer.

Mainframes

As the oldest of the computing environments, the *mainframe* has traditionally been the workhorse that performs all of the data processing for a group or corporation.

The first true business mainframe was the IBM 360. When it was introduced in the 1960s, it was considered the most sophisticated computer of its time. It was also the first computer capable of both scientific and business computing. (It went full circle, hence the name 360.) Later, IBM developed another mainframe architecture, the 370.

The 360 and 370 were pioneers in data-processing departments. Over the years, these systems were upgraded and improved, leading to the 43xx series and eventually to the 3080 and 3090 systems. The 3080 is still widely used today; it is based on the 360 architecture, while the 3090 is based on the 370.

These mainframes are installed in their own air-conditioned rooms, ensuring a constant environment and preventing overheating. The disk drives—commonly called direct access storage devices, or DASDs—are quite large and have enormous storage capacity. Because the 3090 operates with MVS/ESA, more than 1,000 nodes can be connected to the computer system; a network is established to allow the central processing unit (CPU) to accommodate that many nodes. (These nodes are dumb terminals or PCs emulating dumb terminals; in other words, no processing goes on there. A *dumb terminal* is an input and display terminal, with all the processing taking place in the CPU.) The IBM network established is called a *System Network Architecture*, or SNA.

The CPU and DASDs are not the only devices in this network. A network also requires a front-end processor, 3274 controllers, modems, multiplexers, and more as the level of sophistication rises. There is also specialized software, such as the Network Control Program (NCP) in the front-end processor. Designing and implementing such a network is complex, and a staff of applications programmers, systems programmers, communication specialists, and other software and hardware technicians is needed to operate and maintain it.

Initially COBOL was the language most commonly used on mainframes. The mainframe's original mode of operation was batch processing, in which a program executes using the appropriate data files with no intervention by a user or operator. Interactive programming was needed when a user wanted to inquire about a certain part or person. COBOL wasn't up to this task, and the utilities provided by the operating system didn't support the generation of screens and other tasks needed for interactive sessions. This brought about the use of CICS, which allows interactive screens with COBOL programs.

While CICS and COBOL are still a strong combination, more and more mainframes are using fourth-generation languages and database programs implementing Structured Query Language (SQL).

Minicomputers

It's often difficult to say what makes up a mainframe system and what makes up a minicomputer system because they share many of the same features—for example, IBM still uses SNA with its minicomputers. The distinguishing feature is usually cost, the mainframe being more expensive.

The technology of IBM minicomputers started with System 34. System 36 was introduced next, followed by System 38; the latest entry is the AS400.

Systems 34 and 36 used an operating system known as *System Support Program* (SSP). COBOL and RPG II were the primary languages of these systems. System 38's operating system functioned much more like that of a database and used RPG III and COBOL.

Minicomputers don't have the power of a mainframe. Thus, they function as departmental computers in many large corporations and form the central data-processing systems of smaller corporations. One advantage of a minicomputer, however, is the ease of interactive programming.

Like a mainframe, the minicomputer uses dumb terminals or PCs that emulate dumb terminals. Again, all the processing is done by the minicomputer's CPU.

Microcomputers

The PC entered the scene in the late 1970s, creating a revolution in computing. It had an immediate following and was treated like a toy by those who were entrenched in a mainframe or minicomputer environment.

As the PC continued to develop, it appeared that all the exciting improvements were happening in this environment. There is a split between those who view the PC as the ultimate and those who wish to banish it. This war drags on, but we may be closer to a state of peaceful coexistence.

The Integrated Computer Environment

In the past, a computer environment was classified by the type of computer system that met the company's needs. That viewpoint is now fading as it becomes more apparent that integrating various types of computer systems can help meet those needs.

Integrated environments are developing rapidly. The corporate mainframe still exists, but it's often either complemented by a LAN or placed in a subservient role to the LAN. At times it may become part of the LAN by functioning as a repository of data.

Some corporations are actually replacing their mainframes or minicomputers with a LAN (a process known as *downsizing*). LANs are now seen as having tremendous power, rivaling that of a mainframe, because they are flexible and inexpensive.

LAN Configurations

LANs are configured according to their method of operation: peer-to-peer, resource sharing, or client-server.

Peer-to-Peer

On a peer-to-peer network, each workstation can share some, all, or none of its resources with the other workstations.

Resource Sharing

With resource sharing, one or more centralized servers send and receive files and contain the resources the workstations use. The workstations can't access other workstations' resources, and they do all their own processing.

Client-Server

Client-server computing splits an application into client (workstations) and server components—such as a database server. At the front end, the client part of the application accepts input from the user, prepares it for the server, and issues a request to the server. At the back end, the server receives requests from clients, processes them, and provides the requested service to the client. The client then presents the data or other results to the user through its own interface.

A spin off of distributed processing, client-server computing is now the big trend in information systems development. Among its strong points, the client is used to actually run the application program, and the database server—which can be a mainframe or minicomputer—can be used for processing. The entire file is no longer transferred over the network by the file server to the client where the correct record is ascertained. Now the command is issued by the client and the database server finds that correct record and transmits only that record to the client. Both the overhead and the time required for processing are greatly reduced. The horsepower of a mainframe can now be coupled with the flexibility and ease of programming a PC.

Broadband and Baseband Networks

LANs fall into two basic categories: broadband and baseband.

Broadband LANs

Broadband LANs are the exception rather than the rule. These networks differ from their baseband counterparts in that they use coaxial or fiber-optic cable to carry multiple channels of data. A single cable can carry five or six separate communication channels. In that sense, a broadband network is analogous to cable TV: One cable connects the house to the cable television service, but it carries multiple channels.

Broadband networks use analog transmission methods, allowing the cable to handle information at different frequency levels. Each frequency forms a separate, autonomous communication channel. Frequency levels are determined by the number of cycles per second: a frequency between 100 and 300 Hz (hertz, or cycles per second) forms one channel. The frequency between 400 and 700 Hz forms another channel. The number of channels a cable can accommodate depends on how many cycles per second the cable can handle. The higher the frequency limit, the greater the number of data channels permitted (see Figure 1.2).

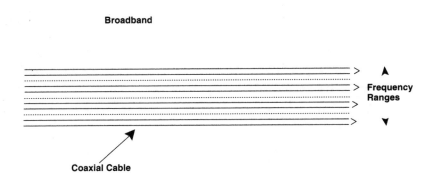

FIGURE 1.2 With broadband, the cable is divided into frequency ranges. Each range is its own communication channel and is independent of the other frequency ranges. In this way, multiple signals—such as voice, data, and video—can be transmitted over one cable.

A broadband network is ideal in an environment such as a university or hospital. Since it provides data, audio, and video transmission, one cable is enough to network the entire campus or facility.

Baseband LANs

Most LANs are baseband. A baseband network uses only one channel on the cable to support digital transmission, which is much faster than analog transmission. (see Figure 1.3). This book is primarily concerned with baseband networks.

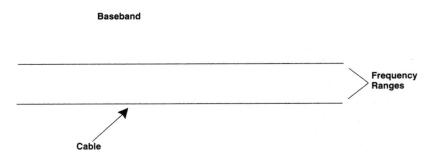

FIGURE 1.3 With baseband, the frequency range of the cable constitutes the one communication channel. Only one signal may be transmitted over the cable.

CHAPTER 2

LAN COMPONENTS

As noted in Chapter 1 a LAN is made up of hardware and software. This chapter will examine the hardware components in greater detail.

The File Server

The file server is the most important piece of hardware on the LAN. It provides a central repository for the network application programs and network data and it can be accessed by all workstations on the network. To handle this workload, the file server needs to be the most powerful microcomputer on the network.

Some network operating systems allow a file server to also function as a workstation to save money. However, using a file server in a *nondedicated mode*—both a file server and a workstation—doesn't deliver the maximum speed and efficiency to your LAN.

When determining the power of the file server, you have to examine a number of its parts, including:

- RAM (random access memory)
- CPU (central processing unit)
- Hard disk or disk subsystem
- Bus architecture
- Expansion slots

RAM

RAM, simply referred to as *memory*, is one area where you shouldn't try to cut costs. The number of megabytes of RAM installed on the file server directly affects the performance of the network. After all, it's the file server's memory that runs the network operating system.

Some network operating systems function as the operating system for both the file server and the network as a whole. Such systems can run on the file server with no need for other software. With other operating systems, such as UNIX and OS/2, the network operating system must be run as a task under the file server's operating system. The file server loads UNIX first, for example, then runs the network operating system as an application under UNIX.

You can use 1–6 megabytes (Mbytes) of RAM just to accommodate the various operating systems on the file server. Some network operating systems implement file and directory caching, where data is read from the file server's hard disk and stored in blocks of the file server's memory (cache blocks) at the same time it is sent to the requesting workstation. The next request from the workstation can probably be serviced by using the data in these memory blocks, so the file server doesn't have to access its hard disk for each data request.

Caching can make data retrieval up to 100 times faster, since data access is at RAM speed and not disk speed; however, more RAM is required. On an average-size network, it's not uncommon to have 4–10 Mbytes of RAM on the file server.

CPU

The file server's microprocessor is extremely important. The more powerful the microprocessor, the faster the network operating system runs. Microprocessors can function at different speeds, with ratings given in megahertz, (MHz). The higher the MHz, the faster the processor.

The 80486 and Intel's Pentium CPUs are very popular microprocessors for file servers. Intel offers different versions of the 80486. These various Intel 80486 chips have speed ratings of 25, 33, 50, 66, 75, and 100 MHz. Intel also designed and manufactures the Pentium microprocessor. This is Intel's top-of-the-line microprocessor; it is used in many IBM-compatible personal computers. Intel also offers the Pentium processor in various models. The Pentium processor has speed ratings of 60, 66, 90, 100, and 120 MHz. The

8088 was the first microprocessor used in an IBM PC (see Figure 2.1). At that time, it had a Norton index of 1. The *Norton index* was a de facto standard for measuring the processing speed of a microcomputer. This rating was determined by running the SI utility from the Norton Utilities software package. The SI benchmark was based on an IBM PC equipped with an 8088 microprocessor, so it had a rating of 1.

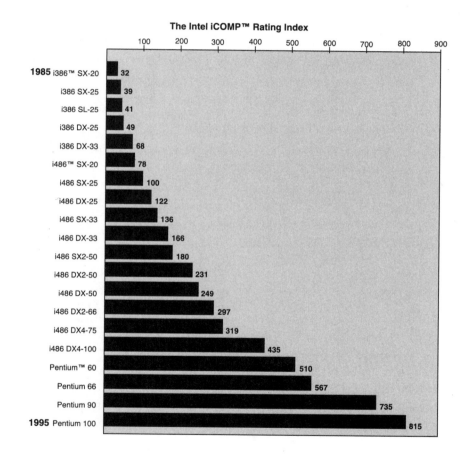

FIGURE 2.1 The evolution of CPUs.

Next came the 8086 microprocessor. It was a little faster, with a Norton index of 3 or 4. The IBM AT and IBM AT-compatible computers followed, with an 80286 microprocessor and a Norton rating of about 10. The 80386 microprocessor was substantially more powerful, with a Norton rating of 16 to 22 and higher, as the chips' cycle speeds increased. At this point the Norton rating scale became obsolete. The AT chips (80286) were no competition for the new chips that were being produced. With the advent of more graphics-intensive software and 32-bit microprocessors, other benchmarks were developed and used in lieu of the Norton rating. Intel uses a rating index it developed, referred to as iCOMP—Intel COmparative Microprocessor Performance. The iCOMP is a comparison of different Intel microprocessors. Manufacturers using the same Intel chip will produce personal computers with different performances.

The iCOMP uses the 25 MHz 80486 SX as its base with an assigned value of 100. All other processors are then measured from this reference point. The Intel 80386 25 MHz SX has an iCOMP value of 39, while the Pentium 100 has an iCOMP rating of 815. This indicates quite a performance difference between the two microprocessors.

The 80286 is being phased out at many companies in favor of the high-end 80486- and Pentium-based file servers.

An AT-class microcomputer with an 80286 microprocessor could accommodate a small network of eight to ten nodes, but with the falling prices of hardware, it just isn't practical. It would be much wiser to take advantage of the extra power of 80386, 80486, or Pentium microprocessors. The file server would then be able to accommodate more nodes as the network grows. Newer network operating systems are being designed to take advantage of the faster CPUs, and some, such as Novell's NetWare 386 and Banyan Vines 386, require at least an 80386 CPU in the file server and a 32-bit microprocessor.

Bus Architectures

The larger the data segment, the faster the computer functions. One advantage of using a 80386 or later chip is its ability to manipulate data in 32-bit segments. The 80286 boosted performance by increasing the data transfer size on the *bus* (the channel over which data moves throughout the PC) from 8 bits to 16 bits. The memory of the 80386 allows data segments to travel in 32-bit segments, increasing the speed of operation even further (see Figure 2.2).

With the 80286, 2 bytes enter the CPU before it actually processes the request. This is known as *multiplexing*. With the 80386, IBM introduced a new bus architecture in the form of Micro Channel Architecture (MCA). MCA is a 32-bit bus, although it usually functions as a 16-bit bus for stand-alone PCs.

File servers using the 80386, and 80486, and Pentium CPUs can take advantage of the MCA's 32-bit bus.

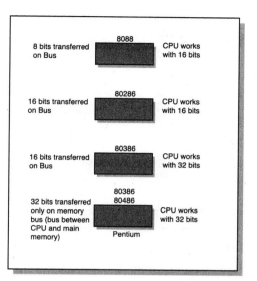

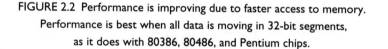

FIGURE 2.2 Performance is improving due to faster access to memory.
Performance is best when all data is moving in 32-bit segments,
as it does with **80386, 80486,** and Pentium chips.

Another common bus architecture is the EISA (Enhanced Industry Standard Architecture) bus. This 32-bit bus remains compatible with the older 16-bit bus, *ISA* (Industry Standard Architecture), while the MCA bus is not. This is a factor to be aware of when purchasing a PC. You need to be sure your network—and you, as the administrator—can cope with a mixed architecture.

Hard Disk or Disk Subsystem

One consideration that is often overlooked when selecting file servers is the size and access speed of the hard disk, the file server's storage device. Most network bottlenecks occur at the file server. The file server's hard disk is often the weakest link in the network chain, causing the file server to fall behind in its ability to service requests. This is usually because the file server cannot access the hard disk fast enough to stay ahead of data requests.

The average access time of a hard disk is measured in *milliseconds* (ms), or thousandths of a second. The shorter the access time, the better the file server's performance. An average access time of 65 ms used to be acceptable in the 1980s, but this is far too slow for the demands placed on the file servers of today. For adequate network performance, the access rates for the file server's hard disk should be no slower than 20 ms.

Another important factor in avoiding bottlenecks is the amount of storage space offered by the file server's hard disk. At one time, a 120-Mbyte hard disk was considered large. Today, it's not uncommon for a file server to have a 650-Mbyte hard disk. Some larger LANs have a disk-storage capacity measured in billions of bytes, while network operating systems being introduced today make it possible to manipulate hard disk drives that can store trillions of bytes. That storage capability rivals a mainframe computer. One trend in disk subsystems is the RAID (redundant array of inexpensive disks) technology. This disk subsystem allows large storage capacity and decreases the access time for reads from the hard drives, helping eliminate the bottlenecks that may occur during peak demands on the file server.

The latest technology introduced for storing and accessing information is the CD-ROM. This is an optical (not magnetic) round and compact storage device. It can store enormous amounts of information on a small disk. The CD-ROM has become popular in multimedia circles, but it can also be connected to a file server. This allows everyone on the network access to CD-ROMs and all the information they contain.

Expansion Slots

The PC chosen for the file server should have a number of free expansion slots, since most network operating systems accommodate multiple network interface cards in the file server. A file server with only one expansion slot is inadequate if network growth warrants adding more NICs to the file server.

In addition, expansion slots may be needed to add RAM to the file server in the form of memory expansion boards. Expansion slots can also be used to add a disk subsystem to the file server. Peripheral devices can be attached to the file server using the expansion slots or can provide more serial or parallel ports.

The computer industry is now developing PCs to be used exclusively as file servers. These computers have multiple 80486 and Pentium microprocessors and enormous RAM capabilities and can accommodate trillions of bytes of disk storage with extremely fast disk access times. Some have separate microprocessors to handle I/O (input/output). These computers are definitely not for every network.

The Workstation

The device the network user comes in contact with most often is the workstation. This is usually a PC used to run applications. Normally, users don't need to know much about the LAN they're using; their primary concern is how to use the PC and the application programs needed to do their work.

Network workstations don't need as many standard features as their file server counterparts; RAM requirements start at 1 Mbyte and are limited only by the department's budget. Workstations are commonly installed with 1, 2, or 4 Mbytes of RAM, whereas file servers usually start with at least 4 Mbytes.

The workstation's microprocessor is the biggest determinant of performance. Workstations usually have a wide variety of microprocessors. More people are buying 80486 and Pentium machines. The graphical user interfaces—such as Windows 3.1 and O/S2—and their ability to multitask and operate concurrent application programs, require more processing power in the workstation. The 8088 and 8086, and even the 80286, are being phased out by many vendors.

The number of expansion slots available can be an issue depending on what must be attached to the workstation. This isn't as important, however, on a workstation as on a file server.

Hard disks and disk subsystems also may not be an issue because many workstations don't have hard disks; instead they rely on the file server for storage. Although this may save a few hundred dollars or more per machine, it isn't always the best approach. If the workstation is equipped with its own hard disk, it can remain up and running even when the file server goes down.

If the workstation does have a hard disk, it might be wise to load an extra copy of the word processor and other applications on the hard disk. Just because the workstation is connected to a LAN doesn't mean the PC is dependent on the network. A user can work all day on a PC and never access the LAN if the PC has its own hard disk. Conversely, a workstation may be totally dependent on a network, if all the applications and data are stored there.

The following PCs can be considered as LAN workstations:

- IBM PCs and compatibles
- Diskless PCs
- Apple Macintoshes
- UNIX-based and other engineering workstations

Before trying to incorporate different hardware designs into a LAN, be sure the network operating system supports that type of workstation. Some operating systems use communication protocols, such as TCP/IP (Transmission Control Protocol/Internet Protocol), that are specific to a certain operating system that executes on the workstation. Mixing diverse workstation operating systems and computer architectures can be very challenging.

IBM PCs and compatibles are normally easy to connect because virtually every network operating system supports them. However, some of the lesser-known PC brands may present problems. These are usually IBM clones of questionable quality or workmanship. When a problem does occur, it usually has to do with the BIOS (basic input/output system) read-only memory (ROM) used on that particular PC. By staying with mainstream IBM-compatible PCs, you'll be less likely to encounter problems.

Apple Macintosh computers may also be networked. In fact, Apple has its own network operating system—AppleShare—and protocol AppleTalk—designed specifically to network Apple Macintosh computers. UNIX-based workstations can also be networked, though with a little more difficulty for users only familiar with DOS.

Two issues warrant further discussion: using IBM-compatibles and Apple Macintoshes on the same network and diskless workstations.

Combining IBM-Compatibles and Macintoshes

Today, IBM PCs and compatibles coexist with Apple computers on networks. At one time, IBM-compatible computers were the dominant PCs in business, while the Macintosh was used as a special-purpose computer, usually designated for desktop publishing. In recent years, Macintosh has made tremendous strides within the business world, and it now supports a wide range of network hardware and applications. Because of this development, it is not uncommon to see IBM-compatibles and Apple Macintoshes side by side in an office.

From its inception, the Macintosh has been able to share peripherals and files on a Macintosh-based network. When a built-in LocalTalk network jack and the

AppleShare network operating system software were provided, all Macintosh users needed to do was plug the computer in. The only limitations were speed [230 kilobits per second (Kbits/sec)], network size (limited to 32 users), and the inability to connect the network to IBM-compatibles or host mainframes.

IBM connectivity proved to be the biggest challenge facing Apple. It got the ball rolling by introducing a line of networking products, including the 10-Mbps EtherTalk and 4-Mbps TokenTalk NICs. Apple also introduced AppleTalk Phase II, a networking specification that allows thousands of Macintoshes to be connected on larger internetworks.

Several networks, including TOPS/DOS, TOPS/MAC, and NetWare for Macintosh, have solved the problem of connecting Apple Macintoshes and IBM-compatibles, although networking the two is neither easy nor advisable. The problems that remain with networking primarily involve file conversion due to the incompatible file formats of the two systems.

Diskless Workstations

The concept of a diskless PC workstation has been around for a number of years. As the name implies, this computer has no floppy or hard disk drives. Most diskless workstations are IBM-compatible machines that have a built-in microprocessor that runs MS-DOS.

These diskless computers look much like dumb terminals and consist of a monitor, a small base unit, and a keyboard. Some units simply consist of a keyboard with the microprocessor and all related circuitry housed inside. Whatever the design, there are no slots for diskettes; diskless computers can do everything a regular PC can do except store data on a local floppy or hard disk.

At one time it was thought diskless computers were going to become very popular for four reasons:

- Security
- Virus protection
- Control of unlicensed software
- Cost effectiveness

Security

A PC that can't copy network files onto a diskette logically makes a good security device. The only way network information could be copied using a diskless workstation would be via a printer or calling the information to the screen and writing it down by hand.

Virus Protection

Just as you might not want certain things taken off the network, there are certain things that you don't want put on the network—in particular, computer viruses. With diskless workstations, all network applications have to be placed on the LAN by the network administrator. Before placing new software on the network, the network administrator can check it for viruses.

Control of Unlicensed Software

Because there are no disk drives, users can't place unauthorized software on the LAN. The network administrator must install applications on the network meaning the licensed use of software can be monitored at all times.

Cost Effectiveness

Because it lacks the extra disk devices, diskless workstations usually cost less than regular PCs. The cost effectiveness doesn't degrade performance; the diskless workstation performs as well as any other PC with a comparable CPU. The only drawback is that all application software must reside on the file server and the diskless workstation can't work independently of the network.

One other point is that the shell, redirector, or requester must be loaded for the workstation to function on the network. If you can't load the shell from a local disk drive, you must use a ROM chip located inside the diskless workstation or on the NIC. The only problem with boot ROMs is that they're tied to a specific version of DOS and a specific release of the network operating system. If the network is upgraded, all the boot ROMs need to be replaced.

Even with these four reasons the diskless PC never gained widespread popularity. They filled more of a niche market.

The Network Interface Card

The network interface card is inserted into one of the expansion slots on the workstation. Each workstation and file server on the network must have an NIC, which is where the cabling is attached.

The NIC's job is to form data packets from the workstation and then transmit them onto the network cabling. (A *data packet* is a predefined structuring of bits that is understood by the network and the protocols it supports.) The NIC also receives data packets from the network cabling and translates them into bytes that the workstation's CPU can understand.

The following questions should be considered when purchasing an NIC:

- Does it have an 8-bit, 16-bit, or 32-bit adapter?
- Does it have RAM buffering?
- Does it have a microprocessor?

Bit Size

NICs are available with eight eight-bit, 16-bit, and 32-bit adapters. What exactly does that mean to the network designer? First, let's consider the microcomputer bus.

The bus is the path over which data is transmitted internally. Older, 8088- and 8086-based PCs had buses that were 8 bits wide, so 8 bits of data could be transmitted concurrently via the PC's internal bus. With the advent of the 80286 CPU, the bus's bandwidth increased to 16 bits to accommodate the transfer rates used by the 16-bit 80286. Many 32-bit, 80386-based computers still transmit data across a 16-bit-wide bus, although they can also manipulate 32-bit-wide data. If the PC has an EISA or MCA bus it can transmit 32-bit-wide data across the bus.

The 32-bit NIC is more efficient and able to improve the workstation's performance. Because the NIC connects the workstation to the network, the data can be sent to and received from the NIC faster with the workstation performance.

RAM Buffering

Another option is RAM buffering. RAM chips integrated into the NIC prevent it from forming a bottleneck on the network and can also improve workstation performance.

The theory behind RAM buffering is quite simple. There are times when the amount of data received is beyond the NIC's capabilities to handle it. This data is placed in a holding area—the *RAM buffer*—until the NIC can catch up to the workload.

The RAM buffer works in much the same way as a print buffer. When a program sends information to the printer, it sends more information than the printer can handle. For performance reasons, it doesn't make sense for the computer sending the data to wait for the printer to catch up. The solution is a print buffer, which is nothing more than memory used to hold the incoming data until the printer is ready. This allows the printer to continue printing and, more importantly, doesn't slow the microcomputer that's sending the data.

Similarly, the RAM buffer allows the workstation to maintain communication with the file server. Without the buffer the communication channel would be broken until the NIC could accommodate more data and then reestablished to finish the transmission (see Figure 2.3).

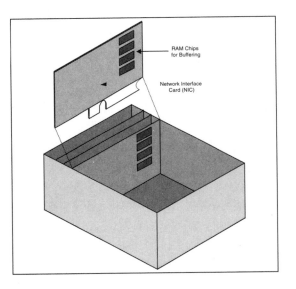

FIGURE 2.3 If the information or data comes in at a rate faster than the NIC can accommodate, it is temporarily stored in RAM until the NIC can process it. This is known as buffering.

NIC Microprocessors

Some NICs are even equipped with a microprocessor. This is one of the latest NIC performance enhancements. A microprocessor allows the NIC to process data without involving the PCs CPU, which then has to do less work. The microprocessor on the NIC and the main CPU share memory (see Figure 2.4).

NIC with Microprocessor

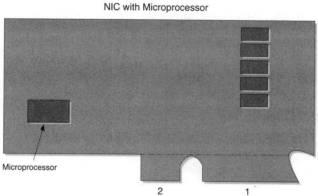

Microprocessor

2   1

FIGURE 2.4 The NICs built-in microprocessor enhances performance by accessing the PCs memory and relieving some of the burden placed on the CPU.

Cabling

Cabling is the LAN's transmission medium; it carries the data packets to and from the file server. The cabling commonly used in a LAN falls into one of three categories:

- Coaxial
- Twisted-pair
- Fiber-optic

Coaxial Cable

Coaxial cable can carry network data at rates in excess of 350 Mbps. It has one central copper wire, and a main conductor, surrounded by insulating material. Over this insulating material is a stranded shield, which is the secondary conductor and acts as a ground. All these components are surrounded by a protective jacket (see Figure 2.5).

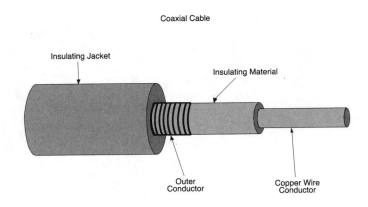

FIGURE 2.5 Coaxial cable. Data travels over the copper-wire conductor and the outer conductor acts as a ground. These two metal conductors are separated by insulating material. The entire cable is protected by a heavy exterior insulating jacket.

Coaxial cable is available in different varieties and thicknesses. It also has different impedances. (*Impedance* determines the amount of resistance offered to electrical impulses transmitted over the wire and is usually measured in ohms.) Each type of network has a specific impedance rating that the coaxial cable must match. The thicker the cable, the more cumbersome with which it is to work. Thick cable is harder to install, especially when it's being pulled through existing conduits and troughs. It's also more expensive. To complicate matters even further, different coaxial cable types can coexist on the same network.

For networked PCs, coaxial cable offers the following advantages:

- It supports both broadband and baseband LANs.
- It can run unboosted for longer distances than twisted-pair cable.
- It can transmit voice, video, and data.
- It has been used for some time for data communication, so the technology is well-known.

Coaxial cable also has some disadvantages:

- The thick coaxial cable may be too rigid to install easily.
- It is more expensive to install than twisted-pair cable.
- The cable itself is more expensive than twisted-pair.

Twisted-Pair Cable

There are several different types of twisted-pair cable.

An unshielded twisted-pair (UTP) cable consists of two insulated, braided copper wires. It's more than just two insulated copper wires wrapped together, however, because twisted-pair cabling must follow exact specifications as to how many twists or braids are permitted per foot of cable. Groups of unshielded twisted-pair cable are often placed within a protective jacket (see Figure 2.6).

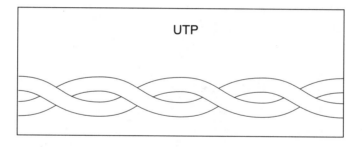

FIGURE 2.6 Copper wire with individual jackets twisted together.

The wiring used for most telephone systems is UTP. This is one of the reasons it is gaining in popularity, since many buildings are already wired with twisted-pair telephones. Also, during construction of a building, extra pairs of UTP are usually installed in anticipation of future needs and at minimal expense. UTP technology for data communications is growing rapidly and can now be used by most networks.

Shielded twisted-pair differs from UTP in that it uses a much higher-quality protective jacket for greater insulation (see Figure 2.7). Thus, it has a longer signal transmission range then unshielded twisted-pair, and is less prone to electrical interference from outside sources. Despite this, the majority of twisted-pair cabling being installed is UTP.

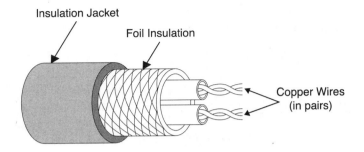

FIGURE 2.7 Shielded twisted-pair consists of copper wire with individual jackets twisted together inside an insulating jacket.

Twisted-pair cabling has the following advantages:

- It's inexpensive.
- Devices are easy to connect.
- It's easy to install.

It also has several disadvantages when compared to coaxial and fiber-optic cable:

- It's more prone to electrical noise and interference.
- It generally has lower data-transmission rates.
- The distance between signal boosts is shorter.

IBM groups its twisted-pair cable into three categories: Type 1 is shielded twisted-pair, Type 2 is shielded twisted-pair with an additional four pairs of UTP integrated into it, and Type 3 is IBM's name for UTP.

Fiber-Optic Cable

Fiber-optic cable (see Figure 2.8) carries data in the form of modulated light beams. As the name suggests, no electrical impulses are carried over a fiber-optic line; those that signify bits are transformed into beams of light. These light beams are modulated to indicate whether a bit is on or off.

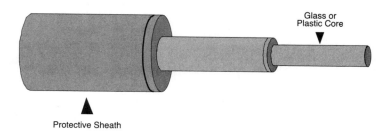

FIGURE 2.8 Fiber-optic cable.

Fiber-optics are used for very high-speed, high-capacity data communication. They enable data transfer at rates exceeding 1 trillion bps. A network that uses fiber-optics exclusively is Fiber Distributed Data Interface (FDDI).

The fiber used in the cables can be composed of either glass or plastic. Plastic fiber-optic is easier to install but has a much shorter transmission distance than glass.

Fiber-optic cable offers the following advantages.

- It is capable of very high-speed data transfer.
- It produces no magnetic or electrical signals; thus, it doesn't interfere with nearby sensitive equipment.
- Because it doesn't carry any electrical impulses, it can't be affected by electrical noise or interference from the LAN environment.
- It can carry a data signal a longer distance than either twisted-pair or coaxial cable.
- It cannot be tapped, making it an excellent choice for security reasons.

Fiber-optic cable also has the following disadvantages:

- More skill is required to install it.
- More skill is required to connect devices to it.
- The cable is expensive.
- It is more costly to install than twisted-pair or coaxial cable.

Work in the field of fiber-optic research and fiber-optic networks is ongoing and a lot more is expected from this technology in the near future.

The Hub

On every network, each workstation must have access to the file server. It would be impossible for each workstation to have its own connection to the file server, so a hub or concentrator is used.

The hub can be thought of as an electrical junction box on a house. Usually only one main electrical power line is connected to a house. This connection runs to a junction box, where multiple circuits are created to serve the house.

LANs function the same way. Not only does the file server attach to the hub, but the workstations are attached as well.

Certain topologies require the hub to be modified. With a linear bus topology, some of the actual cabling serves as the hub or concentrator. With star, ring, and star-wired ring topologies, the hub is a central area in which workstations and file servers can communicate. The information coming into or leaving the network is directed through the hub to its destination (see Figures 2.9–2.12). The hub may be either active or passive. An active hub regenerates the signal and connects the cabling, enabling the signal to travel farther, while a passive hub is simply a cable-connecting device.

Hub for a Star Topology

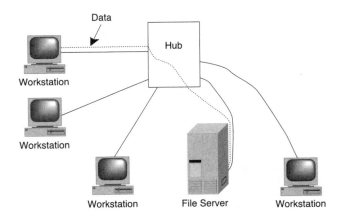

FIGURE 2.9 For a workstation to communicate with the file server, data must first go through the hub. To communicate with a workstation, the file server also sends data through the hub.

Hub for a Tree

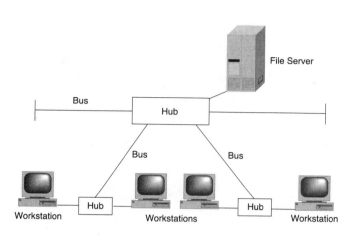

FIGURE 2.10 In a tree design that uses a bus topology, hubs are accessed before transmission to and from file servers and workstations.

Hub for a Star Topology

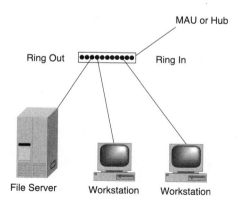

FIGURE 2.11 Inside a hub, a loop or ring is made with only one media access unit (MAU); the Ring In and Ring Out ports on the hub are not used.

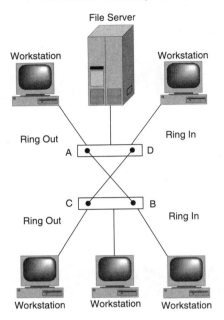

Hub for a Star-Wired Ring Topology

FIGURE 2.12 The signal is connected from the port of the first MAU (A) to the second MAU (B). There, it completes the circuit and connects from the Ring Out port (C) of the second MAU to the Ring In port (D) of the first MAU. Thus, a ring is maintained.

CHAPTER 3

LAN Operations: Why Use a LAN?

There are many reasons to use a LAN. This chapter presents a few of them.

Distributed Processing

Distributed processing is the foundation of LAN theory. We'll examine it here with regard to all the software and hardware used on the LAN.

To illustrate, consider a LAN that consists of only one workstation and one file server. The network operating system is loaded and running on the file server, while application programs and data are stored on its hard disk drives. The workstation is running the PC's operating system as well as the network shell; it also has its own hard disk. All other network hardware is in its place: NICs are in the expansion slots of both the PC and the file server, with cabling connecting the two.

Now that we have a small LAN, let's explore its operations using two examples.

Example 1: Running an Application

The user enters a command to run a specific program on the workstation. This application program could either be on the workstation's hard disk or on the file server's hard disk. In this example, the application (a database program) is on the workstation's hard drive, so no request is sent to the file server.

No request was issued to the network because of the working relationship between the workstation's operating system and the network shell, both of which were able to discern that this was a command for the workstation alone.

But what if the application is on the file server's hard disk system instead? As before, a user calling for a network-based application enters a command on the workstation asking for a specific program. The workstation calls for this program, and the shell determines that the request should be sent to the file server. The file server receives the request and transmits the application to the workstation, where it is stored in RAM.

In this situation, a network request was issued because the workstation's operating system and the shell determined that the application program was on the file server. If the user enters a command that is a function of the workstation's operating system, it is performed by that operating system. If the command is a function of the network operating system, however, it is directed to the file server and the network operating system.

Example 2: Accessing Data

In either situation in the first example, the application program is loaded into the workstation's memory. However, an application program is useless without data.

Let's say the data is stored on the file server's hard disk. When the application program requests data records, the request is directed to the file server by the combined action of the workstation's operating system and the shell. Again, the file server does no processing except to provide data input and output. When the network operating system receives the request, the file server sends the file to the workstation's memory, and that's where the processing takes place.

Once the database records have been changed at the workstation, the records that have been modified are now ready to be stored. The workstation issues a request to update to these records. The request is received by both the workstation's operating system and the shell, which determine that the write must be to the file server. Control passes once again to the network operating system, and the write is performed.

If the data were located on the workstation's hard disk, no requests would be issued to the network. A workstation may be a node on a network, but it can also act independently of the LAN; the fact that it is connected to a LAN does not in any way detract from its functionality as a PC.

These LAN operating principles apply whether you have one or 20 workstations on the network. The only difference is that the file server is much more active when it has to support more workstations, and the overall performance of the LAN could degrade.

Example 3: Client/Server

Client/server application software is the latest trend in the use of computer networks. It is a more specialized version of distributed processing. It further specifies which components of the network do what processing processes. It consists of the user's workstation, or a client, and an additional server, such as a database server that is part of the network. A request for database information is routed to the database server from the workstation. The database server then transmits the reply back to the workstation, or client. The database server helps alleviate some of the processing that takes place at the workstation, or client. Usually, applications increase in performance in this environment. Additionally, the traffic on the network is decreased. Client/server is described in greater detail in Chapter 12.

High-Speed Communication

A LAN can send data through the network at much faster speeds than a mainframe or minicomputer data network. The transfer rate on a LAN ranges from 1 to 100 Mbps, although LANs are being developed that transfer data at the rate of 1 Gbps (*gigabits*, or billion bits, per second). By comparison, the speed of a mainframe is up to 56 Kbps.

The LAN's ability to transfer data rapidly results in more efficient use of the network and the data residing on the network. That's because the faster the data can be transferred, the more work can be accomplished in a shorter period of time.

Electronic Mail

The advent of the microcomputer made it possible for an individual to do data processing at his or her desk, greatly enhancing productivity and the quality of work. However, users still needed the ability to communicate with one another. The telephone wasn't always convenient or efficient, and messages were still generally hand-carried.

With computer networking, the need to communicate was met through the use of electronic mail, or E-mail. *E-mail* is a specialized application program that runs on the network and functions much like the postal system. This communication program interconnects the workstations on a LAN; each user on the LAN has a directory for E-mail, commonly known as a *mailbox*.

The actual electronic message is simply information, in the form of a memo or letter, that you type as if you are using a word processor. This electronic letter is then forwarded to the desired person's mailbox. LAN users check their mailboxes from time to time to see if any messages have been forwarded. Some E-mail applications even notify the addressee when messages are received by displaying a notice on the workstation screen.

Today's E-mail programs are very sophisticated and offer many features that would enhance any work environment. For example, you can use them to arrange meetings or send memos to people in different buildings or across the country.

Metered Applications

Metering of the applications stored on the file server is another feature provided by a LAN. If an office has 20 employees, for example, all those workers aren't likely to need the same applications, and some are likely to use certain applications more than others. A spreadsheet package may be used by all 20 employees, but perhaps only four or five of the 20 may use it extensively. Still, the remaining 15 people use the spreadsheet occasionally, and it should be available to them when they need it. Rather than purchase 20 copies of the software or a site license for unlimited use, both of which can be expensive, you can use metering software.

A metering software package is installed on the file server along with five copies of a spreadsheet package. The system operator tells the metering system how many times the spreadsheet package may be accessed on the network. If five spreadsheet packages are available on the file server, the metering system is set to five. Then the metering system will allow no more than five people to use the spreadsheet program concurrently on the network. If a sixth person needs the spreadsheet, he or she must wait until one of the others exits the software package.

The metering system, therefore, serves two purposes. First, it saves money. Why buy 20 copies of a spreadsheet program when five copies are sufficient? Second, it maintains the legality of the network. The licensing agreements for the software limit the number of users permitted per copy; with the metering system, software licenses are not broken.

Shared Data

Some programs use shared data, whereby many users use the same application at their workstations and all the data to be shared is located on the file server. In this way, several people using the same program can access the same data. This data sharing is a primary benefit of mainframes and minicomputers.

Software packages that use shared data must be able to support multiple users. Multiuser programs are designed to accommodate data that is to be shared; they implement both file locking and record locking to maintain the integrity of the data so one user's data doesn't overwrite another's.

When a user accesses a file, the program locks it so no one can use that file until the lock is removed. The normal sequence of events is that the file lock is activated, the file is modified, and the lock is removed. It happens so quickly that locking is transparent to the user, giving the appearance that the files are being accessed by all users at the same time.

Record locking is more efficient and causes less wait time for the user than file locking. With record locking, when the correct record is found, a lock is put only on that record rather than on the entire file. Thus, the file may be used by the others who are sharing the data; the only record they can't access is the one that's locked. Once the records are processed at the workstation, they are returned to the file server; the records are saved to the file, and the locks are removed.

A file or record lock is normally implemented only when a file is actually being changed. Sometimes when a user locks a file, he or she is the only one who can modify, add, or delete records in the file; however, other users aren't prevented from reading the records in the file. On other occasions, the file is locked so that unauthorized users can't read it. An authorized person can lock a file; others must wait until the lock is removed. The same holds true for record locking.

Multiuser application programs that are bought off the shelf usually handle file and record locking. If an application program is being custom-coded, however, the programmer must know how to design and code programs for multiple users and shared data.

Shared Resources

A major benefit of installing a LAN is that it eliminates duplication of peripherals. Organizations often install LANs for this reason alone.

What kind of shared peripherals can the network support? Any that a stand-alone can support, such as duplicate printers. The network can also support plotters, modems, host 3270 boards, tape backup systems, fax machines, and any other devices the workstations can access.

Printers are primary targets for resource sharing. Let's say 15 of the 30 users on a LAN need to produce letter-quality documents on a regular basis using a laser printer. Without a LAN, there are two options.

The first option is for a user to copy a file onto a diskette and walk it over to a user who has access to a laser printer (this is sometimes referred to as a *sneakernet*). This means either interrupting someone else's work to print the document or waiting until the PC attached to the laser printer is not in use.

The second option is to purchase a laser printer for each of the 15 users who need to print letter-quality documents. This is an expensive way to eliminate the waste of time and inefficiency of sneakernetting.

With a LAN, this problem can be solved efficiently and cost-effectively. Instead of carrying around diskettes or buying a host of printers, you can use a network printer. It's relatively easy to attach one or two, perhaps even three, laser printers (depending on the workload) to the file server. Each user on the LAN can then send a document to the laser printer using the network. Now all 15 people have regular access to a laser printer for the cost of only one or two printers, and the only walking that's necessary is to fetch the printout. This approach is even more efficient when the network printers are strategically positioned throughout the work area.

In all likelihood, the other 15 users will need to print to a laser printer at some point. The LAN solves this problem, too, since everyone on the network can access the network laser printers. This approach saves money and increases office productivity.

Another shared peripheral device is the gateway, which allows the LAN to access a mainframe or minicomputer. With a LAN, there is no need to purchase an emulation board and software for each PC—all that's required is a gateway with the appropriate software.

Several network users might also need access to a modem. Instead of purchasing a modem for each user or swapping the modems between users, you can buy one and let users share it over the LAN. The LAN can also support other communication devices, such as an asynchronous communication server that gives users all over the network access to communication services. The same is true for fax machines.

Better Use of Existing Resources

LANs can use a variety of commercial software packages. Buying off-the-shelf network software saves time and money in development and maintenance, and software packages designed to operate on a PC are more plentiful than those for mainframes and minicomputers. These commercial software packages can usually grow with the needs of the organization and its LAN.

Existing hardware can also be better used in a LAN environment. Consider our discussion of printers as shared resources. The organization may already have two laser printers that can easily be installed on a LAN. Thus, the hardware already on hand can be used to solve the problem of limited resources or to make better use of existing resources.

These aren't the only reasons to implement a LAN; there are many more. And as new situations arise and new technologies are developed, the benefits and features offered by LANs will continue to grow.

SECTION II

NETWORK OPERATING SYSTEMS, SERVERS, AND SOFTWARE

CHAPTER 4

NOVELL'S NETWORKING

Novell is the dominant force in local area networking, estimated to have 65 to 67% of the worldwide network operating system market. Its influence is also apparent in the features of other companies' network operating systems. Novell's mission—to accelerate the growth of network computing—is unchanged from when the company began in 1983, because Novell believes the full power of computing resources is available through networking.

Novell was the first distributed-processing vendor to support multiple platforms. It was also the first to support multiple topologies and to route between those topologies, the first to support all DOS version networks, the first to support OS/2, and the first to provide TCP/IP standard communications products for Apple. Novell was first to provide multitasking DOS for PCs, DOS that is fully executable from ROM, and DOS that uses extended memory. Novell products can also coexist with and connect to Apple, Digital Equipment Corporation (DEC), Hewlett-Packard, IBM, and UNIX environments.

Novell has assembled a wide array of networking products for a variety of computing needs, from small workgroups of desktop computers to large, businesswide environments. It's network operating system is known as NetWare. This software is optimal for managing, sharing, translating, and synchronizing information in network computing. The NetWare operating system defines the capabilities of a network server, managing the sharing of communications services, file and print services, database services, and messaging services.

Unlike many of the products in its class, NetWare doesn't run on any other operating system on the server, making NetWare more integrated and somewhat more seamless.

In 1989, Excelan, Inc., merged with Novell, bringing with it seven years of open systems experience in data communications protocols. These added capabilities have led to Netware's integration of several protocol standards, including Apple's *AppleTalk File Protocol* (AFP), Sun Microsystems' UNIX-based *Network File System* (NFS), and open standards including TCP/IP and OSI. When integrated with the NetWare network operating system, such protocols are the key to seamless, high-speed communications among dissimilar computers.

Desktop systems products are another important aspect of Novell's overall strategic plan. The merger of Novell and Digital Research in 1991 demonstrates Novell's commitment to providing client operating system software that's tightly integrated with network services, such as network management. The resulting product, *DR DOS*, has already set a high standard for enhanced DOS capabilities.

Also in 1991, Novell entered into a joint venture with AT&T's UNIX System Laboratories to form UNIVEL. In 1992 Univel introduced the first version of the *UniWare* operating system, a 32-bit general-purpose UNIX operating system.

In 1992 Novell acquired Annatek Systems, Inc., improving software management and distribution.

In 1993 Novell's acquired UNIX System Laboratories (USL). USL developed the *UNIX System V* operating system, the *TUXEDO* enterprise transaction processing system, and a C++ programming system. This acquisition gave Novell a proven and reliable UNIX application server.

Novell also acquired Software Transformation, Inc (STI), and Serius Corporation in 1993. These companies provided Novell with many benefits offering its customers the development of cross-platform network applications. Fluent, Inc. was also acquired in 1993, bringing full-motion video to enterprise computing.

The year 1994 brought WordPerfect Corporation and Borland's Quattro Pro business unit to Novell.

Open and Integrated Computing

As an open systems company, Novell is dedicated to standards. The *Novell Environment* is the foundation, or infrastructure, on which Novell products are built. The Novell Environment represents Novell's approach to providing network services for application integration in a distributed multivendor environment. The Novell Environment delivers a unified open-software solution that allows new and existing applications to share information and system resources regardless of the applications involved, where they reside, or the vendor platforms.

Working with other architectures defined for distributed network applications, such as IBM's System Application Architecture (SAA), Hewlett-Packard's New Wave Office, and DEC's Network Application Support (NAS), Novell's architecture for distributed network services allows products and applications from several vendors to be integrated into a network computing system.

In the Novell Environment, applications can run either on the user's workstation (the client) or on a server—client applications require user interaction, while server applications run unattended.

A distributed network operating system preserves the user-friendly off-the-shelf applications developed for client systems. It also can preserve applications for a minicomputer or mainframe by downsizing them onto distributed microcomputers.

As a specialized distributed network operating system, NetWare provides services for applications that run on clients as well as services for applications that run on servers.

The network services offered in the Novell Environment can either all run in one processor on NetWare or be distributed across a LAN or wide-area network. Each of these services can be shared by applications and other services—multiple iterations of any service can also be available for sharing.

The Novell environment is an open architecture that supports the standard protocols concurrently. In addition to supporting standard protocols, it supports native file standards, allowing client applications to share a file without partitioning the disk. As an open architecture that supports network management standards the Novell environment allows distributed environments to be managed and controlled centrally.

Performance

At the highest level, NetWare operating systems can provide network services that make NetWare server a better-performing server than those that are host-based. General-purpose operating systems on host-based servers are designed to provide a general-purpose environment for many tasks, and they are usually not optimized for network activity.

Several factors are responsible for NetWare's superior performance.

- *A multitasking kernel*—The NetWare kernel is multithreaded as well as multitasking, allowing the operating system to provide true multiuser capabilities at the server and ensuring good performance under heavy workloads.

- *Elevator seeking*—NetWare's separate disk-read process is responsible for reading data from the server's hard disks and placing it in cache buffers. Incoming read requests are prioritized based on the drive's current head position. This technique, called *elevator seeking*, takes advantage of head movement and results in significantly higher disk throughput under heavy loads.

- *Disk caching*—NetWare stores frequently read files in cache memory at the server, where they can be read more quickly than if they were on the server disk. This process reads information from the disk in large sections instead of reading only requested information, storing the data in memory in anticipation of future requests. minimizing the number of times the physical disk must be accessed.

- *Background writes*—Disk writes are handled by a separate disk-write request in NetWare. Separating this process from disk reading allows disk writing to become a background task that executes during lulls in network activity.

- *Overlapped seeks*—If a NetWare server has several hard-disk channels, using overlapped seeks allows several disks, one per channel, to be accessed simultaneously instead of one at a time. Independently controlling disk drives in this fashion prevents one disk from being idle while NetWare gets information from another.

- *Indexed file allocation tables (Turbo FATs)*—The NetWare file system uses FATs to locate data on the network hard disks. When large files (bigger than 2 MB) are stored on the server, NetWare indexes the FAT to allow fast searches and, in turn, faster disk reads.

Reliability

NetWare products contain a variety of features that ensure system reliability and data integrity. The following features protect everything from the storage medium to critical application files:

- *Read-after-write verification*—Every write to the disk is reread and verified as readable.

- *Duplication of directories*—NetWare maintains a duplicate of the root directory structure. If the directory structure is corrupted, the backup ensures that users still have access to network data.

- *Duplication of FAT*—NetWare maintains a duplicate of the FAT, preventing contamination of the table from rendering an entire disk useless.

- *Hot fix*—This feature detects and corrects disk media defects on the fly.

- *System fault tolerance (SFT)*—SFT provides several reliability features, including *disk mirroring*, *disk duplexing*, and the *Transaction Tracking System (TTS)*.

With *disk mirroring*, two duplicate hard disks are supported by one controller. Every time the file server writes to the primary disk, it performs the same write function to the secondary disk. If the primary hard disk should fail, the secondary disk takes its place.

Disk duplexing is similar to disk mirroring except that duplicate hard-disk controller cards are present. Should the primary controller fail, the secondary controller card takes over.

The *TTS* is designed to maintain the integrity of multiuser databases. The system views each change in a database as a transaction that is either complete or incomplete. If a user is in the middle of a database transaction when the system fails, the TTS rolls the database back to the point just before the transaction began. This action is known as *automatic rollback*. The TTS also has a roll-forward recovery, keeping a complete log of all transactions to ensure that everything can be recovered in the event of total system failure.

Security

Security is built into NetWare operating systems at the most basic levels, rather than being added on as an application of a workstation operating system. Because NetWare uses a specialized file structure, users can't access network files through DOS, OS/2, UNIX, or any other operating system, even if they have physical access to the server.

NetWare products provide security mechanisms at the following levels:

- Account security
- Password security
- Directory security
- File security
- Internetwork security

In 1983, Novell introduced to the LAN market the concepts of usernames, user profiles, and passwords.

User profiles list the resources to which each user account has access and the rights it has while using that resource. Network supervisors can specify the date, time, and location that a user can use to log into the network. Intruder detection and lockout features notify supervisors of any unauthorized access attempts.

Passwords are stored in encrypted format on the network hard disk, and supervisors can require users to change passwords at specified times. Because of the encryption, not even the supervisor knows the user's password. The password keys are encrypted on the cable as they pass from the workstation to the server, preventing unauthorized cable taps from revealing passwords.

When a NetWare server is run in nondedicated mode, the user—although using the server as a workstation—must log into the network. As a result, any access to data, through an application or otherwise, is granted only through NetWare security.

NetWare doesn't discriminate against workstation operating systems where security is concerned. DOS, Windows, OS/2, Macintosh, and UNIX workstations are treated equally, and all security features apply to all supported workstation operating systems.

Standards Support

The NetWare operating system's support of industry standards allows users to easily change over to future technology without making current computing systems obsolete. Standards support also enables interoperability between computing systems, increasing the efficiency and value of the network.

Network computing standards fall into two categories: *application standards* and *communications protocol standards*.

Application Standards

In the past, most networking applications were workstation-based with all application processing taking place in the workstation. Applications of this type rely on the standards for file service established by IBM in the DOS, Windows, and OS/2 environments; those established by Apple for the Macintosh environment; and the de facto standards for remote file service established by Sun Microsystems in the UNIX environment. To network these different environments effectively, NetWare supports the application standards in each.

To allow distributed applications in a multivendor environment, NetWare also supports a variety of server and client (workstation) operating systems. These include DOS, Windows, OS/2, the Macintosh operating system, and UNIX original equipment manufacturer's (OEMs) as client platforms and OS/2, UNIX, VMS, and other operating systems as server platforms.

Regardless of which server and client operating systems are used, client-server applications use *interprocess communications protocols* (IPCs) to establish a network link between the client and the server. NetWare supports multiple-IPC mechanisms, including Novell's *NetWare Sequenced Packet Exchange* (SPX), IBM's *NetBIOS* and *Advanced Program-to-Program Communications* (APPC), Microsoft's *Named Pipes*, AT&T's *Transport Level Interface* (TLI), and BSD *Sockets*.

Communications Protocol Standards

Network operating systems rely on communications protocols to provide a network computing environment. Each of the three types of network protocols—media, transport, and client-server—provide a specific service, allowing users to access shared resources.

Media protocols determine the type of physical connection used on a network. (NetWare supports more than 100 network adapters.) Once a hardware connection has been established between nodes on a network, a transport protocol is needed to provide the next level of network services. A *transport protocol*, as its name implies, allows packets of data to be moved from node to node. NetWare supports Novell's IPX/SPX (Internet Packet Exchange/Sequential Packet Exchange), Apple's AppleTalk, standard TCP/IP, and standard OSI transport protocols.

When both the hardware connection and the transport services are in place, a *client-server protocol* is needed before a user can access network services. This protocol dictates the manner in which a workstation requests information and services from a server. In turn, the same protocol dictates the manner in which the server replies to that request.

These three protocols work together to allow users to request network data and services from specific network nodes, such as servers. A user requesting to open a file, for example, will usually make that request through an application. The network software running on the workstation takes the application's request and formats it according to the rules of a client-server protocol. The request is then routed to the server by a transport mechanism, which uses the connection provided by the network media.

At the server, the software can understand the request because it supports the same client-server protocol. It processes the request, formats the reply according to the client-server protocol, and routes the reply back to the workstation through the transport protocol, which uses the connection provided by the media protocol.

Instead of proposing that all types of networks use the same protocols, Novell designed NetWare products that support several protocol standards. Allowing a network operating system to integrate multiple standards in a single network provides a transition path for future standards, such as OSI, as they emerge.

NetWare Operating Systems

NetWare operating systems provide solutions for a variety of needs. The product line is stratified according to the features and functionality each NetWare product offers.

Personal NetWare is a simple and inexpensive peer-to-peer network operating system for 2 to 50 users who require basic network features and functions. (Typical small businesses using peer-to-peer networks have 10 or fewer users.) Designed for first-time PC network users, Personal NetWare allows users to set up a network and begin sharing resources such as applications, files, and printers.

NetWare 3.12 is suitable for small to medium-size businesses and work-groups within large companies, accommodating both small networks with nondedicated server operation and medium-size departmental networks with dedicated servers. Good performance, internetworking support (both local and remote), and comprehensive management tools make it suitable for advanced networks as well. Replacing version 3.11 version 3.12 increased performance and includes several new features such as e a 5-user NetWare for Macintosh and a basic message handling service (MHS).

For extra fault tolerance there is NetWare 3.11 SFT III, based on NetWare 3.11. System fault tolerance level three has been added, which enables a network to incorporate a backup server. If the main server should fail, the backup server automatically takes over, and downtime due to server failure is virtually eliminated.

Netware 4.02 is the premier network operating system. Version 4.02 has all the capabilities of NetWare 3.12, and more. It provides users with instant and transparent access to networkwide information. It includes NetWare Directory Services, security enhancements, wide area networking improvements, and enhanced administration and management tools.

Network services form the core of a network computing system. They provide everything from the most basic network services, such as file and record locking, to complex services such as SQL queries to a shared database.

NetWare 3.11 SFT III and NetWare 3.12 contain a new set of programming interfaces and tools for network services. With these products, client-server applications run as *NetWare Loadable Modules* (NLMs), providing the additional power needed to support heavily used network services in the server.

NLM applications have full access to NetWare security. The NLM interface provides a standard programming environment, making the applications as easy to develop and test as DOS applications. Because of the modular architecture in NetWare 3.11 SFT III and NetWare 3.12, NLMs can also be loaded and linked to the operating system without bringing down the server.

Workstation Connectivity

Several Novell products give Macintosh, OS/2, and UNIX workstations access to NetWare file and print services.

NetWare for Macintosh 3.0 is server and client software that provides NetWare file, print, and routing services to Macintosh workstations. Macintosh support in NetWare 3.11 is implemented using NLMs, giving users the full power of Novell's 32-bit operating system.

The NetWare Requestor for OS/2 lets OS/2 workstations operate within a NetWare network, while NetWare NFS gives UNIX workstations transparent access to the NetWare operating system. NetWare NFS consists of several NLMs that add NFS server capability to the NetWare server. Once this product is installed, workstations with NFS client services can share files with other NetWare clients (such as DOS, Macintosh, and OS/2 workstations) and print to NetWare printers.

Database Services

Database services are an essential part of Novell's network computing solution. Novell's core database services are the foundation for running business-critical applications such as spreadsheets, accounting packages, and a variety of other custom applications.

NetWare database services allow developers to write customized client-server applications without having to write a record manager or relational database engine. Using these services, developers can easily incorporate the performance, reliability, and functionality of NetWare into their applications, creating an efficient client-server data management system. Novell supplies support for client-server applications with two products: NetWare Btrieve and NetWare SQL.

NetWare Btrieve is a server-based key-indexed record manager that allows high-performance data handling. This de facto LAN record management system has been the database of choice for many vertical application developers.

NetWare SQL provides direct access to Btrieve-based data from multiple desktop platforms and applications. Because NetWare SQL uses Btrieve as its underlying record manager, applications written to either product can share data with each other. Novell also provides toolkits for both Btrieve and SQL.

Messaging Services

The past few years have seen a great deal of growth in the use of electronic messaging, with the network server as the accepted provider of messaging services. Novell's goal is to provide a reliable messaging service that ensures corporate wide communications from a broad range of current and evolving industry standard messaging solutions.

NetWare messaging services are provided by NetWare MHS (message handling service) and NetWare Messaging CONNECT.

NetWare MHS is a messaging engine that allows communication between front-end applications so they can share data and coordinate activities over local- and wide-area networks. NetWare MHS takes advantage of *store-and-forward technology* to improve message delivery between applications or processes running on a network. This technology also reduces communication costs by letting users specify that a message be transmitted at the most cost-effective time. Costs are incurred only for the time it takes to actually deliver the message, not for keeping the communication lines open while waiting for messages. NetWare MHS runs automatically on an unattended PC and uses network resources only when collecting or delivering messages.

Since no single mail system spans all platforms, NetWare MHS is capable of integrating dissimilar mail systems over the corporate backbone to ensure corporate wide mail availability. NetWare MHS is supported by more than 600 registered developers of applications, gateways, and utilities. MHS gateways from third parties provide connectivity to X.400, IBM's PROFS, UNIX systems, DEC's All-in-1, VMSmail, MCI Mail, Western Union's Easylink, telex, fax machines, and voice-mail systems.

Communication Services

Novell offers a comprehensive set of communications products that are fully integrated with the NetWare environment. NetWare Communication Services are a family of Novell products that give users access to host resources and wide-area networks. It's the first completely integrated LAN communications system designed to support any combination of LAN-to-host, LAN-to-LAN, or remote LAN access services.

NetWare Communication Services are implemented as NLMs and run on top of NetWare. They can be configured to run alongside file, print, or any other NLM-based services on a single server, or they can be installed with NetWare Runtime on a server dedicated to communications services.

NetWare Communication Services products give users complete hardware independence. They are designed to support the most popular desktop operating systems, including DOS, Windows, Macintosh, OS/2, and UNIX workstations. In addition, users can access host resources and wide-area networks through a variety of external connections, including SDLC, Token Ring, X.25, ISDN, T1, and asynchronous lines.

Novell's communications products provide:

- LAN-to-IBM host connectivity
- Dial-in/dial-out connectivity
- Communications services management

LAN-to-IBM Host

Novell has developed NetWare for SAA to satisfy its customers' needs to access IBM mainframes and AS/400 minicomputers, both of which store data and run mission-critical applications.

NetWare for SAA, a set of NLMs built on NetWare and the NetWare Communication Services platform, gives workstations on NetWare LANs comprehensive IBM and AS/400 host connectivity. It integrates with and uses NetWare's performance, flexibility, security, name services, management, and administration features. NetWare for SAA can support up to 508 concurrent host sessions and can connect to multiple IBM hosts from a single server, providing service on multiple Token Ring, SDLC, or QLLC/X.25 host data links simultaneously, and it supports the five most popular desktop operating systems— DOS, Windows, Macintosh, OS/2, and UNIX.

NetWare for SAA supports IBM's AS/400 PC support utility, allowing NetWare clients to access AS/400 applications transparently. It also supports IBM's NetView management system, with a *RUNCMD interface* that enables the host computer to control NetWare servers—loading and unloading NLMs, for example—directly from the host. This is in addition to the complete NetView monitoring capability already provided. NetWare for SAA can also be managed remotely from anywhere on the network with Novell's Windows-based NetWare Communication Services Manager.

NetWare 3270 LAN Workstation for DOS gives network users access to SNA host computers through NetWare for SAA. The NetWare 3270 Vector Graphics Option works with LAN Workstation for DOS to give DOS workstation users on a LAN access to IBM mainframe graphics applications. NetWare 3270 LAN Workstation for Macintosh and NetWare 3270 LAN Workstation for Windows give Macintosh and Window users access to SNA hosts through NetWare for SAA. In addition, a wide variety of third-party emulators are available for Windows, Macintosh, OS/2, and UNIX clients.

Dial-In/Dial-Out

Remote access is becoming a necessary consideration in LAN development. More and more businesses and individuals want the flexibility of dialing into networks from remote locations and sharing resources for dialing out of the LAN. Novell has three dial-in/dial-out products: NetWare Asynchronous Communication Services (NACS), NetWare Access Server, and NetWare Asynchronous Remote Router.

NACS 3.0, an NLM built on NetWare 3.11 and the NetWare Communication Services Platform, allows users to dial out of the LAN through a modem pool. Users can also share access to other asynchronous services, including locally connected minicomputers and X.25 networks. Remote users can also dial into an NACS server and access individual workstations on a LAN. The NACS can be managed remotely by Novell's NetWare Communication Services Manager from anywhere on the network.

The *NetWare Access Server* enables as many as 16 remote users of DOS and Macintosh workstations and ASCII terminals to dial into and access all the resources available on a NetWare LAN, including files, databases, application software, electronic mail, and host services provided by SNA mainframes and UNIX minicomputers. Users can also connect to the NetWare Access Server over the LAN; meaning Macintosh users can run both DOS applications (via the Access Server) and Macintosh applications simultaneously on their workstations. It also allows DOS users to use the NetWare Access Server as an application server.

The *Asynchronous Remote Router*, a low-speed wide-area networking option that connects two networks, provides a transparent link enabling users to access data and services on remote networks as if the data and services were available locally. It provides connections with other remote networks at speeds up to 19.2 Kbps.

Communication Services Management

The NetWare Communication Services Manager is a Windows-based application that provides extensive network management capabilities. NetWare Communication Services—including NetWare for SAA host services and NACS asynchronous and X.25 services—can be configured, monitored, and maintained remotely from anywhere on a network. It provides a comprehensive set of network management tools for fault, performance, and configuration management.

Internetworking

Novell's internetworking products tie local NetWare networks into wide-area networks, helping customers as their networks grow and computing resources expand. Novell offers three such products: NetWare Link/64, NetWare Link/T1, and NetWare MultiProtocol Router.

NetWare Link/64 and *Link/T1* let customers interconnect geographically remote NetWare networks. NetWare Link/64 is for customers who need interconnect capabilities at speeds of 9600 bps to 64 Kbps. NetWare Link/T1 is for those who need speeds up to 2.084 Mbps.

The NetWare MultiProtocol Router allows customers to connect an Intel 80386- or 80486-based system into a multiprotocol router supporting IPX, IP, and AppleTalk. It connects Ethernet, Token Ring, LocalTalk, and ARCnet networks in any combination and provides transparent access to the servers, printers, and mail systems. Users can remove the routing function from the file-server processor to improve server performance.

Network Connectivity Options

Novell offers users TCP/IP connectivity for DOS, Windows, OS/2, and Macintosh users with its LAN Workplace products. With these products, users can access NetWare servers and TCP/IP host resources simultaneously.

NetWare for VMS is a client-server application that enables a DEC VAX/VMS system to function as a NetWare file and print server that enables

DOS, Windows, and OS/2 users to transparently share data, applications, and printer services with VAX terminals users.

NetWare FTAM is an OSI server that allows a variety of FTAM clients to access the NetWare file system. This standard protocol-based product is a key to enabling multivendor interoperability with NetWare systems. NetWare FTAM implements all seven layers of the OSI protocol suite and enables file transfer between NetWare and any other complementary OSI system, regardless of the hardware or software platform being used. In addition, it allows FTAM clients to send files to NetWare print queues.

NetWare Name Service

NetWare Name Service (NNS) is available separately and runs on NetWare 3.12. This naming service enables NetWare users to access resources on multiple servers with a single login. For network supervisors, NNS simplifies the task of maintaining a consistent user environment. For network users, NNS offers transparent access to the computing resources they need, no matter where those services are located on the network.

NNS lets network supervisors define a group of servers, called a *domain*. Rather than logging into a single server, these users log into the domain. Network supervisors manage all servers in the domain from their own workstations. Any changes they make to the user environment are automatically distributed to every server in the domain.

Print Services

Print services in NetWare are provided through a print-server application that is bundled with the operating system. The NetWare print server allows users to share as many as 16 printers per print server on the network, with the potential for multiple print servers on a single network. Printers can be attached to either the server or any workstation on the network. Printers attached to the server are managed by the print-server software, while those attached to workstations are managed by *terminate-and-stay-resident* (TSR) software that runs on the workstations.

Personal NetWare Features

As mentioned earlier, Personal NetWare is a peer-to-peer network for small businesses or workgroups. Each PC on the network can be configured as a client, a server, or both. A *server* is a PC that shares resources (up to 50) with other PCs on the network.

Personal NetWare is easier to administer than the other peer-to-peer networks on the market offers the following administrative features:

- Supervisors can control access to shared resources by assigning up to three definable access rights.
- Regardless of the number of servers the user needs to access, only one account per user is required.
- The entire network can be managed from any PC on the network.
- Shared resources can be moved without affecting users' access to the resources.

Personal NetWare doesn't have the same reliability features as other NetWare products regarding SFT Levels 1 and 2. It does, however, have the following features that maintain operation:

- *Auto-reconnect* automatically restores network connections after a power failure or surge.
- Distributed and synchronized user accounts allow the network to operate even if only one server is functional. If users' accounts have been administered when a portion of the network goes down, the user account databases are resynchronized when that portion becomes operational.
- A network connection utility verifies that network adapters, cabling, and IPX software are installed correctly and are operational during installation.

Personal NetWare and standard NetWare can coexist on the same network. A workstation can be part of both networks accessing NetWare file servers as well as the resources of other workstations on the Personal NetWare network.

NetWare 2.2 Features

NetWare 2.2 is an older Novell product, but it is still available. NetWare 2.2 consolidates *entry level systems* (ELS) NetWare Levels I and II, Advanced NetWare, and SFT NetWare into a single networking product stratified by the number of users it supports (between 5 and 100). It has the following features:

- SFT Levels I and II.

- Disk analysis is done by a process called *ZTEST*, which verifies the media of certain areas on the hard disk that are critical to the operating system.

- It is media-independent, allowing network supervisors to integrate different and often incompatible types of networking hardware within a single network. NetWare 2.2 provides an internal router that allows the server to connect up to four different networks, making them appear as one logical network.

- It includes the NetWare DOS *Open Data-Link Interface* (ODI) client drivers, which support multiple protocols (such as IPX and TCP/IP) through a single network adapter. User workstations can communicate with servers using different protocols through a single network station adapter. Previously, such functionality required multiple adapters in the workstation. This solution saves both money and slots in the DOS workstation.

NetWare 3.11 SFT III Features

NetWare 3.11 SFT III has the following features:

- Full 32-bit operating system takes advantage of the 80386, 80486 and Pentium microprocessors.

- It is 80486-aware. When this product is installed in a server with a 80486 microprocessor, special instructions are executed that allow it to take advantage of the 80486's features.

- NLM architecture allows additional software components to be loaded and unloaded while the server is running. NLMs include drivers, utilities, and applications.
- It supports up to 4 gigabytes (Gb) of RAM, up to 32 TB (terabytes) of disk storage, and up to 64 volumes per server.
- Files can be up to 4 Gb and can span multiple physical drives, enabling the server to store large databases and applications that once could be stored only on mainframes and minicomputers.
- Network volumes and files can span up to 1024 physical disk drives.
- It includes NetWare *Remote Management Facility* (RMF), enabling network supervisors to manage remote servers from their own workstations over LAN connections or phone lines.
- Includes SFT Level III.

NetWare 3.12 Features

Version 3.21 has the same features as NetWare 3.11 SFT III, excluding SFT Level three, but it has increased performance and better message system handling.

NetWare 4.1

NetWare 4.1 is Novell's most advanced network operating system. It allows the user to see an entire multiserver network as a single integrated system. It builds on NetWare 3.12 by adding the following features:

- NetWare directory services
- New administrative tools
- New security features
- Multiple language capability
- Increased WAN performance

CHAPTER 5

MICROSOFT'S NETWORKING

Microsoft has three network operating systems:

- LAN Manager
- Windows NT
- Windows for Workgroups

LAN Manager

LAN Manager was Microsoft's first premier client-server platform. It was designed to provide the best possible performance for network processing in a client-server environment.

In its earlier versions, LAN Manager required the OS/2 operating system on its file server. Since then, Microsoft has licensed LAN Manager to other vendors, including AT&T/NCR, DEC, Hewlett-Packard, SCO, and others. Because these companies have developed their own versions of LAN Manager, the product no longer depends on having OS/2 running on the file server, making it more operating system-independent in that it can run on OS/2, UNIX, and VMS.

LAN Manager's architecture has two primary benefits: network-optimized system code is provided to handle network requests, and the operating system provides mainframe-style multitasking support to protect data, processes, and the server itself from destructive incompatibilities. All LAN Manager implementations—OS/2, UNIX, and VMS—offer the same powerful combination using multitasking operating systems compatible with industry standards.

Safeguards for Multitasking

LAN Manager approaches client-server computing using two very important safeguards—memory protection and preemptive scheduling. All major mainframe and minicomputer systems use multitasking architectures that incorporate these safeguards. Without this additional protection to prevent applications from interfering with one another, problems within one application—or the interaction of two otherwise well-behaved applications—could not only disrupt an application's normal operation, but could corrupt valuable data as well. Some situations could even cause the entire server to crash.

Memory Protection

Microsoft understands that the key to safe multitasking is memory protection at the hardware level. Running multiple applications simultaneously requires that memory be protected so one program can't accidentally overwrite the code and data of another.

LAN Manager uses the protected mode of the *80x86 microprocessor* to maintain system integrity for multitasking. If one program attempts to overwrite the code or data of another, the microprocessor causes the system to terminate the guilty program.

Memory protection saves resources and money because one server can be used for a variety of purposes. One example is a server that provides file-server functions and runs a client-server database and communication services.

Preemptive Scheduling

With applications and processes vying for the server's CPU time, it's important that the operating system provide a reliable method of applications scheduling. LAN Manager approaches this problem with a mechanism known as *preemptive scheduling*. Preemptive scheduling allows the system scheduler or dispatcher to remove an application from the CPU and assign the CPU to another application according to a dynamic multilevel priority scheme.

This approach offers three advantages. First, it ensures a fair division of CPU time among all the processes running on the system. Second, because the decision to relinquish control of the CPU is made at the operating-system level rather than at the application level, the system is protected from crashing if one process gets stuck in a loop. Finally, this approach frees developers from having to worry about sharing CPU time—they can write each application as if it were the only one running on the system and let the operating system manage CPU access.

Client-Server Applications

Microsoft LAN Manager's open architecture supports thousands of network applications written for MS-DOS and the NetBIOS protocol. It is also the platform for more than 200 applications designed specifically for client-server computing. These programs include powerful database, spreadsheet, accounting, and communications applications for a client-server network.

Some of these programs designed for client-server networking include Microsoft SQL Server, DCA/Microsoft Communications Saver, LAN Manager for MS-DOS and OS/2 Clients, and LAN Manager for Macintosh.

Microsoft SQL Server

Microsoft SQL Server brings multiuser database management services to today's corporate networks, offering a strong platform for the delivery of mission-critical applications. In addition to providing centralized control, integrity, and security of data, it enables a wide range of client applications and tools to share information safely and effectively.

Open Data Services is a new feature of Microsoft SQL Server. It ties clients and servers into corporate data sources, providing critical links with enterprise information systems. The services offer a programmable platform for server applications that access any data source, and since SQL Server is tightly integrated with Windows-based clients, users of this system can access and work with strategic corporate information.

Microsoft SQL Server is supported by more than 125 front-end tools including the leading spreadsheets, databases, development tools, and computer languages. You can select from such corporate standards as Paradox, dBASE IV, DataEase, Microsoft Excel, and Lotus 1-2-3. To create custom client-server applications for the Microsoft Windows operating system, next-generation tools such as PowerBuilder, Object/1, and the Microsoft Visual Basic programming system can be used.

DCA/Microsoft Communications Server

DCA/Microsoft Communications Server (Comm Server) provides an easy and flexible way to create links between LANs and IBM SNA networks. Comm Server allows Windows-, DOS-, and OS/2-based clients on a LAN to communicate with computers that use IBM SNA protocols. Its architecture lets users choose either standard, full-screen 3270 terminal emulators or leading graphical (Windows or Presentation Manager) emulators from companies such as DCA, Wall Data, Software Associates, and Eicon Technology. Since Comm Server handles most of the protocol requirements for host connectivity, memory demands on client PCs are low.

Using CommServer, windows users enjoy the benefits of many LAN Manager features, including:

- Direct login to the network from the Windows environment.

- Persistent network connections or automatic reconnect if the user is accidentally disconnected. Network connections are automatically reestablished when users log into the network or after a connection is lost.

- Remote access through the Windows environment over a modem to servers, using the *LAN Manager Remote Access Service* as a gateway.

- Dual redirection for connecting to LAN Manager or NetWare servers through the Windows environment. Users can easily access LAN Manager and NetWare servers simultaneously with the Windows File Manager interface.

LAN Manager for MS-DOS and OS/2 Clients

In addition to support for Windows-based clients, LAN Manager supports the use of MS-DOS- and OS/2-based clients. Using MS-DOS and OS/2, users can choose how they wish to access the network functions—either through the MS-DOS or OS/2 command line or through a subset of the LAN Manager administrator's full-screen window-oriented user interface. This graphical interface offers drop-down menus, dialog boxes, and mouse support for point-and-click control. Users can browse through the network, find available servers, view resources, and control their own printing. Like the administrator's interface, the MS-DOS and OS/2 LAN Manager client interfaces are consistent with those of Microsoft Windows.

The auto-reconnect feature is also available for MS-DOS and OS/2 clients.

LAN Manager for Macintosh

LAN Manager also supports Macintosh clients with the *Services for Macintosh* program. This option for LAN Manager data-based servers ties Macintosh workstations to the LAN Manager network and lets Macintosh and PC users share files and printers using their workstations' own standard interfaces.

As on Apple networks, the standard AppleTalk and Macintosh Chooser and Finder are used for access. For example, a Macintosh can connect to files on a LAN Manager server via the Chooser, while a PC user in the Windows environment can connect to the same files via File Manager.

Other features of the LAN Manager Services for Macintosh include:

- *Automatic file-name conversion*—Macintosh users can create files with long file names, while PC users see the same files with standard eight-character-dot-three-character FAT file names. Files are converted between AFP, FAT, and high-performance file system formats as required. Macintosh users can also access a PC-created data file as if it had been created by another Macintosh user. For example, by double-clicking on a Microsoft Excel spreadsheet data-file icon from a file created on a PC, a Macintosh user can launch Excel and load the file.

- *Integrated administration*—LAN Manager Services for Macintosh is fully integrated into the LAN Manager data-based server. PC and Macintosh users share a common user account database and are administered using the same tools.

- *Easy installation*—A single floppy disk installs all services on a LAN Manager-based server. Macintosh software is not required on the client workstations, and additional hardware is not needed. The server setup program copies the appropriate files to the server and configures the Macintosh service automatically or according to administrator specifications.

High-Performance File Sharing

The advent of the 80386 and 80486 microprocessors gave PCs processing power equivalent to that of minicomputers, making these microprocessors the CPUs of choice for many file servers. Microsoft LAN Manager is designed to get optimal performance from these microprocessors. During installation, LAN Manager configures itself for 80286-, 80386-, and 80486-based file servers.

For maximum performance on 80386- and 80486-based file servers, LAN Manager automatically installs a high-performance 32-bit network input/output subsystem designed to provide the fastest possible file sharing within a network environment. This subsystem consists of 80386- and 80486-specific kernel extensions and an 80386 version of the OS/2-based high-performance file system, called *HPFS386*. HPFS386 provides fast access to large disk volumes and high performance in a server environment in which many files may be open simultaneously. Features of the HPFS386 include support of extended file attributes, long file names (up to 254 characters), and enhanced access and audit control. At its highest level, HPFS386 includes highly contiguous file allocation and caching of directories, data, and file-system structures for fast lookup in large directories with minimal disk access.

Printer and Peripheral Sharing

LAN Manager provides several services for controlling and managing network printers and other shared peripherals.

Administrators can easily manage multiple print priorities using LAN Manager. Several print queues can feed the same printer, and one queue can feed multiple printers. For example, two queues could be mapped to a group of printers, each with a different priority. One queue could be designated for short letters and the other for long mailing-list printouts. This procedure would ensure that print jobs for letters took priority over other jobs.

Print jobs can also be routed to the first available printer or to a specially configured printer—one with special paper or a specific font cartridge, for example. Printing can also be designated for a specific time of day, such as after peak-use hours.

Users can be notified of printing status with messages such as "Your job is finished" or "Printer out of paper."

Ultimately, administrators have ultimate control over the configuration and status of printers, queues, and individual print jobs. They can view local or remote print queues and delete, pause, continue, reprioritize, and restart them. Printing processors, such as PostScript interpreters and graphics print programs, can be installed for additional print-processing capabilities. For security purposes, access permission to printers can be controlled in the same way as those used for file access, and users can view and control their own print jobs.

The UNIX Connection

Microsoft extends client-server computing into multivendor environments with *Microsoft LAN Manager for UNIX Systems*. This is a portable adaptation of Microsoft's high-performance full-featured LAN software that allows machines based on UNIX and other operating systems, such as DEC's VMS, to act as servers for PC client applications running under Windows, MS-DOS, and OS/2.

Designed specifically for client-server computing, LAN Manager for UNIX Systems combines the best qualities of stand-alone PCs (ease of use, favorable price/performance ratios) with the traditional strengths of minicomputers (security, management, and administration).

LAN Manager for UNIX Systems allows users to share applications, data, and resources from OS/2, UNIX, and VMS servers without having to learn a variety of server operating commands. It shares common client software, interfaces, and administration commands with all other LAN Manager implementations meaning that even with a variety of servers running under OS/2, UNIX, and VMS, users can work with familiar front-end spreadsheet and database systems without knowing which operating system is on the server.

With topology and transport independence, LAN Manager for UNIX Systems gives the system integrator the freedom to choose from Token Ring or Ethernet, TCP/IP, NetBEUI, OSI TP4, or even more than one network interface card and network transport within a single system. Software developers can take advantage of a robust set of common LAN Manager application programming interfaces (APIs) to develop applications that are compatible with all LAN Manager implementations. In addition, LAN Manager for UNIX Systems provides for some advanced UNIX features such as the ability to act as a bridge to the NFS, Remote File System, and Andrew File System.

LAN Manager for UNIX Systems provides the same performance, administration, and security features as the LAN Manager products for OS/2 and the forthcoming Windows NT. It is offered by AT&T/NCR, Data General,

Groupe Bull, Hewlett-Packard, ICL, Olivetti, SCO, Siemens-Nixdorf A/G, Unisys, and other leading vendors.

The DEC Connection

LAN Manager technology is a key component of DEC's Pathworks networking product line, allowing PC users to connect to a VAX server. DEC will soon offer full support for LAN Manager APIs on Pathworks for OS/2, VMS, and Ultrix servers.

Wide-Area Networks

In the 1990s we have seen a trend toward large, integrated, multivendor networks, including the enterprise network and the wide-area network. Microsoft has three products that allow smooth transitions to wide-area networks: Comm Server (discussed earlier), Microsoft TCP/IP, and LAN Manager Remote Access Service.

Microsoft TCP/IP: Network Transport Protocols

Microsoft's network strategy for LAN Manager calls for hardware-independent industry-standard protocols that allow performance and interoperability in a variety of computing environments. This strategy includes the industry-standard *NetBEUI transport protocol*. This small fast protocol is ideal for local-area connections.

For systems requiring wide-area connections, the Microsoft TCP/IP included with LAN Manager is a routable transport protocol that provides wide-area, multivendor connectivity for LAN Manager networks. PC workstations running Windows, MS-DOS, or OS/2 can seamlessly interconnect with LAN Manager implementations on OS/2, UNIX, and VMS platforms—as a result, LAN Manager LANs can be linked using standard TCP/IP routing into a single integrated wide-area network. Distant users of the network can access any of its servers and resources as easily as local users can.

LAN Manager Remote Access Service

LAN Manager Remote Access Service can be installed on any LAN Manager-based sever to give remote PC users full access to network features. The service allows home users, business travelers, and off-site administrators to access the corporate network as if they were working on-site.

With the Remote Access Service users of remote workstations running Windows, MS-DOS, or OS/2 can access LAN Manager using standard modems. For example, a sales manager working at home on a Windows-based PC can use LAN Manager Remote Access Service to check an inventory on an SQL Server database running on the network at the company's manufacturing plant. After confirming the inventory figures, the manager can send E-mail to the manufacturing manager requesting that production levels be raised to meet high sales figures.

No dedicated gateway PC or special hardware is required to install LAN Manager Remote Access Service. Once users connect to the dial-in server, they can use their remote computers in exactly the same way as locally connected PCs.

Security features are provided to ensure proper access to the LAN. LAN Manager security is fully implemented before remote users are allowed access to the network. In addition, users don't send their passwords over the telephone line during login—doing so would make the password vulnerable to wire taps. Instead, a special procedure that changes with every login is used.

If tighter security is desired, administrators have a choice of call-back options. The server can be instructed to hang up and call back either a previously established number or one supplied by the user during a connection.

Interoperability with Novell Networks

Existing Novell NetWare systems can add LAN Manager servers without losing functionality or undergoing an immediate all-or-nothing transition. Using the LAN Manager dual redirector software, Windows and MS-DOS users can access and copy files between LAN Manager and NetWare servers simultaneously. There is, however, limited communication between the NetWare and LAN Manager servers.

LAN Manager Administration Services

LAN Manager provides a comprehensive set of network management, administration, and diagnostic tools that make it easy to control and manage users, workstations, servers, applications, resources, and security. LAN Manager also features tools for distributed administration.

Centralized Administration with Domains

Managing a growing network can become a formidable task. New users must be created and given access to multiple servers and made a part of multiple user groups. Existing users are constantly changing groups, access rights, and physical locations. Traditionally, each transition task had to be performed at every server on the network, making administration difficult and time-consuming.

LAN Manager allows the LAN administrator to administer a group of servers machines, known as a *domain*, as a single entity. Domains allow administrators to control all user and group account information at one central location rather than having to run around to individual servers on the network. By doing this, administrators need only add a new user account or change membership in a user group one time, because the new account automatically becomes available to all servers in the domain. Administrators can also control, via user groups, all network resources from a central point, and users need only one password to access all the resources they have access to within a given domain. Domains also allow centralized login control, validation, and automatic tracking of logged-on users.

All servers within a domain share a common database of user and group accounts that the administrator can manipulate in one action. This database is managed by a central server, which functions as the primary domain controller. The domain controller is the primary site for the database and is where the administrator sends updates. An automatic copying mechanism replicates the accounts database and all subsequent changes to the other servers in the domain, enabling each server to respond to new sessions using purely local, but up-to-date, information.

The domain system's database is also the basis for a login validation system, validating users and passwords at login time and maintaining a central list of logged-in users. By doing this, the administrator can determine which users are logged into a domain without checking each server for active sessions. The centralized login service also has a mechanism for reporting login information to the user, including the last login time and the number of bad password attempts since the last successful login. This feature enhances security by helping to detect unauthorized access attempts.

Delegating Tasks

LAN Manager allows the administrator to delegate various tasks or administrative functions to assistant administrators, known as *operators*. This enables administrators to delegate a safe subset of administrative privileges without creating a security risk.

Four types of network operators can be defined:

1. *Accounts operators* manage user and group accounts.
2. *Print operators* manage printers and print queues.
3. *Communications operators* manage communications devices and queues.
4. *Server operators* administer the server, manage sessions, and send messages to users.

Disk and file operators aren't necessary because this administrative function can be delegated using the *change permissions resource access control*, which grants a user full administrator file privileges for a given file, directory, or disk drive.

Replicator Service

LAN Manager provides a replicator service that lets the administrator selectively copy a set of files stored on one server to other servers on the network. Replication can be used to distribute any administrative or application-related files, such as network utilities, application executables, application or system configuration profiles, corporate phone lists, or style sheets, macros, templates, and dictionaries.

This service could be used to replicate a network utility automatically to a selected group of servers. Whenever the utility is updated on the export server, the files are automatically copied to the import servers. The LAN administrator, therefore, needs to update files in only one place.

Remote Administration

LAN Manager's remote administration allows a network administrator to control any LAN Manager-based server from any workstation on the network or, with Remote Access Service, over a telephone line. Remote administration provides full administrative functionality, as though an administrator were working at the server console. As a security feature, an audit record is generated whenever a remote administration connection is established.

Network Statistics, Error Logging, and Alerting

The LAN Manager administration facilities provide valuable information to help the administrator configure, monitor, and troubleshoot the network more effectively. LAN Manager maintains a complete set of in-memory statistics and a disk-based error log that track all network activity—information that can be very useful in diagnosing and improving network performance.

Detailed informative messages are sent to designated users or administrators when events of interest occur. Alerts, such as "Printer out of paper" or "Disk is full," are sent in cases of printer or disk problems. When alerts are sent, all pertinent data is recorded, including the server name, date and time of the alert, a description of the problem, and the recommended action.

NetView

IBM's de facto standard for SNA management is NetView. LAN Manager can connect to NetView using the DCA/Microsoft Communications Server.

Security

LAN Manager allows administrators to control and monitor access to network data and services at each of the network components.

User Login

The LAN Manager security system provides a centralized login service that works with the database maintained by the domain system. This service validates usernames and passwords at login time.

Account Control

The user account subsystem gives network administrators a wide range of security mechanisms that can be used to control and manage user access to the network. They include:

- *Valid login times*—Permitted login times can be specified in weekly intervals, such as every Monday, Wednesday, and Friday between 9 a.m. and 7 p.m.
- *Valid workstations*—By default, a user can log in from any workstation on the network. The administrator can, however, restrict a user to a limited number of workstations.
- *Account expiration date*—Individual accounts can be set to expire on specific dates. This is useful for temporary employees and in classroom environments.

Forced Logout or Grace Period

When a user's account expires or the login time limit is reached, the system can either be set to force the user to log out immediately, grant the user a specified grace period before automatic logout occurs, or ignore the expiration and let the user continue working.

Password Control

LAN Manager uses the U.S. government data encryption standard for encrypted passwords and a sophisticated authentication algorithm—the login dialog is different for every login attempt, giving the best over-the-wire security in the industry.

Network administrators can also use several system wide settings to control the use of passwords, including:

- A minimum password length specifying a required number of characters.
- A maximum password age, forcing users to change their passwords at specified intervals.
- A minimum password age to prevent users from altering their passwords until a specified interval has passed. This also deters users from flipping between two passwords in an attempt to defeat the maximum password age restriction.
- A unique password history to ensure that a password chosen by a user is different from as many as eight of the user's previous passwords.

Intruder Protection

All network operations that require validation of a password are delayed for two or three seconds after the first time an incorrect password is entered. This helps defeat password-finding programs, known as *dictionary attacks*, that repeatedly try to log in using random passwords.

Account Lockout

To prevent repeated attacks on an account, an administrator may activate account lockout. After an administrator-specified number of unsuccessful login attempts, the account under attack is disabled and can only be reactivated by the administrator.

Resource Access Controls

Microsoft LAN Manager provides two types of resource security: user level and share level.

User-level security combines the LAN Manager user account definitions with the network resource access permissions to give administrators fine-grained control of all server resources, including files, directories, print queues, peripheral devices, and named pipes. User-level security is the default mode and is recommended for most environments.

The *share-level security* feature works by assigning a unique password to each shared resource—only users who know the password can use that resource. Share-level security is appropriate in environments where tight security is not required.

Access Control List

With user-level security, whenever a user tries to access a particular resource, the LAN Manager security system checks the user's name against the *access control list* for that resource to see if and what type of permission has been granted. A user must have both a valid network account and the necessary permissions to access a network resource.

The access control list also enables the administrator to define and grant permissions to groups of users. Creating groups of users with similar resource needs makes it easier to grant access permissions. For example, all employees in the payroll department can be made members of a group called *Payroll*. The administrator can then grant the appropriate permissions to that group instead of individual members. New users added to Payroll automatically inherit the group's permissions. By using a combination of group designations and permissions, a system of interlocking permissions can be devised to manage the resources of a large network.

Local Security and Restart Protection

Security at the server console is enforced in a number of ways. A *restricted access mode*, implemented through the *Net Console feature*, allows administrators to limit user access to server functions at the console. With Net Console running, users may query only the status of printer and communication queues; delete, pause, and continue their own print jobs; list server resources; and view the status of peripheral devices. Net console requires the administrator's password to enter and exit restricted access mode.

On 80386- and 80486-based servers, the HPFS386 file system provides local security (via built-in file protection) that protects the server from unauthorized access. While Net Console severely restricts user access to server options, local security allows users to access only those files and programs that they have the necessary permissions to use. This form of local security extends the network's user-level security to the server itself, so file access permissions apply equally to users on the console, users on the local network, and even remote users. Because full network security is enforced, no additional security at the server console is necessary. Files remain inaccessible to users without the proper permission.

Network Auditing

An *audit-trail facility* enhances security by letting administrators keep track of selected server resources. Any network resource, such as a directory, individual file, named pipe, or print queue, can be designated for auditing.

Resource auditing can provide data on the type of access (open, close, read, or write), username, accessing workstation, date and time of occurrence, outcome of access, and descriptive information about the event. Server auditing can keep track of when the server was started, stopped, paused, or continued; all logins and logouts; and all remote administration connections. The administrator can audit changes to the user and group account database and to the access control list.

Diskless Workstation

Another feature of LAN Manager is the *diskless workstation*. The LAN Manager *Remote Program Load* (RPL) service enables diskless workstations to start Windows, MS-DOS, and OS/2 system software over the network, by creating an RPL database on a server and describing each diskless workstation's remote start requirements. Individual diskless workstations can have their own requirements, or the administrator can specify that multiple machines have the same configuration information.

Maintaining Reliability

Protection from Disk Failure

A fault-tolerance subsystem is provided to guard against data loss as a result of defective disk media or failure of the disk-drive subsystem. Fault monitoring detects errors during hard-disk read and write operations and issues alerts when errors are detected. Error correction helps recover and restore data.

Disk Defect Mapping

When the HPFS or HPFS386 file system is used, a *defect map* is created for the hard disks. This map contains a table of defective disk sectors, which are marked as permanently unusable and assigned to new physical locations on the disk.

If a defective sector is detected after the original defect map is created, a *hot fix* is applied to the defective media by assigning an alternative disk sector on the fly and marking the defective sector to prevent future use. Only defective sectors, rather than entire tracks, are relocated, preserving as much disk space as possible and preventing a hot fix from fragmenting files unnecessarily.

Disk Mirroring

Disk mirroring pairs a server's hard disk drive with a concurrent on-line backup drive. The drive controller writes to the primary drive and backup drive simultaneously so that the backup always contains a copy of the data. If the primary drive fails, the backup drive takes over and protects against data loss. This mirrored pair appears to the operating system as a single hard disk drive.

Drive Duplexing

Drive duplexing works just like drive mirroring except that fault tolerance extends to the drive controller. Two drive controllers are paired with two hard disk drives to provide added protection against failure of the controller components.

Protection from Power Failure

Protection against server crashes because of power failure is offered by a variety of uninterruptible power supplies, which perform a controlled and orderly shutdown of the server.

Windows NT Server

The newest addition to Microsoft's network operating systems is the Windows NT Server. It has much of the functionality and features of LAN Manage, but, the Windows NT Server is based on the Windows NT operating system. It is not just LANManager ported over to Windows NT, but is instead a whole new network operating system. It goes beyond what LAN Manger can do, supporting symmetric multiprocessing and *RAID* (Redundant Array of Inexpensive Disks) level 5. It also has a feature called *trusted domains*, which allows for one workgroup to view files in another workgroup.

Windows for Workgroups

Windows for workgroups is a peer to peer network. It doesn't have as much functionality or as many features of LANManager or Window NT Server, and it is primarily used for small workgroups that need to share files, applications, or resources—such as a printer or fax. Windows must run in enhanced mode and is fully integrated with the Windows NT Server so the two network operating systems can coexist on the same network. This combination can increase the functionality of the network. In addition, it lends peer-to-peer resources to another dedicated network server network.

CHAPTER 6

IBM's NETWORKING SYSTEMS

IBM's LAN local-area network systems business strategy is based on the concept of "the LAN as a System."

IBM states that the hardware and software used in a LAN is more than just a collection of parts called servers and clients. Instead, it is a single logical grouping of applications, data, and hardware resources—viewed as a system, the whole is greater than the sum of its parts. A LAN user, according to the business strategy, should have a consistent view of system resources—printing a document is always done the same way whether the printer is locally attached or on a server. The data location is transparent to the user and location changes can be made without affecting the way a user deals with the data. The types of security control and software maintenance associated with business applications on mainframes are available to LAN-based systems.

Today's business environment is fueling the concept of the LAN as a system. In the past, hardware was more expensive, so sharing printers and file space on a larger dedicated server was a cost-effective alternative to replicating these resources. Today's emerging business environment differs from that of the 1980s in many ways:

- For the same cost, hardware capabilities today are substantially greater than they used to be.
- PC use is expanding to business-related applications.
- Business organizations are becoming flatter and the "empowered employee" is emerging in large—as well as small enterprises.

IBM LAN Systems Business Strategy

IBM's understanding of the LAN system creates fundamental implications for its business strategy. These implications include:

- *Access to data anytime, anywhere*—IBM LAN system solutions provide both relational database and transaction processing support that permit the applications using them to work on a variety of hardware platforms.

- *Investment protection*—IBM LAN system solutions are built on an Operating System/2 (OS/2) platform that permits running older PC application programs to run on the LAN providing adequate functionality along with newly acquired or written programs. The underlying OS/2 programming interfaces are common for both the server and client systems, meaning that application function distribution can be shifted among machines over time without a complete redesign.

- *Industrial-strength LAN*—The OS/2 LAN server was designed with levels of data protection ranging from periodic replication ability to fault-tolerance features for disk mirroring and duplexing. Support for uninterruptible power supplies and the ability to provide warning information are also included.

Customer Base

IBM's LAN systems business strategy is also driven by the needs and expectations of five different customer segments: a *medium-large* segment based on size with three subsegments based on LAN implementation strategies—autonomous workgroups driven to solve specific problems, such as *bottom-up* driven to combine multiple workgroups, and *top-down*, to create an enterprisewide application focus. The *fewer than-50 employees* segment has two subsegments based on individual ownership versus multiple-investor ownership.

The *medium-large* top-down environment is characterized by an enterprise-wide focus with centralized control and management. The medium-large autonomous workgroup by contrast is a functional control, management, and decision-making environment. Medium-large bottom-up represents a multiple workgroup environment with a mix of central and functional control. Clearly, all three environments may exist in a single business.

The small single-investor environment is heavily driven by cost and prewritten software. The small multiple-investor environment has many of the same cost concerns but may place increased emphasis on value-added remarketing offerings. Investment in both development and support programs is related to the differing requirements of the following customer sets:

- *Coexistence and value add*—The need for coexistence with current applications and network operating systems is strong across all of the segments, but of less importance in small home offices. The OS/2 LAN server provides the current level of support and the emerging Distributed Computing Environment (DCE).

- *Application development productivity*—While application development productivity is of significant value for the inhouse efforts of selected medium-large companies, the products of independent software developers and value-added remarketers are necessary for the other segments. IBM supports these independent developers.

- *Investment protection and resource management*—These needs transcend virtually all environments. The product functions embodied in OS/2, LAN Server, and the NetView family are designed to meet those needs.

IBM's LAN System Development Priorities

The LAN as a System

Like the minicomputer and mainframe systems of the last 20 years, the LAN provides centralized security, administration, and management functions. Beyond these functions, the LAN has also evolved to allow flexibility and diversity that users have come to expect. Treating the LAN as a system means providing a manageable environment with a single-system image. The goal is to ensure that LANs no longer appear as sophisticated, expensive, and complicated products, but instead are easy to use and manage.

With a single-system image, the user's *graphical user interface* (GUI) appears to be the first, last, and only interface in the user's computing universe, while in reality, it may be an integrated piece of a huge worldwide network comprising thousands of resources. A single-system image also means that organizations can manage a heterogeneous network as a single entity.

Connection Flexibility

IBM has designed a blueprint for optimum network flexibility while providing for the strongest network connections. The *Multi-Protocol Transport Networking architecture* (MPTN) provides for communications on almost any network protocol. A variety of network interface cards and cable connection mechanisms that support the *Network Device Interface Specification* (NDIS) can be used with the MPTN architecture.

Data You Need, When You Need It

For mobile users, IBM has developed the full-function dial-in/dial-out remote LAN access for LAN Server. *IBM LAN Distance* enables users with portable systems to connect to a LAN by telephone. This provides transparent access to LAN applications and services from anywhere in the world. LAN Distance clients supporting both OS/2 and DOS or Windows can access LAN Server, NetWare, and NFS servers. This feature can significantly enhance LAN efficiency for employees who travel on business and need access to resources and data.

System Management

IBM's strategy for distributed system management is to solve the business issues associated with managing changes, configuration problems, software distribution, and assets. IBM is delivering a distributed systems management family, called *LAN NetView*, to address the problems of distributing information and data that will satisfy both IS and end users.

Open Systems

In response to customer demand, the computer industry has shifted from proprietary technology to open systems. While everyone agrees that this shift is necessary, the definition of *open* is being debated.

IBM's approach to building open systems is based on the following characteristics of open environments:

- Applications and data can be moved from one vendor's computer system to a different vendor's computer system.

- Computing systems and products from different vendors can work together to form an application solution.

- Standards are complied with, whether they are set by standards-making bodies, de facto industry standards, or common specifications/technology endorsed by the industry.

Strategic Direction

IBM's strategic direction encompasses a set of fundamental notions:

- Distributed system technologies involving vendor products are required for success in the business enterprise.

- Scalable hardware and software offerings that permit an *add-on* versus a *replace* philosophy are required to support changing needs in the business environment.

- System management capabilities that take advantage of the underlying operating system capabilities are prerequisites for integrating applications and information in the business enterprise.

- Software development (especially applications) requires a new paradigm to replace the historical labor-intensive, technology-sensitive approach. Object-oriented technology and transparent communications technology enable such a paradigm shift.

Distributed Systems

While distributed systems technologies are being developed, IBM and others in the industry are already working on new technologies such as objects, distributed objects, multimedia, image, wireless computing, mobile systems, symmetrical multiprocessing, and microkernel-based systems. Using distributed systems as the base, these new technologies are incorporated into an exciting new computing environment for end users, administrators, and application developers. With IBM's distributed system technology, this family will be extended to increasingly insulate end users, administrators, and application developers from the specifics of the network, including connections, protocols, service providers, and hardware. The network will continue to be scalable, enabling users to choose product solutions that address current needs while offering the flexibility for system growth. As new technologies, such as objects and distributed objects, are developed and enhanced, IBM will incorporate them into the family to interoperate with current products, providing upward compatibility.

Scalability

IBM's approach to scalability enables users to expand their environments by adding, rather than replacing, products. Each product family member is simply an *add-on* to the previous level. The next generation of IBM products will address customers in markets of all sizes. At the same time, these products will protect existing investments in hardware, software, and skills, thus enabling growth without the need to change or replace systems.

Future *entry products* will offer a low-cost load-and-go environment that requires no server and minimal administration. This product level is designed for organizations that require easy-to-use personal productivity applications. It will support file and print sharing and an electronic mail capability—as a group these are sometimes called *peer-to-peer communications*—that allows people to collaborate on the same information whether they are in the same room or miles apart.

Workgroup products will offer all the functions of the entry product-level, plus advanced system management options and additional connectivity. This environment provides a server and is designed for larger organizations needing higher-performance, fault-tolerance functions in the server, more rigorous system management capabilities, and more connection choices, providing a straightforward growth path from the entry product.

Enterprise products will include a set of extensions to the workgroup environments aimed at accessing enterprise data and integrating workgroups with enterprise applications. This product line will include global directory services, full systems and network management, host information access, and mechanisms to give a single-system image to multiple heterogeneous LAN systems. Global security will be implemented with the *OSF/DCE Security Service*, which specifically addresses the challenge of maintaining security in a distributed environment. In addition to stringent security services, IBM's enterprise products will include a backup/restore capability, access control, and software license management.

Systems Management

To enhance *LAN NetView*, IBM is working with other industry suppliers to encourage the development of systems management applications. NetWare Services Manager from Novell and LANlord/2 from Microcom are two examples.

LAN NetView products will combine open architecture and technologies from selected sources, including X/Open, the Open Systems Interconnection (OSI) System Management Model, and IBM SystemView to help customers manage heterogeneous network environments. LAN NetView includes industry-standard protocols such as CMIP (for standardizing management communications between systems) and XMP (for providing a common programming interface) for system management applications. Using these protocols should increase the number of distributed applications available by making it easier to develop powerful applications that will appeal to a variety of users.

Transport Technology

To provide application transparency, IBM is developing and supporting programming interfaces such as the industry-standard Sockets and X/Open's transport interface.

The Sockets interface, first introduced in UNIX, has become a de facto industry-standard API for communications. With this interface, users and their existing applications can operate consistently and transparently across multiple network environments, including TCP/IP, NetBios, IPX, OSI, and SNA. In addition, a single network adapter card can be used with multiple protocols — meaning that with one network adapter, users can participate in LANServer, NetWare, and TCP/IP networks simultaneously and transparently. These future developments will be achieved using the MPTN blueprint.

Object-Oriented Technology

With the magnitude of current industry-wide software backlogs and escalating software maintenance costs, many companies realize that they must shorten their application development cycle to remain competitive. IBM's strategy is to offer products that provide a basis for developing object-oriented distributed programs.

From the user's perspective, object-oriented technology will make using computers more intuitive. The drag-and-drop capabilities of OS/2 and AIX illustrate how easily users can manipulate the system in an objected-oriented environment. While end users benefit from this easy-to-use and learn environment, application developers can work faster because of highly reliable code.

Distributed Computing Environment

As previously stated, IBM strategic planning involves the use of *Distributed Computing Environment* (DCE). DCE permits applications that allow a network of multivendor systems to appear as a single system with user access to many different resources on a network. DCE is based on technology licensed from the *Open Software Foundation* (OSF) and is endorsed by leading computer manufacturers, such as IBM, DEC, and Hewlett-Packard, that participate in the OSF.

Since the architecture accommodates numerous operating system and hardware platforms, any DCE-enabled process running on one computer can interoperate with a DCE-enabled process on a second computer—regardless of the computer's manufacturer or operating system.

IBM Products

LAN Server 4.0

This is IBM's premier network operating system. It is shipped in two versions: *Entry* and *Advanced*. Both versions have the capacity for the following functionality and features:

- Taking full advantage of the OS/2 base operating system's capabilities of providing a virtual memory-based, preemptive, multitasking application environment.

- The implementation of a *single system image* providing the client system user with transparent access to server resources.

- Support for a Remote *Initial Program Load* (IPL) capability for medialess clients.

- The ability for OS/2 and NetWare clients to coexist.

The following features, available on both versions, were added to LAN Server 4.0 from its previous release:

- Simple install

- Auto adapter detection and identification

- Increased network adapter support

- Network SignON Coordinator/2, which provides a simple method of logging on to a variety of systems and keeping passwords synchronized across multiple locally attached workstations and central site hosts

- TCP/IP support with the MPTN/2 LAN transport

- TCP/IP support for DOS

- A graphical user interface for administrative services

- REXX API

- The new *DOS LAN Services* (DLS) Requestor for DOS/Windows workstations, which offers full CLI support and *DOS redirected install* (CID) enablement.

- Networked Dynamic Data Exchange (DDE) and Clipboard—Windows and OS/2 requestors can share data between applications across a LAN using DDE.

The following enhancements are for the advanced version only:

- Direct Access Storage Device (DASD) limiting

- Pentium exploitation

- Symmetric Multi-Processors (SMP) compatibility

Both versions have an abundance of productivity aids. *LAN Server 4.0 Entry* is a solution for small and medium-size businesses, where shared resources must be available to OS/2, Windows, and DOS clients. The LAN Server's requestors provide limited peer support, providing the ability for other clients to informally share local resources with client LAN Server 4.0 requestors.

LAN Server 4.0 Advanced is ideally suited for large businesses or small businesses where enhanced performance is required. LAN Server Advanced is also the platform for LAN Server extensions, which enhances its capabilities.

OS/2 WARP CONNECT

As this book is being written, IBM is preparing to announce its new version of OS/2 Warp—OS/2 WARP CONNECT. This will be a major offering for IBM's LAN Systems. OS/2 WARP CONNECT promises to bring many new features to the networking environment. At this time IBM has not officially announced these features, but they are assumed by many in the computer industry to include the following:

- Base Product
  - OS/2 Warp version 3
  - IBM Peer for OS/2
  - IBM LAN Server 4.0 requestor
  - NetWare client 2.11 for OS/2
  - LAN Distance Remote version 1.1
  - Network SignOn Coordinator
  - TCP/IP version 3.0 (including Internet Access Kit)
- Utilities
  - AskPSP
  - Diskette images for connectivity products
  - Single Component Installs for connectivity products
  - View/print publications
- BonusPak for OS/2 WARP
- Lotus Notes Express

OS/2 WARP CONNECT should be able to do the following with regard to LAN systems:

- Peer Networking

- Allow sharing of local resources (files, applications, printers, modems, etc.) where informal sharing is sufficient
- Enable PCs to function as peers while simultaneously accessing servers on the LAN
- It should have product interoperability with the following:

  OS/2 LAN Server

  PC LAN Program 1.3

  Microsoft Windows for Workgroups

  Windows NT

  Microsoft LAN Manager 2.x

  LANtastic 6.0

- Networking
  - LAN Server Requestor

    Provide access to shared computer devices, i.e., CD-ROMS, printers, modems

    Provide graphical drag-and-drop administration of a LAN server
  - NetWare Client for OS/2

    Provide native Novell NetWare 4.x and 3.x connectivity in an OS/2 environment
  - LAN Distance Remote for OS/2

    Network SignON Coordinator

    Coordinate single-user id and password access to multiple systems.
  - Network Communications

    TCP/IP for OS/2

    Provide dial-up and LAN access to the Internet

- Benefits of OS/2 Warp Connect are the following:
  - *Performance*—provides users with significantly improved performance, easier installation, and a snappier user interface.
  - *Compatibility*—protects customer investments in DOS and Windows applications, while opening up a whole new world of 32-bit OS/2 software programs.

- *Value*—provides a complete client for LAN Server, NetWare, and TCP/IP, as well as peer-to-peer capability and productivity applications.

- *Ease of use*—enhances ease of use through an improved more visually appealing interface, streamlined installation, and a total packaged connectivity solution.

- *Reliability*—builds upon the proven and stable OS/2 2.x code base to create a networking package that business customers can count on.

CHAPTER 7

BANYAN VINES

Banyan Systems has asserted itself as a leader in enterprisewide, PC-based networking systems. Its network operating system, *VINES*, is designed to simplify the use and management of distributed networks. (*Distributed networks* have multiple file servers, hosts, and locations, while the users, programs, and data are in different geographical areas.)

Banyan claims that VINES is the top-rated solution for multiserver networks. VINES software integrates any number of users, sites, systems, and applications into a single manageable network. Users can have traditional screens displayed on their workstations, and they simply need to make a request of the network and, if security allows, VINES fulfills the request. Using this system frees users from having to make burdensome entries and trying to find the data or program on the network, leading to Banyan's claim that the entire VINES network and its resources are transparent to the user.

Enterprise Network Services

The key to making networks easy to use and manage is Banyan's Systems's concept of *enterprise network services* (ENS). The services in ENS reduce physical complexity, making a large multinational network as friendly and logical as a small office network. Enterprise network services include:

- Directory services
- Network management services
- Intelligent messaging services
- Security services

These services interoperate across a distributed environment to create one logical system with global access and control.

Directory Services

VINES *Directory Services* delivers easy and consistent access to all network resources from any location. Connections between users, resources, sites, and servers are completely transparent. The software that provides these advantages is StreetTalk III.

StreetTalk III

StreetTalk was designed for growing distributed networks. This network directory can support any number of sites. As new users, printers, servers, gateways, and applications are added to a VINES network, StreetTalk permits a unique name for each. The name, network location, and characteristics of each resource are stored in the distributed StreetTalk database, which every service and application on the network uses to locate network items. Behind the scenes, once a request is made for a resource, StreetTalk informs the requesting party where the resource is located and enables a connection to be established automatically.

This network directory service can uniformly integrate a diverse mix of hardware and software across broad geographical areas and make them function as a single machine. It is fully integrated with every service on the VINES network. VINES mail, print, file, gateway, security, user profiles, and administrative services all refer to StreetTalk to determine a user or resource location and can store network-related information. A single distributed network repository for this information means that a local update automatically updates services and applications throughout the network—multiple services or applications never have to be alerted that a user or resource has moved or that a login account has expired.

StreetTalk can also provide for hands-free administration by automatically and instantly integrating new locations with the existing network. When a new location is added, it simply must be plugged into the network—StreetTalk does the rest. Its services interoperate worldwide, if needed, recognizing additions and instantly integrating new locations into the network.

StreetTalk eliminates the threat of a single point of network failure, because its directory services run on every server in a VINES network. Each StreetTalk service maintains a piece of the database with the names and characteristics associated with the users and resources it supports. Collectively, these distributed services interoperate to form a single system.

Easy and Consistent Access

Access to any VINES resource, from any location, is effortless—users identify themselves just once to the system when they log in and never need to identify themselves to a remote service or to issue a special password again. Integrated with StreetTalk, VINES services and network applications know where a user is located, what the user's security privileges are, and where to direct print jobs. Whether a user logs into the network from the office, on the road, or at home, the user's network environment remains the same. Logging into one specific server is no longer required, because the network and all its resources are one simple system.

Flexible Control

As new users, devices, and services are added to the network, they are assigned StreetTalk names. StreetTalk's three-part naming scheme lets you assign logical names and groupings such as:

- Pat Blake@Sales@Echo Corp
- Account Rec@Accounting@Echo Corp
- Color Printer@Marketing@Echo Corp

This hierarchical naming scheme supports flexible administration. Salespeople and their resources can be placed in one group, while marketing people and their resources are in another. Within these groups, a local administrator can be assigned to manage the group's file and print resources. At the same time, local administrators can be prohibited from managing resources not associated with their specific group. In short, users can have local support without compromising broader network control.

Network Change without Network Disruption

Network change is a fact of life. StreetTalk acts as a shield to protect users from frequent changes. When a user or resource moves, the change is recorded just once by StreetTalk. Users, servers, and applications throughout the network are instantly updated because they all use StreetTalk to navigate through the network. The users' workstations never have to be modified to accommodate a network change. StreetTalk does that while enforcing data integrity and simplifying network management.

Instant Access to Information

StreetTalk's companion service, *StreetTalk Directory Assistance*, makes available the names and descriptions of network users and resources. STDA supports a variety of queries and quickly performs global directory lookups and searches. Like the familiar White Pages, STDA lets you browse rapidly through alphabetized listings of network entries and like the Yellow Pages, it lets you look for items by category and can be a powerful inventory tool for administrators.

Management Services

VINES Network Management Services spans the entire network, allowing a small central staff to control user activities, network changes, security, applications, and hardware and software performance across an entire enterprise network. Integrated with all other VINES network services, Network Management Services provides uniform interfaces so detailed information about a variety of network activities can easily be viewed. You can add users, control file and print functions, secure resources, install new options, and upgrade VINES system revision levels.

With the VINES Network Management option, the administrator can view real-time statistics about varying clients, connections, and activities across multiple sites and servers.

Another option is the VINES Assistant. The Assistant delivers an advanced set of 60 administrative utilities that save time, avert problems, and maximize network performance. This add-on also includes 26 PC-based administrative utilities, historical data-gathering and analysis tools, and 33 new support utilities for the server console, with a menu interface tying all these options together.

Security Services

VINES Security Services provides consistent fine-grained security across a variety of network resources. Administrators can secure distributed files, printers, gateways, and applications through a single security paradigm. These services are integrated with every other network service and are enforced transparently with every network activity.

Security Services additionally places control of security at the source— that is, with the owner or administrator of the resource. Every VINES system directory, file, printer, and host gateway has an associated *Access Rights List* (ARL) that specifies the users that are authorized to access that particular service. Only the owner or administrator of a resource can make this determination, resulting in tighter network control. If you're responsible for securing a variety of network resources, ARLs give you a consistent way to exercise those controls.

In addition to resource-by-resource control, VINES Security Services gives administrators control of each user's login environment. The administrator can determine who can log into the network, when they can log in, how long they can be logged in, the physical locations from which they can log in, and how often they must change their password.

Messaging Services

Intelligent messaging can set itself up and work with all network servers, automatically adapting to network changes. It supports messaging applications from Banyan and other leading third-party E-mail interfaces and mail-enabled applications and is fully integrated into StreetTalk III, resulting in users being added only to the StreetTalk directory. It is also integrated into Network Management, resulting in single-point monitoring of all E-mail.

Communication Services

VINES Communication Services provides network transparency. Any number of LAN, leased-line, dial-up, X.25, SNA, and TCP/IP connections can be used to link local and remote workgroups seamlessly into a single system.

Time Services

VINES Time Services synchronizes enterprisewide services and applications, making network events consistent across time zones and international boundaries.

All these services are available in English and German, French, Spanish, and Hangul (a Chinese character set).

VINES Products

The basic VINES LAN operating systems come in four software packages: VINES 10, VINES 50, VINES 100, and VINES 250.

These network operating systems support many clients—including PC-DOS, Windows, OS/2, and Macintosh—and their native interfaces. All network resources appear as extensions of the user's workstation. DOS and OS/2 users access network resources with their operating system commands, while Macintosh and Windows users access network resources through native graphical interfaces.

VINES 5, *VINES 10*, and *VINES 20* let users share printers that are attached to client workstations as well as those attached to the file server. Both PostScript and standard text printers are supported. Twenty print services per server are available, eliminating the server-printer distance conflict, so that printers can be placed where they are most often used.

VINES File Store

Banyan's *VINES File Store* (VFS) lets DOS, Macintosh, OS/2, and Windows users communicate freely and share files, supporting the native file-storage environment for each client type, including: DOS naming conventions, Macintosh AppleTalk Filing Protocol, and OS/2 Extended Sequence Message Block protocol definitions. File access is always through the user's familiar client interface.

VINES SMP

Another VINES network operating system is *symmetric multiprocessing* (SMP). As the only network operating system that uses more than one CPU in a multiprocessor network server, the combination of VINES SMP and multiprocessor file servers allows consistent response time to be maintained as users, services, and applications on a single network server increase. SMP also provides a high-performance development environment for building distributed client-server applications.

VINES SMP is resource-efficient—with symmetric multiprocessing software, servers don't have to be added when computational loads increase; a processor added to the existing system is not all that is needed. Managing symmetric multiprocessing is easier, too because SMP automatically allocates tasks to available processors, so time is not spent monitoring the workload processing flow. No modifications are needed to run VINES services, options, or applications on a multiprocessor server.

VINES SMP can either be installed as a complete network operating system, ready to run on any Banyan-certified system with multiple processors, or as an upgrade option. Upgrading is simple and delivers increased processing power without the hardware and software costs or the administrative overhead of adding a new server.

VINES' distributed network architecture and SMP technology form a strong foundation for client-server computing, giving applications significantly better performance.

This software is designed to operate on advanced symmetric multiprocessor systems, which allow any task to be assigned to any processor—There are no idle processors when there's work to be done. Any processor can run a file system process, associated I/O activity, or client-server application. Because SMP accepts a task as soon as a processor is available, resources are allocated efficiently and consistent performance is ensured for all network users. In work environments with CPU-intensive applications, users can expect significantly improved performance.

VINES Option for Macintosh

This software package is for use with VINES 5.0 and provides comprehensive Macintosh client support within a VINES system network. It provides transparent access and resource sharing with AppleTalk networks via Token Ring, Ethernet, and LocalTalk through all supported LAN and wide-area network topologies using VINES encapsulated routing for AppleTalk.

The full suite of VINES system network services, including directory and security, is available for the Macintosh. With Vines an unlimited number of

Macintosh users can access and use the same file and print resources currently available to DOS, Windows, and OS/2 users.

Macintosh users connect to the VINES system using the Chooser. To the Macintosh client, a VINES system file server looks like a typical AppleShare file server . VINES system file services appear (under their StreetTalk names) as accessible AppleTalk Filing Protocol (AFP) volumes easily available from multiple zones.

The security features currently provided to DOS, Windows, and OS/2 users are also available to Macintosh clients with VINES Option for Macintosh as Banyan gives Macintosh users a VINES system utility to control and manage directory and file access rights. The VINES system fully supports AFP access rights and security features without the need for restrictive configuration settings, and Macintosh users can view and set access rights privileges for folders simply by using the **Get Privileges** command.

VINES Option for Macintosh offers print-spooling capabilities that allow Macintosh clients located anywhere on the network to print to a *Printer Access Protocol* (PAP)-compatible PostScript device, such as an Apple LaserWriter. LaserWriters can also be shared with other client workstations on a VINES network and DOS users have batch PostScript and plain text-printing capabilities when outputting to PAP-compatible PostScript printers.

Disjointed AppleTalk networks can be connected using a procedure called *tunneling*, which simplifies the setup and maintenance of AppleTalk networks within a VINES internet. VINES Option for Macintosh supports encapsulated AppleTalk routing (tunneling) through VINES system networks. The AppleTalk routing configuration is set up through the server console, and AppleTalk packets are encapsulated in VINES system packets, enabling AppleTalk users to access its resources via the VINES system network. Banyan servers can connect disjointed AppleTalk networks, allowing access to resources anywhere in the VINES network.

To give Macintosh users access to the VINES system file services, VINES Option for Macintosh supports AFP versions 1.0, 1.1, and 2.0.

An implementation of the AppleTalk protocol stack is incorporated directly into the VINES system kernel. This implementation provides basic routing functionality as well as communications with printers, file servers, and other resources over LocalTalk, Token Ring, and Ethernet. VINES Option for Macintosh supports both the original AppleTalk protocols (Phase 1) and the newer AppleTalk protocols (Phase 2).

VINES Server-to-Server Options

Banyan *VINES Server-to-Server* options allow information to be transmitted between departments and facilities. Seven Server-to-Server options are available:

- VINES Server-to-Server LAN
- VINES Server-to-Server WAN
- VINES Server-to-Server X.25
- VINES Server-to-Server TCP/IP
- VINES Server-to-Server SNA
- VINES Server-to-Server ISDN
- VINES Server-to-Server T1

Bridges and routers are not required to support this broad spectrum of inter-server connection types, because the VINES system does it all when configured with the Server-to-Server software option.

Using the *Dynamic Routing Algorithm* to help ensure network integrity and reliability VINES system software automatically redirects interserver traffic through an alternate route when a server is removed from service or a communication link fails. The algorithm also includes *Automatic Fastest Path Routing*, which is a unique capability that uses network bandwidth.

VINES Communications Gateway for 3270

The gateway service allows access to any IBM SNA mainframe from a variety of PCs on a VINES network. A single gateway can support PCs running DOS, Windows, and Apple Macintosh computers. (The Macintosh Client and Windows Client versions of the VINES Communications Gateway are sold separately.)

VINES Communications Gateway for 3270 includes the following software:

- The Gateway software, which runs under DOS on a dedicated PC and provides the interface between the VINES network and an IBM mainframe.
- The DOS 3270 Client software, which runs on any PC network client and provides 3270/SNA terminal and printer emulation.

VINES Communications Gateway for 3270 gives users simultaneous access to mainframe applications and flexible PC-based applications. The gateway software supports SDLC and 802.2 Token Ring connections using the DCA's Intelligent Synchronous Communications Adapter (ISCA), SDLC Adapter, or DCA IRMAtrac Token Ring or IBM Token Ring adapter.

The gateway supports concurrent access for 8 to 128 users, depending on the package. Concurrent user upgrade packages allow the network to grow.

Intelligent Communications Adapter Cards

The Banyan *Intelligent Communications Adapter* (ICA) consists of two serial communications cards that let a VINES network server connect to a variety of different host computers, public and private data networks, dial-in PCs, and other VINES system services.

With ICAs, communications protocols can be mixed and matched on a single card. The cards offer the use of six serial ports.

The ICA cards can be installed in 80386 and 80486 computers and are available as Banyan ICAplus or Banyan ICA. The *ICAplus* card can communicate over fractional T-1 lines at speeds in increments of 64 to 384 Kbps, while the *ICA card* allows communication at 64 Kbps.

Using an ICA or ICAplus card in a VINES system server eliminates the need for multiple types of communications boards. A single ICA or ICAplus card can simultaneously support a mix of protocols, including asynchronous, HDLC, SDLC, bisynchronous, X.25, and X.29. In most instances, ICA cards are less expensive alternatives to bridge, router, and gateway solutions, which require dedicated PCs.

The mixed-protocol support of the ICA cards provides flexibility in configuring a VINES system server. As a network evolves and changes, the flexibility of the ICA card lets you change protocols without replacing the card. For example, one card can support an IBM SNA mainframe connection, an X.25 network connection, two DEC VAX minicomputer connections, and two PC dial-in connections. Later, if the network needs an HDLC connection instead of an X.25 connection, one of the communications ports on the ICA simply needs to be redefined.

Support for UNIX Clients

Banyan also offers the *Enterprise Network Services* (ENS) software to the UNIX community. ENS can be layered on your choice of SCO UNIX host. Banyan's *ENS for HP-UX* and Banyan's *ENS for AIX* does the same for HP-UX and AIX hosts. This network server lets PC and UNIX users share files and printers through such standard UNIX protocols as TCP/IP and NFS, running your choice of UNIX applications and the enterprise network services on a single sever.

VINES and NetWare

Banyan also has ENS for NetWare that are fully compatible with NetWare and NetWare applications.

CHAPTER 8

UNIX NETWORKS

UNIX networks differ from NetWare or Windows NT networks in several ways. UNIX is its own multiuser, multitasking operating system. NetWare and LAN Manager can run as tasks on UNIX. UNIX can also function as a host, or centralized operating system, like that of a minicomputer giving both dumb terminals and PC terminal emulations, access to the UNIX host with all processing taking place at the host. Finally, UNIX workstations can access a UNIX host and the host can function as a server. These concepts make UNIX unique in the computer networking world.

Additional considerations for UNIX include its uses of a different file structure and transfer method than that for DOS, Windows, and OS/2 networks and that UNIX networks need to operate over networks that implement TCP/IP as the communication protocol.

Origins of UNIX

When UNIX is mentioned, many people think of a cumbersome, slow, and complex operating system. This is true to some extent: It is an old operating system that dates back to 1969. It was developed at AT&T Bell Laboratories. Then, Ken Thompson and Dennis Ritchie rewrote the UNIX operating system using the C programming language. Using C gave UNIX its cross-platform capability (ability to run on many different computers), but the actual core of the UNIX operating system has changed little since its conception.

In the mid-1970s AT&T made UNIX a commercial product and then sold source code licenses to several different computer manufacturers. This is why today, there are a number of versions of UNIX exist in the marketplace.

An operating system controls the resources of a computer and allocates them to the applications running on that computer. To accomplish this, the operating system (in this case UNIX) has a shell and a kernel. The kernel allows for time sharing among all the computer users and resources of the computer, particularly the CPU. The shell, meanwhile, interacts with the user, the person at the workstation, enabling you to run programs, copy files, log in and out, and perform other tasks included in that shell. The shell may be displayed as a command prompt line or incorporate a *graphical user interface* (GUI). The shell and the applications communicate with the kernel.

One point that differentiates UNIX from other PC-based operating systems is that everything in the UNIX system is a file—a sequence of characters or bytes. There is no organizational methodology imposed on these files—a directory is just a file that points to other files. The software that accesses the UNIX system gives meaning and layout to these files.

UNIX as a Platform

UNIX provides great flexibility when it comes to networking and data communications. With UNIX many options are open to the developer of a communications network, but there is a mystique about UNIX with regard to its complexity, forcing some people to shy away from it.

UNIX as a Host

UNIX was first used on a minicomputer, which has terminals connected to it, either by modem or through RS-232 connections with all processing taking place on the minicomputer's CPU. The terminals originally attached to the UNIX host were dumb terminals, making it a centralized computing system, like that found on IBM's minicomputers. The terminals issued commands to application programs that were running concurrently under the UNIX operating system. It then became possible for one minicomputer to communicate with another minicomputer. This process opened a whole realm of interconnectivity.

UNIX as a Server

A computer that operates under the UNIX operating system can also function as a server for a local area network. Novell and Microsoft are just two of the software manufacturers that produce *network operating systems* (NOSes) that run under UNIX. Novell has a version of its popular NetWare that operates under UNIX and Microsoft has a version of LAN Manager that operates under UNIX. Both of these products usually run as another application program under UNIX. In this way UNIX host can also be a file server in a LAN.

Using FTP

File Transfer Protocol (FTP) is software that operates in conjunction with UNIX and the communications protocols of TCP/IP. The FTP is actually a utility to the TCP/IP protocol suite, facilitating the transfer of files between devices on a UNIX/TCP/IP network.

Using NFS

Network File System (NFS) is a network operating system for sharing file systems and directories across TCP/IP-based networks developed by Sun Microsystems. NFS is an application-layer protocol that uses the lower-level transport protocol of TCP/IP.

The NFS protocol enables you to access a remote directory and its files as if that directory were on your local UNIX computer. The application running on your UNIX computer accesses these remote files as if they were local. The NFS uses file redirection, making the accessing of remote computers' files transparent.

CHAPTER 9

LANTASTIC

LANtastic is a network operating system developed and marketed by Artisoft, Inc. Founded in 1982, Artisoft is located in Tucson, Arizona, and has offices around the world. Although the company develops both software and hardware products, its network operating system—LANtastic—has made it a leader in peer-to-peer networking and the multimedia market. Artisoft's strategic planning has targeted businesses with fewer than 500 employees.

LANtastic Version 6.0

The latest network operating system from Artisoft is LANtastic version 6.0. LANtastic is a peer-to-peer network that can be either DOS or Windows-based, rather than a client/server network. It supports as many as 300 PCs and operates on an 802.3 Ethernet LAN. Version 6 supports the following features:

- *System Manager* features immediate despooling, enhanced printer display, new NET PRINT switches, new print resources parameters, automatic login to servers, one-command multiple-server login, hot keys to menu items, and an enhanced NET HELP display.
- *NetBIOS* in LANtastic transfers data between servers and workstations faster than in previous versions. Because NetBIOS operates in the background without any user interaction, users notice a faster network.

- *Resource-caching* speeds the process of looking up and opening files by keeping user access information in a server's RAM instead of reading it each time from the server's disk. The server can quickly read access control list information for each network resource from RAM, reducing the frequency with which the server has to check the information before allowing or denying a user request.

- *Random-access caching* speeds access to data on disk by allowing server computers to search files more quickly.

- *Delayed record locking* allows a server to hold onto a user request for a record that is already locked and in use by someone else. After the record is unlocked, the user request is completed. Without delayed record locking, the user request for a locked record would be denied and the attempt would have to be repeated, meaning additional instructions have to be carried out, resulting in a slower response time.

Other new features allow users who have System Manager privileges to accomplish a number of network tasks—including installation of the network software—from their own PCs. They can also manage the entire network by copying accounts from one server to another using either a command-line or menu interface, or they can set up servers by running the batch file on their shared drives. In addition, they can log users out of a server and prevent others from logging into a server, making tasks such as backups easier because the System Manager can log all the users out of the server and then disable logins until the backup is complete.

Another feature, *immediate despooling*, allows users to print faster because printing starts as soon as the print command is issued rather than waiting for the print job to be spooled onto the server's disk. The print job is still stored on the user's disk, however, so if for some reason the job isn't completed, the file won't be lost. Users can also pause printing, restart the print job, or print multiple copies. The improved printer queue display tells users when their jobs will print, how long they'll take, and when they will finish.

Four new *NET PRINT* switches have also been added:

1. The */NOTIFY* switch sends a print-completion message to users and their workstations; this is convenient for users who are not in the same room as the printer.

2. The /NONOTIFY switch disables this feature.

3. The /DIRECT switch lets users with a shared printer print their own files faster by sending them directly to the printer without first copying them to the server's despooling area.

4. The /DELETE switch tells the network to delete the file from disk immediately after it is printed using the /DIRECT switch.

New print-resource parameters grant greater control over printing of ASCII files and let users specify the number of lines (up to 255) to be printed before a form feed. Combined with LANtastic's other print features, this allows users to format the printing of text-only files with great precision.

Automatic login to servers allows faster, easier access to a server's resources. After users have logged into a server, they no longer have to enter their user names and passwords to access other servers. The ability to log into several servers with a single command saves the user from entering multiple *NET LOGIN* commands.

Security on a LANtastic Network

LANtastic's use of usernames and passwords makes it possible to limit a user's access to certain hours and days of the week. Users can be granted any or all of the following security rights:

- Read files
- Write files
- Modify files
- Create files
- Delete files
- Rename files
- Make directories
- Delete directories
- Look up directories
- Execute programs
- Change file attributes

E-Mail with Chat

Electronic mail is a built-in feature of LANtastic. It can either be used to send *real-time* text messages between two computers for immediate interaction, or it lets the user send and save messages to read later. A feature called *LANPUP* alerts the user to incoming mail.

LANtastic's sound capabilities can be used with optional Artisoft Sounding Board Adapters to send voice messages across the network using a telephone-style handset provided with each adapter. Like E-mail this feature can be used to carry on a real-time conversation, or it can save the voice message in digital format for playback later.

Uninterruptible Power Supply

An *uninterruptible power supply* can be attached to the server and integrated into the LANtastic networking software. If a power failure occurs, the LANtastic program warns network users that the power has failed, gives them time to log out, and then closes network files so no work is lost.

Remote Control or Shutdown of Any Server

Network administrators can use the *NET RUN* command to remotely assign tasks to any available server on the network. That way, the fastest machine can handle a time-consuming data sort. A user with manager privileges can remotely shut down a server or schedule its shutdown, at which time the system automatically warns users of the upcoming shutdown. Managers can also lock users out of a server when necessary.

Dedicated Server

The *ALONE* command sets up a dedicated server to optimize performance. This stand-alone server can be started with one command. By sidestepping DOS, ALONE allows multitasking on a network server without impairing performance.

Audit

LANtastic's audit feature monitors and records all access to subdirectories and printers. It tells the network manager who used a PC, printer, or other shared device, when it was used and for how long it was used. If someone tries to enter a directory to which that user has been denied access, this feature notifies the manager and provides detailed records for security and billing purposes.

CD-ROM Networking

LANtastic is considered by many to be the best supporter of CD-ROM drives with Microsoft extension software. Many LANs require that Microsoft extension software be loaded on each computer accessing the CD-ROM drive but the LANtastic system requires that the software be loaded only on the computer that has the CD-ROM drive attached.

LANtastic for Windows

LANtastic supports Microsoft Windows' *real*, *standard*, and *enhanced* modes on both nondedicated servers and workstations. With the LANtastic for Windows program, the user can take advantage of Windows' pull-down menus, icons, and on-line help for the *NET* and *NET_MGR* functions. By having multiple windows open, the user can simultaneously monitor print queues and handle E-mail and multiple servers.

The LANtastic for Windows utility program supports the Dynamic Data Exchange (DDE) standard. With DDE, users can use LANtastic's E-mail to send data from a spreadsheet or database window without leaving the application.

LANtastic for NetWare

LANtastic for NetWare adds peer-to-peer capability to a Novell NetWare LAN. With this program NetWare users have access to the central server and can share each others' programs, data, and peripherals, such as hard disks and even CD-ROM drives.

Features of both network operating systems are available to users—they can choose either LANtastic's print spooling or NetWare's print spooling, making this combination useful when customizing a network.

LANtastic for NetWare operates on top of Novell using Novell NetBIOS, which must be loaded for this program to function.

LANtastic for Macintosh

This software transparently integrates, for an unlimited number of users, a Macintosh network and PostScript printers into the LANtastic network operating system environment. It also allows real-time file sharing between the environments. Both LANtastic and Apple's LocalTalk networks are peer-to-peer networks.

The LANtastic for Macintosh system establishes a PC as a dedicated gateway between the Macintosh and LANtastic networks. PC servers on the LANtastic network are set up as logical drives on the gateway PC and appear as slightly modified Macintosh computer icons to users on the Macintosh network. In this way, Macintosh users see PC files and directories as they would standard Macintosh files and directories and can use the Chooser to select printers attached to the LANtastic network.

For PC users, the LANtastic for Macintosh system establishes a dedicated gateway PC where users can access PostScript printers on the Macintosh network and where they can see Macintosh files that have been saved onto the gateway hard drive. PC users can see and access any PostScript printer attached to the Macintosh network from their own LANtastic interface.

LANtastic for Macintosh allows both groups of users to access the other group's files, as long as they're of the same application program file format. File attributes and record locking are supported in both directions.

LANtastic Z

LANtastic Z allows the interconnection of two computers via serial or parallel ports—the same ports usually used to connect printers and modems. In this way a user on a home computer can share his or her office computer resources via modem as if they were directly linked using cable. A two-PC network can be formed with any LANtastic Z using combination of desktops, notebooks, or laptops (even computers that don't accept an adapter card).

This is not a file-transfer program or a typical serial or zero-slot LAN; it has the same features as the standard LANtastic network operating system.

Multimedia

Artisoft is a leader in voice technology as well as CD-ROM. The Artisoft Sounding Board Adapter (mentioned earlier in this chapter) allows users to send voice messages across the network.

This product supports the Windows 3.1 Object Linking and Embedding (OLE) protocol. With this support, users can incorporate sound into their spreadsheet, database, or word processor—any application that supports Windows OLE. It also supports Microsoft multimedia extensions.

Artisoft Hardware

Peer Hub Concentrator

When placed in the expansion slot of a PC on the network, this card allows five other PCs to connect to it. It acts as a concentrator on an Ethernet 10BASE-T network.

Network expansion and management are simplified with this card concentrator. The software associated with the peer hub allows the network manager to view the status of all ports on the concentrator and activate or disable each port individually.

Central Station II

Central Station provides slotless Ethernet connectivity for PCs and peripherals. The Central Station connectivity processor adds expansion flexibility without taking up a slot in the computer.

Using a Central Station a laptop can be brought into the office and plugged into the Central Station PC port. This connection provides full access to the network and disconnects without disturbing the network.

Flexible connections are what Central Station is all about. This connectivity processor is compatible with both LANtastic and NetWare.

Adapters

Artisoft markets the *NodeRunner/SI* series of Ethernet adapters. All NodeRunner/SI adapters run on most Ethernet network software compatible with NE-2000 drivers. These adapters have an intelligence feature that detects and responds automatically to the type of slot and installed memory attached to it. Additional *Interrupt Request* lines allow for flexibility in installations. In a diskless workstation, the adapters allow the diskless workstation to boot across the network from the server (Artisoft's *EPROM chips* are needed to do this). The NodeRunner/SI series consists of the following four adapters:

1. NodeRunner/SI 2000 C—for thin Ethernet cable
2. NodeRunner/SI 2000 T—for unshielded twisted pair cabling
3. NodeRunner/SI 2000 A—for thin or thick Ethernet and UTP cabling
4. NodeRunner/SI 2000M/TC—for Micro Channel or thin and UTP cabling—this is not self-configurable

Power Suite

Power Suite is the LANtastic network operating system bundled with additional software for a comprehensive networking environment. The additional software packages include *Lotus's cc:Mail* for E-mail, *Lotus Organizer* for group scheduling and a personal calendar, and *Cheyenne BitWare* and *BitShar* for fax, data communications, and modem sharing. Additionally, *NETCOM's NetCruiser* is included for Internet access.

Dedicated Server

This product is a what it name implies—software that operates as a dedicated network server. It is used in conjunction with a LANtastic network peer-to-peer system to enhance performance of the network. It combines the best of both worlds. The dedicated server is based on Novell's *NetWare 4 Runtime* implementing true 32-bit processing power.

CHAPTER 10

ADDITIONAL LAN COMPONENTS

Chapter 3 listed the essential hardware components of a LAN. This chapter presents a few additional hardware items that will enhance a network. While this is not a comprehensive list, it should give you some idea of what's available.

Uninterruptible Power Supply

An *uninterruptible power supply* (UPS) provides power to devices when the regular power supply fails. The UPS runs off of rechargeable batteries and can keep a server operating for 15 to 30 minutes, enough time to warn any users still on the network that the server is coming down. UPSes come in a variety of sizes and power ratings, so you should be able to find one that meets your needs.

The UPS can run and interact with the network in several ways. One setup is to place it between the regular power supply and the server (see Figure 10.1). In this capacity, if the power fails, the UPS will automatically supply power to the server and continue to do so until its batteries run out, at which time, the server will have a power outage and be brought down incorrectly. To prevent the server from going down incorrectly, the UPS may have an alarm that goes off when it kicks in, warning whoever is nearby of the power failure. When this type of UPS is inactive (in other words, when regular power is supplied), the batteries are constantly recharging.

FIGURE 10.1 The UPS is situated between the file server and the regular power supply.

The UPS can also be integrated into the server, placed again, between the server and the regular power supply. When a power failure occurs in this setup, however, other functions take place: the UPS, which is programmed with the server, automatically supplies 20 minutes of auxiliary power. After 15 minutes of providing power, the UPS—with the aid of the server—notifies the users that the server is going down in a few minutes. It then issues commands to bring down the server correctly, without corrupting any files. If the power resumes before the 15-minute deadline, everything returns to normal and the UPS's batteries are recharged.

Also available are very small, inexpensive UPSes that enable workstations to have their own auxiliary power. These systems prevent users from losing hours of work when a power outage occurs.

Fax Server

When you want to fax an item, you probably get up, walk to the fax machine, wait your turn, and then fax the document—assuming the receiving machine's number isn't busy. After transmission is complete and you've received a transmission status report, you walk back to your office.

Enter the *fax server*. This is a fax machine that is incorporated into the office LAN. Let's repeat the earlier scenario, this time using a fax server (see Figure 10.2): You create a document that you need to fax to a client. Instead of getting up and walking to the fax machine, you stay at your desk. Instead of waiting, you simply send your documents to the fax machine as if they were E-mail. If you were in a word processor, you could stay in that application and send the document to the fax machine. It's that simple.

When a fax is received by the server you're notified on your terminal that a fax is waiting. After bringing the fax into your workstation, you can read it on your monitor or send it to the network's printer. No longer do you need to run to the fax machine to see if your fax has come in yet; no longer does someone have to walk around distributing faxes. And since your fax is printed on a network printer, your hard copy is better than those from a fax machine.

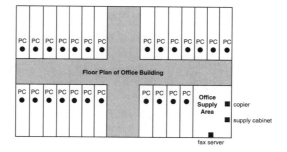

FIGURE 10.2 Every PC is on the same network as the fax server.
Each workstation can access the fax server.

Print Server

It is possible to set up a PC on the network with the sole purpose of handling printing (see Figure 10.3). This is a dedicated PC that can support as many as five printers: one connected to each of the three parallel ports, LPT1, LPT2, and LPT3, and one each for COM 1 and COM 2 (serial ports). More than one print server can exist on a network. Plotters can also be attached to the print server or can be part of a dedicated plotter server.

Some new devices perform print server functions but don't require a dedicated PC. These are boxes with serial and parallel ports attached to them; the box plugs into the network and functions as a print server, just as a dedicated PC print server would.

Backup Server

A *backup server* is a dedicated workstation used to create backup copies of the files on the server's fixed disk. Attached to the workstation is a backup device, which normally uses either magnetic tape or optical disk (see Figure 10.4).

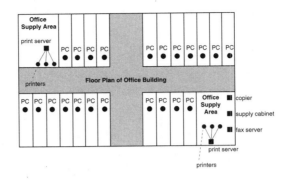

FIGURE 10.3 The print server places printers at either end of the office floor; the result is less traffic and greater convenience.

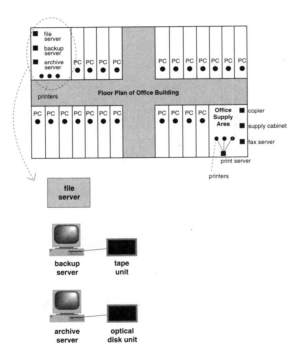

FIGURE 10.4 The backup server and archive server are attached to the network rather than to the file server.

Tape backup units seem to be the most prevalent backup device; they come in several forms, including streaming tapes and digital tapes. Some units use a single tape that can store 1.2 Gbytes or more. Some units use numerous tapes to create a sort of carousel effect: When one tape fills up, another takes its place. This type of backup system can store large amounts of data.

Backup units differ in their method of operation. Some require the network to be still—with no server input/output—while the files are being copied. Others allow the network to function normally while they back up the server's files. Some backup units can back up the users' hard disks at their workstations.

By programming the tape to start at a predefined time and to do either a full backup or an incremental backup, the LAN administrator can program the backup unit so that he or she need not be present during its operation.

The backup server is considered to be a node, or a workstation on the network; therefore, it must be logged into the network and pass security.

Archive Server

Similar to the backup server, the archive server uses a mass storage device (see Figure 10.4). Optical disks are commonly used for archiving because archived files are usually kept in storage longer than backup tapes. With optical disks, the data also is harder to corrupt.

The archive server works by finding files on the file server that have not been used for a specified time and copying them to the optical disk. Those files are then deleted from the file server's fixed disk.

Asynchronous Communications Server

The *asynchronous communications server* allows users on a network to access and share modem pools, minicomputer ports, and X.25 services from anywhere on the network.

Modem pools are a way for all the modems on a network to be shared. They are no longer dedicated to a single workstation (see Figure 10.5).

With the proper third-party applications, network users can dial out of a LAN and access services such as CompuServe or the Internet, as well as X.25 services (see Figure 10.6).

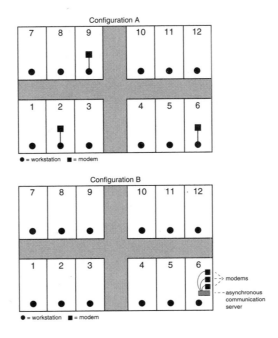

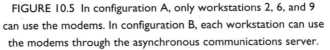

FIGURE 10.5 In configuration A, only workstations 2, 6, and 9 can use the modems. In configuration B, each workstation can use the modems through the asynchronous communications server.

With *terminal emulation software,* users can access minicomputers, such as those operating under UNIX, asynchronously.

Access Server

An access server allows users of DOS, Macintosh, and ASCII workstations to dial into and access all the resources available on a LAN, including network files, databases, application software, E-mail, and host computer services. The remote machines function as if they were workstations on the LAN, with the ability to access all services on the LAN (see Figure 10.7).

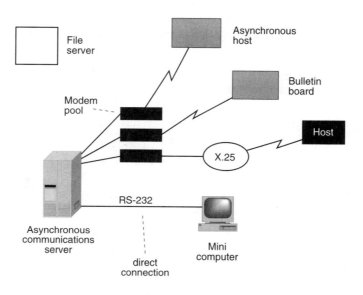

FIGURE 10.6 Users can access the server by modem,
through X.25 or by direct connections.

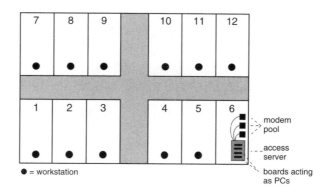

FIGURE 10.7 Remote workstations can enter the networks
through modems connected to the access server.

To save time, processing is done on the LAN, rather than at the remote machine.
To demonstrate the time savings, imagine a user logging into the network from
a remote site using a 9,600-bps modem. He or she starts an application that

calls for a record. Unfortunately, the record is in a file with a million other records, and the entire file must be transferred to the remote site. Each time the user requests a record, the entire file must be transferred. This is not an acceptable way to process information. Instead, processing takes place at the LAN. This can be done in a number of ways, as we'll discuss shortly. Now all that has to be transferred electronically are the keystrokes and the monitor's display. This can be done using either a stand-alone PC or an access server.

Using software and a modem connected to the stand-alone PC, the remote user dials into the modem, and the software that runs in conjunction with the modem and PC allows the remote machine to take over the network PC. This way everything happens on the network PC, and the remote machine is virtually a dumb terminal.

An access server can be more efficient, provide more services, and offer better security than a local processor. This device is a high-end 80386- 80486- or Pentium-PC with specialized software and boards installed. The boards are actually PCs (see Figure 10.8).

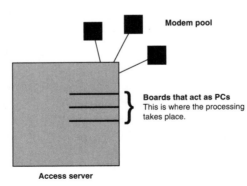

FIGURE 10.8 All modems connect to the access server.

Again, all processing is done by the boards in the access server. Many remote machines can connect to the access server simultaneously, using asynchronous modems and dial-up telephone lines.

There are other ways to access the access server remotely. X.25 connections available from public and private X.25 packet-switching services can be used as can multiplexer connection or a direct connection via an RS-232 null modem cable (see Figures 10.9 and 10.10).

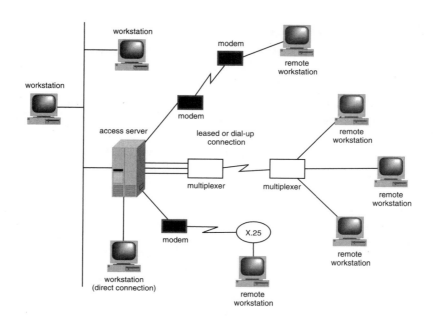

FIGURE 10.9 Alternative remote access methods.

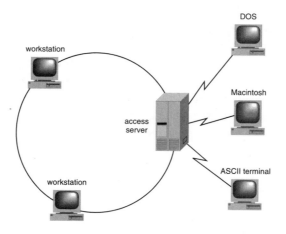

FIGURE 10.10 The access server provides for different access workstation platforms, such as DOS, Macintosh, and Windows.

Application Server or Batch Offload Workstation

Some network operating systems, in conjunction with third-party software, provide batch-processing capabilities. If your program is processing a *batch job* (multiple records and requests), your workstation is tied up until the job is complete—sometimes this can take hours. An offload workstation allows the user to tell the server which workstation will be processing the batch job, and then route that job to the workstation. This frees up your workstation during batch processing.

CD-ROM Drives

With the advent of multimedia the CD-ROM has become very popular. Today enormous amounts of information can be purchased on CD-ROM. Anything from encylopedias to maps of the world to the world's best golf courses are available on CD-ROM. Many times it is advantageous for the users of a network to have access to the information on CD-ROM. However, attaching a CD-ROM drive to each PC and buying multiple copies of the CD-ROM is not cost-effective. Instead a CD-ROM drive or a CD-ROM carousel or juke box can be attached to the file server. Now everybody on the network can have access to them, perhaps through a dedicated PC.

Depending on the network operating system special software may be needed to facilitate this method. It is important to remember that access times for a CD-ROM drive are much slower than that of a hard drive. One additional thing to remeber is that transfer rates of data from a CD-ROM are not nearly as fast as the transfer rate from a hard disk, although a faster CD-ROM drive spin usually increases the data transfer rate. Single spin drives are basically items of the past. Double spin drives are popualr at this time, but as of this writing, newer quad-spin CD-ROM drives are being developed and released. Just like other products within the computer industry, the performance of CD-ROM and overall usage will continue to increase.

Gateways, Bridges, and Routers

These interconnection products allow a LAN to communicate with either another LAN or a host. These are covered in more detail in Chapter 24, "Interconnectivity."

CHAPTER 11

ELECTRONIC MESSAGING

Electronic mail may be one of the most commonly used applications on a LAN. But E-mail no longer means one user simply sending a message to another; today's E-mail packages are much more sophisticated, often integrating calendar and scheduling features into the software.

With the calendar feature, the user can record the day and time of meetings without scheduling two appointments for the same time. When the user schedules a meeting for a certain time, the calendar system asks how long the meeting will be. The user keys in an estimated length, and the system checks that day and time for conflicts. A conflict exists if the time allotment exceeds normal working hours or overlaps with another meeting.

Another useful feature of the calendar system is that users may have the ability to view another user's calendar on a limited basis. (Often, only the user's secretary has this viewing access.) Other users may see time that's already allotted, but they can't see the reason for the allotment. They have no idea if the time set aside on Tuesday from 1:00 to 2:30 is for personal use or for a meeting with the CEO; the important thing is that they know when the other person is available.

The scheduling feature goes hand in hand with this aspect of the calendar feature. You probably know how frustrating and time-consuming it can be to get several people together. The scheduling feature takes care of it for you.

For example, say department head 1 wants a meeting with department heads 2, 3, 4, and 5. Department head 1 enters the scheduling feature and inputs the names of the other department heads and the anticipated length of the meeting. The scheduling feature checks the calendars of everyone involved and finds the earliest time at which their schedules coincide. It then schedules the meeting and marks the calendars of the participants.

Another important feature of the new breed of E-mail packages is that they can be integrated into an IBM mainframe and communicate with a mainframe E-mail package such as Professional Office System (PROFS). Many E-mail programs can send mail from one network to another, even if the receiving network is halfway around the world. The latest popular use of electronic mail has been with dial-up services such as CompuServe, America OnLine, and Prodigy. One of the hottest items for electronic mail at this time is having an electromic mailbox on the *Internet* (a system of networks connecting major research universities and defense installations. These services are accessible from your workstation with the proper communications software and the software.

Various standards affect the use and development of E-mail. They include:

* CCITT X.400
* CCITT X.500
* Message Handling Service (MHS)
* Simple Mail Transfer Protocol (SMTP)

CCITT X.400

It's important to make a distinction between two products when referring to a message handling service: the one referred to by the International Standards Organization (ISO) and the name of a software program from Action Technologies.

The ISO placed MHS capabilities and standards in a specific layer of the OSI model for internetwork communications (OSI is explained in more detail in Chapter 15). The OSI designates layer 7 as the one containing MHS. The purpose of MHS is to provide a standard for electronic messaging.

The ISO used standards established by the CCITT (Consultative Committee for Telephony and Telegraphy) to develop the OSI's standard MHS. These standards are referred to by the CCITT as *X.400*, which consists of the following categories:

- X.400: System model and service elements
- X.401: Basic service elements and optional user interfaces
- X.408: Encoding information and conversion rules
- X.409: Presentation transfer syntax and notation
- X.410: Remote operations and reliable transfer system
- X.411: Message transfer layer
- X.420: Interpersonal messaging user-agent layer
- X.430: Access protocols for teletex terminals

Virtually all LAN developers have announced support for the X.400 standards.

The X.400 MHS has three basic elements (see Figure 11.1):

- *User Agent (UA)*—This is the software component of the X.400 MHS. It provides the connection or interface between the network user and the X.400 MHS, allowing the user to send and retrieve messages.
- *Message Transfer System (MTS)*—The MTS operates in support of the network users and determines the screen display the network users will see. The user agent interacts with the MTS.
- *Message Transfer Agent (MTA)*—The MTA consists of the messages sent by users. Commands and instructions that create store-and-forward functionality are also provided. This function can store messages until a requested delivery time and date and can convert the message into a form the recipient can understand.

The X.400 MHS can, upon request, provide a variety of network and internetwork functions that enhance electronic communications. These functions include:

- Notice of verified delivery or nondelivery with an explanation
- Time and date stamps for submission and delivery
- Multiple-destination deliveries
- Alternate recipients
- Delivery priority (nonurgent, normal, or urgent)

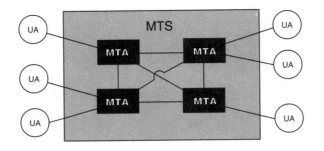

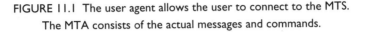

FIGURE 11.1 The user agent allows the user to connect to the MTS.
The MTA consists of the actual messages and commands.

The X.400 MHS recommendations have three sets of standard protocols developed by the CCITT: P1, P2, and P3.

Protocol P1, defined by X.411, contains rules for routing information between two MTAs. These rules govern formatting, or how the information is to be packaged. The data to be sent is in what may be referred to as an *envelope*. Other fields associated with the envelope known as *content elements* perform the following:

- A unique message identifier indicates where the message originated and the name of the sender.
- Describe how the information should be displayed.
- Describe the destination address and destination user.
- Delivery instructions and instructions for any return receipt information, if required.

Protocol P2 is defined in the X.420 specification and defines the type of services requested, such as:

- Allowing only authorized users to send messages
- Specifying the type of notification required of the recipient (such as an immediate reply to a message)
- Providing subject information (This is especially useful for companies that receive large volumes of messages.)

Protocol P3 provides rules for changing the existing parameters for E-mail routing and delivery, including:

- The need for a password
- A need to alter the maximum size of a message
- The need for a test (before the actual delivery) to determine if a message can be delivered

CCITT X.500

The CCITT X.500 set of recommendations, when implemented, will facilitate worldwide E-mail by providing the basis for a common directory. The inability to solve the problem of incompatible post-office-box addresses in the E-mail services of different networks is a major limitation of the x.400. The X.500 recommendations respond to this problem by creating a standard for a global directory of E-mail users.

Once implemented, X.500 will have a major impact on worldwide electronic messaging. For example, a user on a network in Harrisburg, Pennsylvania, will be able to routinely send messages to a user on an IBM mainframe in Frankfurt, Germany.

X.500 uses a hierarchical directory structure. Users access the X.500 directory through a directory user agent, which communicates with the directory using the directory-access protocol.

Message Handling Service

In October 1986, Action Technologies began offering its MHS software to developers. In early 1988, Novell began bundling MHS with NetWare 2.1 without charge. Novell now owns MHS and is developing products from other vendors to support it.

MHS contains X.400-like services, including:

- Management of access to user agents
- Nondelivery alert
- Content type
- Delivery notification
- Multiple destinations

- Message relay and forwarding
- Workgroup addressing
- Dead-letter notification

When a user requests transmission of a message, MHS takes the message and places it in an envelope that contains control information similar to the x.400. Accompanying the message is a message control block, an 18-line ASCII file that contains information on the desired destination, a date and time stamp, the priority requested, and return notification requirements. MHS messages consist of three parts: a header, the text of the message, and an associated parcel (consisting of any binary encoded data). This three-part architecture allows messages to be sent along with lengthy reports or data files.

MHS provides gateways to other networks and can even convert messages to the appropriate format for those networks. Since it is compatible with the X.400 standards, the MHS store-and-forward mode of operation allows messages to be sent with delivery dates and times. This means that electronic messages can be scheduled to be sent at a certain time.

Users don't see or use MHS directly. Instead MHS enables programmers to develop application programs, including E-mail and scheduling programs, that work in conjunction with it. Since different application programs will share this common interface, in the near future, programs can use MHS to communicate directly with other programs on different networks.

MHS messages can start executable programs. An entire scheduling and program-execution system can be made to function over different networks at different times, 24 hours a day. For example, say a manufacturing company has plants nationwide and one central supply area. Each plant can run a program showing the inventory used, with the data from these reports sent to the central supply area. At this location, all the information is collected and placed in a database. A report can then be generated telling the superintendents in charge of material disbursement what needs to be shipped and where to ship it. All this can be done without human intervention.

Simple Mail Transfer Protocol

SMTP was developed for the U.S. Department of Defense as an easy-to-use mail system for the Internet. SMTP, which is part of the suite of protocols known as *TCP/IP*, is often used to transfer mail between two network workstations that are connected remotely.

CHAPTER 12

NETWORK SOFTWARE

As the title implies, this chapter is about software that runs on a local area network (LAN). Almost all of the applications, or programs, on the market for stand-alone PCs can be used on a LAN. In addition, there are network-specific applications designed to operate in a multiuser environment such as a LAN. Many of these applications are single-user programs that were changed to accommodate the needs of a network. Certain considerations must be taken into account when installing or purchasing software for a LAN. These considerations include:

- Software licensing
- Site licensing
- Databases
- Shared data files
- Group software
- Network software

Software Licensing

Software licensing is an area of great concern and debate within the LAN community. One problem is the lack of legal uniformity—one software licensure may be entirely different from the licensure for another software package—however, certain matters are clear.

Single-user software is designed to be used either on a single machine or by only one user at a time. Using such software in a networking environment, where multiple users can access it is clearly illegal. It can, however, be used on a LAN. One way to do this is by using *metering software*, which limits access at any given time to only the number of licensed copies that are installed on the LAN.

For example, the software may be placed on a LAN that has 20 users, all of whom need access to a spreadsheet at some time during the week. None of the 20 users, however, needs constant access. The company has five legal copies of the spreadsheet program, so the metering software is set to five. Each request to use the spreadsheet goes through the metering system. When five users have accessed and are using the spreadsheet program, user number 6 is denied access and must wait until one of the other users is finished. Thus, the metering system maintains the legality of the LAN.

There are other ways to share software programs—specifically, network versions of a particular software package—on a LAN. Now that LANs are a major element within the data processing departments of corporate America, software developers are designing special versions of their software for LAN use. These LAN-specific packages are sold in increments of the number of users serviced—a word-processing package may be purchased that serves 5 users or one that serves 16 users. Buying a network version helps ensure smooth operation on the LAN and does away with the need for multiple copies of software.

Site Licensing

Site licensing is another way software developers allow software to be sold. A site license gives an unlimited number of users at that site access to the software on the LAN.

Why should the software run on a LAN rather than on stand-alone PCs? Some of the reasons include compatibility, uniformity, and a common knowledge base.

Compatibility

Word-processing programs, spreadsheets, and databases are the three most commonly used software applications. Compatibility between various applications is an issue—not all word processors can read or write the formats of other word processors. The same is true of most spreadsheets, databases, and other software. Thus, if Susan is using one word processor and Jerry is using another, they can't exchange documents. Even if Jerry's word processor could import text from Susan's word processor, the formats may be incompatible. Using the LAN version will ensure compatibility by reducing the number of different packages available.

Uniformity

Now assume that Susan and Jerry have the same word processor. However, Jerry has an older version of the program. Susan can now do things Jerry can't, even though Jerry has the same program. Using the LAN version will ensure uniformity and consistency among users.

Common Knowledge Base

Reducing the number of application packages supported on the network will increase the administrator's efficiency. The network administrator will be an expert on a few popular applications and can provide users with better support.

Databases

Database software is the workhorse of the LAN. Word processing may be used extensively, but database processing places a greater load on the network. It seems that everyone on a LAN can use a database program to some extent, and many applications are written in database languages. Because of the drain database programs create on a network, sharing data files should be considered as an option.

The Database Engine

We've already discussed client-server computing on a LAN, but this is a good place to mention that many front ends can access the back end, or *database engine*. This is a software product that may be used on the network in conjunction with a database. The front end can be a spreadsheet program, a custom programmed application, or a time-management program. The database engine, or back end—a centralized repository of data—services the requests of these various front ends, or clients. This database engine finds the requested data in the requested database file and transmits only the requested data, not the entire file to the front end. This can be more efficient in transaction time and network traffic and management than the more conventional method of operation, where the server sends the requested database file to the workstation and permits the front end to find the requested information in the requested database file.

Shared Data Files

File and record locking make file sharing possible.

File and Record Locking

File and record locking allows data to be shared on a LAN without putting the data files at risk of being damaged. Locking usually occurs on network and site-licensed software and custom programmed applications for multiple users.

Locks are generally used when files are edited, updated, or modified. File locking is initiated when users access a file from the application program. The first user to access the file is the one who gets the lock and control of the file. The user who establishes that lock is the only one who can write to the file; other users can read the file, but they can't write to it. Once the lock is removed, the file is ready to be locked by someone else.

Record locking is similar but more detailed. Because the user locks a record in the file instead of the entire file, other users can modify the file but not the record that's locked. Record locking is preferable to file locking because several users can place record locks on a single file.

Some programmers are going a step beyond record locking to *field locking*, which allows users to modify any field of a record except the one that's locked.

Some of the new fourth-generation languages available for network development make instant onscreen updates possible. This is known as *real-time computing*. For example, if a user is running an inventory application on a LAN and wants to know how many RR2s are in stock, the inventory program shows that 23 RR2s are available. But at the parts counter, a sales clerk just

sold an RR2. Because the program is designed to update the inventory immediately after a sale at the counter, once this transaction is complete the supervisor
screen indicates that only 22 RR2s are now available for sale. The screen updates
itself without the user's intervention. This is often called a *screen refresh*.

Group Software

Some programs now allow multiple users to work on the same project. All the
users see the same screen, and each time a user modifies the project, the others
see the effect of that modification in real time. An example of groupware is
the software product For Comment, which allows multiple users to work on
the same document.

Like client-server software, this is a growing area that will take LANs into
the next stage: network computing.

Network Software

As mentioned earlier, single- and multiuser software can exist on the same
LAN. However, there's more to networking software than just loading it on
the file server. Many software programs, unfortunately, aren't compatible with
a well-managed network.

The following guidelines help define programs that should work well on
a network:

- The network manager can use variables within the application's setup
  program to define the directory location.
- The network manager can create user setup files and defaults that the
  application stores in a centrally managed database.
- The user can log in several times simultaneously and from different work-
  stations.
- No hardware key is needed to log into or use the program.
- The network manager can define temporary locations.
- The user is kept from the command line, but the network manager can
  set command-line parameters.

- Password security is closely linked with network operating system security.
- To ensure license compliance, user log files are not used.
- Network printing features include printing to a queue, printer setup strings within a print job, and direct close-and-print queue communication.
- Is the network using DOS alone or is the network using DOS and Microsoft Windows?

Directory Location

Software developers shouldn't make any assumptions about where a program will be located on the server. A LAN administrator must be able to place the application in any subdirectory of any volume on the server. Under no circumstances should the administrator have to place a program on drive G: or H:.

Directories should be established by variables in the application's setup program. These variables identify program and data directories, enabling the program to identify file locations without a search path.

Alternatively, the LAN administrator can create a subdirectory for the program's data and a subdirectory for the executable program. The executable program is then defined in the network's search-path statements. The user goes to the data subdirectory and enters the name of the application program. The network operating system then runs through its search paths and executes the program. As you can imagine, it doesn't take many applications for the search paths to become too large.

Other alternatives do exist and are addressed under Network Management in Chapter 13.

User Setup Files

For ease of use and better network management, a program should let the LAN administrator create unique setup files that configure the program to the workstation. This setup is run each time the user accesses the program.

The setup files allow individual users to specify colors, file defaults, printers, and other parameters. By allowing this, users always have their own operating environments, regardless of where they log in. To save management time and disk space, these files should be kept in a central directory rather than in the individual users' directories.

User Login

A user should be able to log into a program from several locations concurrently. This may not be a very secure way to have a program installed, but in some instances it may be necessary. For example, Susan logs into a program and starts a report on one workstation. She may then go to another workstation and log into the program again to do another task.

Some programs track each user as he or she logs into the program, preventing that user from logging in more than once. Other programs use a temporary file that doesn't allow duplicate names for logins. Depending on the application and how it's used, this may not be a factor.

Hardware Key

A hardware key, also known as a *dongle*, contains firmware code and connects to a parallel port. Some software developers use dongles as a form of copy protection to ensure licensing compliance. The software randomly checks for the dongle's presence and if it is not found, the program stops running.

Users wishing to access such programs must have dongles attached to their workstations, although this requirement creates more work for the LAN. If Susan's workstation has a dongle and is malfunctioning, she can go to another user's workstation, which has no dongle and log into the network. She then starts the program. Since the workstation has no dongle, however, Susan can't do anything with the program.

Temporary Files

These files are frequently used for temporary settings, memory overflow, and spooling of print jobs. One problem with temporary files is that they're often written in either the program directory or the data directory, which can cause file name conflicts with other files. Another problem is that certain naming conventions for temporary files may require too much network savvy on the part of the user.

An application's setup program should let you define the location of the temporary files on a per-user basis. A user's home directory is an ideal location for these files. Temporary files should never be in the same directory as program files. Some programs don't erase the temporary files once they're no longer needed so either the user or the LAN administrator needs to make sure these files are deleted. Rights to the program directory can be set to read-only, and each user can have a home directory with full rights to create and delete temporary files.

WordPerfect brings up a naming-convention problem and tests the user's network savvy. This word processor uses the user's initials in the temporary file name. If a user logs into WordPerfect a second time concurrently with the first time, the program will ask the user if another copy of the program is running. If the user answers affirmatively, the program will then ask the user to enter the name of another drive and directory in which to store the temporary files; if the answer is no, the second login will overwrite the first login's temporary files. Because users don't usually know the network drive letters or directory names, they do not have this option.

Command Line

Many programs let the user drop, or *shell out*, to the command line to run utilities or enter DOS commands. On a single-user version of the software, this may be fine, but sometimes it's better to prevent the user from reaching the command line. Some LAN administrators feel that if users reach the command line, they can wander around the network drives, compromising network security. Applications that exit to the command line should let the LAN administrator disable the feature on a user-by-user basis.

Passwords

Passwords are normally used when a user logs into the network. Many application programs require passwords upon execution, but it is inconvenient for users to enter a password every time they access an application.

User authentication for an application should be done in conjunction with the database of network operating system logins. The application can then determine the user's name and interrogate the application's login-name database to see if that user is authorized to use the program. This eliminates the need to enter a login name or password when entering a program.

The application should also have menu-item security based on user authentication. Because a user normally doesn't need access to every item on a menu, a simple method of restricting access should be in place. Applications should show only those menu items the user has permission to use.

User Logging

Some programs, in an attempt to limit the number of users because of a licensure agreement, keep track of who is using the applications by writing the users' names to a log file. This method can, however, place an extra burden on the LAN administrator in that it may not be clear how many users are actually using a program. If Susan exits the program incorrectly by a reboot or power-down, the log file doesn't erase her name, so it will keep her from running the application again. To be able to use the program, Susan must have the LAN administrator clear her name from the log file.

Printing

Printing is one of those activities that always seems to cause trouble on a network. Some applications make the printing problem worse; a good network application will let the user print to a queue.

When users print from a stand-alone workstation to a directly connected printer, they can download fonts to the printer once a day. The only way to deviate from these fonts once they're loaded is by powering down the printer. On a network, however, the printer accepts jobs from many users with a variety of printing demands. Therefore, the network applications must provide a flexible printer setup.

Because making assumptions about the printer status is risky, all setup strings (codes that put the printer in a certain state) should be transmitted as part of the print job and should immediately precede the data to be printed. The programs should always reset the printer to its default state when the job is finished.

Applications must have default settings for all the printers they will use. Additionally, they should allow the user to choose the desired printer from within the application.

Windows

Many applications today operate under the Microsoft Windows environment. This can be an issue for the network manager, because memory on workstations can be more of a critical issue. Windows allows *multitasking*—the ability to have more than one application program operating at one time. This feature uses memory making the question of a hard disk an issue. Windows uses the hard disk for memory writing and retrieving (swapping), a type of virtual memory. Should this disk be the file server's or should each workstation have its own hard disk? Should Windows be launched or started from the file server, or should each workstation launch its own version of Windows. The Windows environment brings many more questions into play, such as *OLE*, object linking and embedding, and *DDE*, dynamic data exchange. Complete books have been written just on these subjects.

SECTION III

MANAGING AND TROUBLE-SHOOTING LANS

CHAPTER 13

NETWORK MANAGEMENT

LAN administration can be exciting and challenging. This chapter lists some of the duties of a LAN administrator. The best place to start is to establish procedures for the network.

LAN Management Procedures

As with minicomputer and mainframe systems, certain procedures need to be established and followed when a LAN is used. This will help ensure the smooth operation of the network and data integrity.

These procedures include but are not limited to:

- Backup
- Archive
- Disaster recovery
- Security
- Virus protection.

Another LAN management task, troubleshooting, is covered in more depth in Chapter 15.

Backup

As discussed earlier, it's wise to have a backup server on the LAN. Without backups, the loss of data on the file server could put a company out of business. The importance of backups is never fully appreciated until something happens to the data.

With that thought in mind, be aware that a backup policy should be devised and carried out *without exception*. Many LAN administrators use a rotational tape sequence covering a three-week period: A copy of the network's data exists for three weeks prior to the current date. This is known as the *backup window*. (Two weeks or four weeks might also be appropriate, depending on the amount of data and the time span desired for the backup window.) After three weeks, any data that needs to be retrieved is done by other procedures (such as archiving and historical files).

This process continues for three weeks, then starts over again. Many people familiar with minicomputer and mainframe systems refer to this cycling as the Son, Father, and Grandfather. Three generations are created, each corresponding to a week of backup. This procedure is fairly simple (see Figure 13.1):

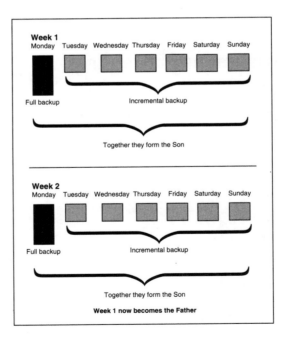

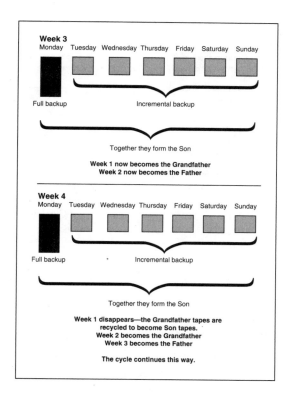

FIGURE 13.1 Rotation sequence.

On Monday of the first week of the cycle, all the data on the LAN is backed up. This is the Son tape. On subsequent days, only the data files that were modified since the last backup are backed up. This is an *incremental backup* (see Figure 13.2).

Each day's backup is done on a separate tape. Therefore, the entire cycle would use 21 tapes.

On Monday of the second week of the cycle, another full backup is done of all data files on the LAN. On subsequent days of the week, a backup is done of only the data files that were modified since the last backup. During this second week, the Son tapes become the Father tapes; the second week's tapes become the new Son. This is where the rotation is applied.

On Monday of the third week of the cycle, the data files are backed up onto yet another set of tapes. The Father set of tapes is now the Grandfather, the Son tapes are the Father tapes, and the new tapes become the Son.

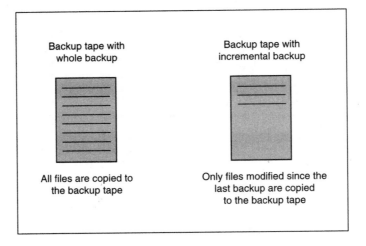

Backup tape with
whole backup

Backup tape with
incremental backup

All files are copied to
the backup tape

Only files modified since the
last backup are copied
to the backup tape

FIGURE 13.2 The difference between incremental and complete backups

The cycle is now complete: three weeks' worth of data has been backed up. Now let's look at what happens during the next cycle.

On Monday of the first week of the new cycle, all data files on the LAN are backed up. On subsequent days, an incremental backup is done. Again, the Father becomes the Grandfather, the Son becomes the Father, and the new backup becomes the Son. Notice that a three-week window exists; for example, you can't retrieve a file that was on the Grandfather tape from the third week of the first cycle.

The cycle outlined here is a three-generation rotational tape sequence, but a number of variations exist. Full backups could be done on Friday, for example, while on the other days only incremental backups would be performed.

Some LAN administrators do more than one incremental backup a day. They may do one in the morning, one in the afternoon, and another at the end of the day. This helps ensure that any file can be retrieved. Say you create a spreadsheet in the morning and save it. The incremental backup is done later that morning, saving your spreadsheet. After lunch, you retrieve the spreadsheet and modify it substantially. You realize that your changes weren't necessary, but by that time the original spreadsheet is gone. With the incremental backup done that morning, however, you can retrieve the original spreadsheet.

After the backup system is online, test it by making a backup, erasing the data, and then restoring the data. If the data is restored to the disk in readable form, the system is working. If not, you'll need to ascertain the problem and get it resolved. Nothing is worse than going to a backup tape that has been corrupted.

Two backup copies should be made: one to stay on site and another to be put in a safe place off site. Some LAN administrators the backup tapes in a fire- and waterproof safe rather than make duplicate copies. This is not always a good solution because while the tapes may not burn in a fire, the temperature inside the safe could render them useless.

Historical files are often made in addition to the backup. The backup procedure just outlined has a window of only three weeks in which to retrieve a file. Some LAN administrators do a full backup every month and store the tapes rather than copy over them. This method isn't failsafe, but it can help when some form of a file needs to be retrieved. Other LAN administrators use other time frames for historical files.

Archiving

Archiving is different from creating a backup. Both involve copying files to a storage medium; when a file is archived, however, it is then removed from the file server's disk to free up disk space.

Files aren't archived and removed at random. Every so often—say, every six months—any files that haven't been used during that period are archived and removed from the file server.

Unlike backup tapes, archive tapes are not rotated; they are indexed and stored. The index tells the LAN administrator what period the tape covers and the directories and files it contains. A good indexing system allows the LAN administrator to easily find an archived file. Archiving with an index means a user can come back a year or more later, ask for a certain file, and have it restored to the network.

Determining whether a file has been used involves looking at the time stamp associated with the file. Every file contains the date and time of its creation. Whenever the file is modified, this stamp changes to reflect the date and time at which the file was modified. If a file hasn't been modified for six months, the date and time will be six months earlier.

The LAN administrator can check file dates manually, but that would be tedious and time-consuming. An alternative is to use archiving software that automatically checks the date and time stamp and then archives, indexes, and deletes the appropriate files. This software can be set to work at different time intervals. If six months is the time limit, for example, the archive software checks for a date of six months or older. Compact discs are often used to store archived files because; they're more durable than tape and hold larger quantities of files.

Disaster Recovery

Where LANs are concerned, a disaster can range from a fire, flood, or earthquake to fault tolerance or user error on a large scale, such as when a user inadvertently or maliciously erases an entire directory of data files. Disaster recovery, therefore, should encompass true disasters, fault tolerance, and improper network usage.

True Disasters

When a true disaster strikes, a company can be saved if backup and archiving procedures were followed. If they were followed, a set of backup tapes should exist off site so they can be loaded onto a file server at some other location. While a true disaster can severely hurt a company, at least the data and program files can be restored.

When a disaster plan is devised, the alternate file server and network should already be arranged. That may entail borrowing space and time on another company's network or putting a small network into operation at another site.

Fault Tolerance

The level of fault tolerance desired is determined by the cost the company is willing to absorb. Basic fault tolerance is achieved by using redundant devices, such as duplicate disk drives, duplicate controller cards and disk drives, or a duplicate file server. If the primary file server goes down, the secondary file server takes over.

Improper Use of the Network

This type of disaster is best controlled by having good network security, but security plans aren't foolproof. Again, the best recourse is to perform the backup and archiving procedures regularly.

Security

A LAN administrator must keep the network secure from unauthorized access. This means limiting access to network users and eliminating network access by noncompany employees.

The security features found on most network operating systems can be used to limit access to confidential and sensitive information. These features give the user certain rights depending on his or her location on the network. The LAN administrator should also require the use of a password during the login procedure.

The following is a partial list of what the administrator can do to help keep the network secure:

• Prevent users from placing their passwords in a batch file for automatic login. Batch files can be viewed by unauthorized users.

• Require that passwords have a minimum number of characters.

• Require that users change their passwords at regular intervals, such as every 30, 60, or 90 days.

• Require the use of unique passwords when they're changed. In other words, a user can't choose the same password twice.

• Prevent users from logging into the network from several workstations concurrently.

• Instruct the users never to walk away from their workstations while they are logged into the network. If they leave their area, they should first log out. An unattended workstation is an open invitation to an unauthorized person.

• Assign temporary users a network account with an expiration date.

• Lock out a particular network account after a predetermined number of password attempts.

In addition, the LAN administrator should be notified whenever an employee is terminated or voluntarily leaves the company so that employee's network account can be disabled or deleted.

A good way to prevent people from accessing the network remotely is by using a callback modem. When this modem receives a call, it requires that a password be entered and then it calls the user back. It has a table listing all authorized users, their passwords, and their phone numbers.

Finally, the administrator should see to it that the file servers, fixed disks, and backup servers are in a secure area to avoid theft or copying of data.

Virus Protection

Computer viruses have become a real threat to the computer industry. Once it infects a LAN, a virus can wreak havoc. Viruses range from relatively benign, showing "GOTCHA" on the screen to quite malevolent, corrupting data files. The corruption can infiltrate the backup files even before the virus is detected.

The most insidious aspect of viruses is the way they spread. If a LAN accesses another LAN across the state, the virus can be transmitted from one to the other and the newly infected LAN can in turn infect another LAN.

Viruses usually take one of the following three forms, athough there may be others:

- A *worm* is a program that reproduces itself without necessarily infecting the host program. It runs amok, filling RAM or fixed-disk space with little clones and overwriting programs and data in the process.

- A *Trojan horse* is a program that carries a potentially damaging item: a virus. An excellent example is a virus checker that carries and distributes a virus.

- An actual *virus* is a program that inserts itself into, or attaches itself to, an executable (.COM or .EXE) file or system (.DRV or .SYS) file, then infects other files the same way. When the virus attaches to an executable file, it runs every time the program is invoked. Memory-resident viruses can sit in RAM, redirect DOS calls from a modified or relocated vector table, perform some task, and route the DOS call back to its intended destination. They can turn .COM files to garbage, delete track 0 from the hard disk, slow down the system, jam the printers, and use up computer time.

Although viruses are frequently blamed for everything that goes wrong on the network, the problem may not be a virus. The following symptoms indicate that a network may be infected with a virus:

- Programs that are used every day begin to run more slowly. The user can best determine if a program has the same response time it used to have.

- Disk access is ill-timed or more frequent than normal.

- Program load time increases. For example, a program that used to load in 60 seconds now takes 3 minutes.

- The workstation locks up more frequently.

- Hardware and software problems occur after a component is added to the system.

- Users receive unusual or humorous error messages.

- Available disk space decreases rapidly.

- TSRs that used to work now execute improperly or not at all.

The best way to treat a virus is to prevent it from getting onto the network. Here are a few precautions you can take:

- Make and follow a backup procedure.

- Get a good virus checker. Several types are available: a *scanner* checks files for known virus signatures, a *monitor-type checker* looks at DOS calls, and another type takes snapshots of the disk and compares the files at various times.

- Don't let users download files from bulletin boards.

- Buy software only from reputable sources.

- Don't allow users to place copied programs on the network.

- Don't loan out disks, especially original program disks.

- Make your .COM and .EXE files read-only with the DOS *ATTRIB* command.

- Have a stand-alone workstation that tests disks before their contents are placed on the network. It's better to infect a single stand-alone workstation than an entire network.

Now let's look at some of the other responsibilities of a LAN administrator.

Hardware and Software Maintenance

The LAN administrator must troubleshoot software for users, perhaps deciding that outside training services are needed for certain applications.

When a new release of an application is issued, the LAN administrator installs it on the network.

The LAN administrator also maintains the functionality of the network's hardware, whether it's a network interface card or a file server, when a hardware problem occurs, it must be remedied. The LAN administrator may do all, some, or none of the actual hardware repair or installation, depending on whether a contract exists with an outside company specializing in hardware maintenance. All hardware should be documented, and a journal should be kept. Documentation will be discussed later in this chapter.

Distributed Network Management

Distributed network management provides for centralized management of a network or internetwork. The centralized console can communicate with any device, be it a bridge, concentrator, or router on the network, providing valuable information for the LAN administrator.

The protocol that allows communication between the console and network device is known as *SNMP*. Another distributed management protocol, the Common Management Information Protocol (CMIP), can be used, but SNMP is by far the leader in the installed base of networks.

An SNMP implementation consists of three components:

- *Network agents*—These are devices to be managed, such as routers and bridges.
- *Network Management Stations (NMSes)*—These are host computers that manage the network.
- *The SNMP protocol*—This specification describes not only how the agents and managers communicate but also the types of information they can exchange.

Agents must include SNMP agent software. The agents or devices use this software to monitor network information—such as the number of connections or the speed of transmission—at their specific locations.

An NMS is a PC workstation on the network that is dedicated to the management of the network using the SNMP protocol. The NMS must contain SNMP management software, which may be considered the front-end program. The NMS polls and requests from the agents or devices information that is placed in a database and the SNMP software so the LAN administrator can view it.

NMSes also feature *graphical user interfaces* (GUIs), but SNMP doesn't dictate any specific GUI. Some SNMP management software uses Windows as the interface.

SNMP is not the management software that resides in the NMS; it is the communication agent that carries messages from the agents. SNMP allows administrators to monitor and analyze networks and isolate faults. The agents have software that places messages into the SNMP protocol.

SNMP is actually a protocol suite consisting of three specifications: *RFC 1157* (the SNMP), *RFC 1156* and *RFC 1158* (the *management information base*, or MIB), and *RFC 1155* (the *structure of management information*, or SMI).

The MIB defines the kinds of information—variables—that vendors must implement to be SNMP-compliant. The base MIB defines only the minimum set of variables (approximately 100), including information such as the number of packets transmitted, the number of errors, and the last connection opened and closed.

Each agent or device on the network includes an MIB and each NMS has a database containing all the MIB variables.

MIB information is either device-specific or device-independent. Vendors can add information to the base MIB to differentiate their products; these additions are referred to as *enterprise branches*, *enterprise extensions*, or *proprietary extensions*.

Although adding vendor-specific extensions to the MIB gives SNMP more functionality, it may create compatibility problems. In an attempt to overcome these problems, the Internet Activities Board (IAB) Internet Engineering Task Force is adding elements to the base MIB, and vendors are forming alliances to make sure their products are compatible.

RFC 1156 is a document that defines the original MIB, called MIB-1. MIB-2, which is defined in the RFC 1158 document, has additional variables and is backward-compatible with MIB-1.

The SMI defines the structure and language for organizing all the SNMP network management information. All such information and SNMP controls must be represented in one of the forms defined in the SMI specification.

Note that it's possible to manage a non-SNMP device or network with an SNMP manager by installing proxy agents in that device or LAN. Proxy agents are usually developed by third parties and are most useful when you have a proprietary network management protocol, such as IBM's NetView, that you want to use in an SNMP-managed environment. The proxy agent translates proprietary protocols into NMP-readable protocols.

In 1988, the IAB endorsed SNMP as the standard network management protocol for TCP/IP networks.

Other Administrative Tasks

Network Planning

The LAN administrator must know the status of the network at all times and stay abreast of company plans for data processing with regard to the LAN. By doing these two things, the administrator can plan and budget for network growth, whether that means adding a few new workstations, adding another server, connecting to a wide-area network, or connecting to a host system. This maintains controlled growth and avoids the problems that occur when development is rushed.

Maintaining Network Performance

While this is a LAN management duty, maintaining the performance of the network usually implies that something is wrong—This topic is covered in Chapter 14.

Maintaining the User Interface

The LAN administrator must maintain the user interface of the LAN. This often involves using a menu program to create menus with enough power that users need never go to the command line. The users don't need to know all the DOS and network commands—everything they need to do they should be able to do from established menus.

Documentation

An important part of a LAN is its documentation. Items that should be documented are the configuration of the network, problems that have occurred on the network, resolution of those problems, and changes in hardware or software. Documentation should be in an easy-to-reach and easy-to-understand format.

Procedures should also be documented, as should the purchase date of all products along with the model and serial numbers. In other words: *when in doubt, document it.*

CHAPTER 14

LAN TROUBLESHOOTING

Troubleshooting is a task that all LAN administrators must perform at one time or another. Depending on their skill level and experience, administrators may be able to troubleshoot the network on a small or large scale. In either case, experience is a great teacher when it comes to troubleshooting a network.

Many LAN administrators spend a great deal of time troubleshooting network problems. One user calls to report that he or she can't print; another calls complaining that he or she can't log into the network. Yet another user calls, irate, because the workstation is frequently hanging—the LAN administrator must diagnose these problems. Once the root of the problem is found, solving the problem is fairly easy. Many times, all that's needed is to replace faulty hardware or software.

The LAN administrator can solve the problem in one of two ways: by using a structured, rigorous methodology or by *shotgunning*; the latter method involves educated guesses and arbitrarily replacing components to see if the problem disappears, while using a *structured methodology*, requires definitively knowing what the problem is before fixing it. Most experienced LAN administrators use both approaches in a staged fashion. For a new LAN administrator, a structured approach is recommended, until experience provides the knowledge base needed to make educated guesses.

This chapter outlines a three-step process for finding the cause of a problem. The first stage involves doing some quick checks without specialized equipment. These checks can often reveal the cause of a problem, but they rely on the administrator's experience and ability to recognize areas that have changed on the network. The network documentation is very helpful at this point. Besides showing how the network originally operated compared to how it operates now, the documentation indicates whether this or a similar problem occurred before and, if so, how the problem was resolved in the past.

For example, if users are complaining about large file transfers failing, an administrator might suspect a malfunctioning bridge because he or she knows that other bridges have failed recently. It would be a safe bet to suspect the bridge and direct efforts toward that device.

If these quick checks don't isolate the problem, go on to stage two. The second stage involves taking a closer look at the network for special indicators or symptoms. Specialized tools are often needed to identify symptoms that point to the cause of the problem.

Using the bridge as an example: If a bridge has never gone bad and this particular bridge has been on the network long enough to be considered stable, more information needs to be collected before suspecting the bridge. A new path to bypass the bridge could temporarily be added, then if the problem disappears or lessens, it can be safely assumed that the bridge is at fault. If the bridge starts dropping frames because of high traffic loads, equipment is needed to help increase the load and measure the bridge's ability to forward frames to detect the malfunction.

The first two stages require some familiarity with normal network operations so that abnormalities will be apparent. Establish network baselines in your documentation—typical values for such factors as traffic load, CPU use, types of applications, types of protocols, number of users, and amount of traffic per user.

The third stage requires going outside the company either for specialized equipment or a person who specializes in network troubleshooting. This can be expensive and should be done sparingly.

Let's look at the three stages of the troubleshooting process in more detail.

Stage One: Quick Checks

Many network faults are the result of a component failure or a change in a component. The key to stage one is collecting enough accurate information to determine whether that's the case—without spending so much time on it that the quick check is no longer quick.

It is important to fully understand the problem being diagnosed. Missing vital information at the beginning of a check can lead to an incorrect diagnosis and an inappropriate fix. An understanding of the problem will also help determine whether a more thorough check is needed.

The goal of this stage is to identify and eliminate potential causes of the problem. The best way to do this is to talk to the users. Solicit their input and complaints. Ask them to re-create the problem, if possible, so you can witness it firsthand. Find out if the problem is widespread, with several people affected or if only one person is experiencing the problem. Check to see if the problem is preventing users from working or whether it's simply a performance problem that is causing delays or interruptions.

Always be aware of the kinds of work the users do and the applications they use. For example, if a user is having trouble printing a document, the problem could be that he or she isn't executing the print command properly. Familiarity with users' work and applications allows some problems to be fixed quickly.

Sometimes performing one or two simple tests is required to ascertain the severity or scope of the problem. You may get the system back up and running more quickly by simply replacing or swapping a component or two. If this doesn't work, some information has still been obtained without wasting much time.

Phase One is when experience and documentation are crucial. Is anything about the problem similar to a previous problem? For example, assume several adapter cards have gone bad in the past. They started creating errors shortly before they failed completely—as documentation should show. Now a user is having trouble attaching to the network. After asking some questions and finding out that he or she is getting error messages similar to those associated with the cards that failed in the past it becomes apparent that the problem is solved, remedied, and documented.

Most problems encountered on the network have probably happened before, making it possible to identify the problem just by going over the network's history in your mind. If you're new to the network, you can use the documentation to see if the current problem is similar to an old one.

Many network failures occur after something has been changed or modified. Changes in topology, configuration, applications, and users can all cause a network to fail. If thinking through past experience with the network or its documentation doesn't shed any light on the problem, begin thinking about the present. Has anything changed on the network? Were new components added? Did any of the users change? Were any connective devices reconfigured?

When it is suspected that the problem may be caused by recent network changes, verify the correct operation of any suspect components and their connection to the network. Incorrect configurations or connections are often inadvertent.

Some problems occur when people other than the LAN administrator make changes to the network. When asking users about the problem at hand, be sure to ask them if they recently made any changes. Also ask what they were doing just prior to the problem because changes may have been made inadvertently.

If past experience and network documentation don't isolate the problem and there haven't been any recent changes, it's time for stage two.

Stage Two: A Closer Look at the Network

In the second stage, the network is divided into workable segments so you don't have the entire network to contend with. Each segment can then be examined and either ruled out or found to be the cause of the problem.

Because more information must be gathered during this stage, specialized equipment—such as a protocol analyzer—may be needed.

Most network problems are directly related to the network components. The following is a list of some of the components that may need to be examined more closely:

- Workstation
- Network adapter
- Wiring concentrator
- Cabling
- Server
- Host
- Bridges
- Routers
- Gateways
- Protocol stacks

Ask at least the following questions when gathering information:

- *Do any stations work?* Find out if other users near the one who voiced the complaint are also having problems. If so, the server, host, or interconnection devices along the path to the server or host can be suspect. If not, focus on the workstation, the cabling, and any wiring concentrators that connect to the workstation.

- *Is there any traffic on the network?* A protocol analyzer can help answer this question by showing the amount of traffic on the network. Little or no traffic indicates a major component failure—the type of traffic that does exist can help determine which component may be at fault. If the traffic is unusually high, see who is generating the traffic and why (make sure the traffic is legitimate). Also check for "chattering" components—those that repeatedly transmit data after they should have stopped.

- *Can the station operate as a stand-alone device?* This question determines whether there is a PC malfunction or a network component malfunction. If the workstation can operate in stand-alone mode, the problem may be the adapter card or the network configuration on the workstation. If the workstation can't operate in stand-alone mode, troubleshooting of the PC will be required.

- *Can the station connect to the network?* If any type of connection is made to the network, several possibilities can immediately be eliminated because the workstation hardware is functioning and the physical connection to the network is fine. If the workstation can't connect, the first thing to do is check the wiring. This is best done using a media tester—sometimes referred to as a *time domain reflectometer*—to isolate a wiring problem. If the wiring is good, the problem lies in the workstation.

- *Is the adapter on the workstation functioning?* Determine this by swapping adapter cards, provided the workstation can connect to the network.

A *symptom* is a piece of information that points you in the direction of the problem. Table 14.1 shows some common symptoms of network problems.

Stage Three: Bringing in a Specialist

If all the segments and components have been examined and the problem still hasn't been isolated, it's time to call in a specialist. This person should be highly trained, have specialized equipment, and have a broad range of experience with network troubleshooting.

TABLE 14.1

User Complaints

Poor performance or slow response

Can't connect to the server

Lost connection with the server

Can't run an application

Can't print

Recent Changes

New user

New component

New application

Revision of an application

Revision of a component's software

Revision of the workstation operating system

Reconfiguration of components

Reconfiguration of the network operating system

Abnormal Behavior

Traffic heavier or lighter than usual

Different protocol mix

Different application mix

More protocol errors than usual

Server usage heavier or lighter than usual

Response time slower than usual.

SECTION IV

LAN STANDARDS, ARCHITECTURES, ACCESS METHODS, AND PROTOCOLS

CHAPTER 15

NETWORK ARCHITECTURES, STANDARDS, PROTOCOLS, AND ACCESS METHODS

The goal of a network is to incorporate the many hardware and software components into a useful functioning system. Unfortunately, this task isn't as simple as it sounds.

In an effort to bring hardware and software together, LAN architectures and standards are continually developed. Various standards organizations are attempting to lay a foundation on which to build LANs and data communications as a whole. Different devices from different manufacturers form the basic components of a LAN, so these devices must be able to communicate with one another (be *interoperable*). The computing industry is being encouraged to develop products that adhere to these emerging architectures and standards. A computer manufacturer cannot be forced to adhere to a standard, however; the standards can only be recommended.

Terminology

In this book, *protocol* refers to the predefined manner or set of rules by which a function or service is performed. A *standard*, meanwhile, is defined by rules and written specifications.

Many standards exist, including a few that computer manufacturers have created on their own. Because only one manufacturer can use its own standards, however, they are not standards in the true sense of the word. Products from other manufacturers may have to communicate with equipment produced using proprietary standards, and this is where most of the problems arise. One company's equipment may not be able to communicate with another company's equipment because of incompatible protocols or standards. Protocols regulate what is known as the *data format*, or the manner in which data is exchanged between layers. Many standards have been created by recognized standards organizations; these will be discussed later. The objective is to find some order in the chaos and allow diverse components to communicate with one another.

An *architecture* combines the existing standards and protocols needed to create a functioning network. In other words, the network defined by the combination of standards and protocols is called the *network architecture*. A network architecture is, therefore, also a standard—it defines the rules of a network and how its components can interact.

Characteristics of the various network architectures that have been developed meet the high-level objectives that the computer industry embraces. These consist of:

- *Connectivity*—This allows hardware and software products to be connected and form a unified networking system.
- *Modularity*—This permits the use of a relatively small set of mass-produced general-purpose building blocks in a wide array of network devices.
- *Ease of implementation*—By following industry networking standards, implementation will be simplified, and a variety of configurations that meet the needs of all users can be easily installed.
- *Ease of use*—This lets users take advantage of the communication facilities without concern for or knowledge of network structure or implementation.
- *Reliability*—This provides appropriate error detection and correction facilities.
- *Ease of modification*—This allows the network to evolve and be modified easily as user needs change or new technologies become available.

Architecture also determines the topology of the LAN.

Network Topologies

The workstations and file server in a LAN must be connected via a transmission medium or cabling. The physical layout of the network is called its *topology* and can be compared to a topographic map depicting the terrain—the "lay of the LAN." Topology of the LAN describes how it is constructed.

There are three basic topologies with various derivations. The most common topologies are the *star*, *ring*, and *linear bus*.

The Star Topology

The star network has a central hub connected to all the workstations, or nodes, and the file server via cables. All network traffic passes through the hub. and each workstation is a spoke emerging from that hub, like a wagon wheel (see Figure 15.1).

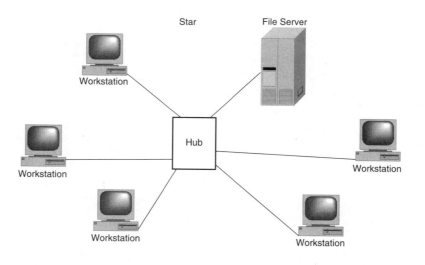

FIGURE 15.1 In a star, the controller may be a hub
to which the file server would be attached.

The star topology offers several advantages over the others (see Table 15.1). One is ease of maintenance—since the only area of concentration is at the hub, the cable layout is easy to modify. Diagnostics are also much easier to perform on a star topology. A defective cable line is easy to find, for example, because there is only one node for every cable accessing the hub.

TABLE 15.1 Advantages and disadvantages of the most common network topologies.

Topology	Advantages	Disadvantages
Star	Cable layouts are easy to modify. Workstations can be added to the network easily. Centralized control/ problems resulting from defective communication lines are easily identified.	Large amounts of cable are required. More cable means greater expense. A centralized hub means a single point for potential network failure.
Ring	Less cable is needed overall. Shorter cable means lower cabling costs. No wiring closet space is required.	A single node failure causes network failure. Fault diagnosis is more difficult. Network modification/ reconfiguration is more difficult and disrupts network operation.
Linear bus	It uses the least amount of cable. The wiring layout is simple. It has a resilient architecture; its simplicity makes it very reliable. It is very easy to extend.	Fault diagnosis and isolation are difficult. The trunk can be a bottleneck when network traffic is heavy.
Star-wired	Fault diagnosis and isolation are relatively easy. The modular design makes the network easy to expand.	Network configuration can be technically complicated. The cabling system is complicated.
Tree	It is easily extended. It simplifies fault isolation.	The structure depends on the root; if the primary bus fails, the network fails.

Conversely, a star LAN has certain disadvantages. The one-node-per-cable feature that makes diagnostics easier also increases the amount of cabling required, increasing the cost of setting up the network. A bigger problem is that because all the data must pass through a central point, if the hub fails, the entire network fails.

The Ring Topology

The ring topology connects several workstations on a single transmission medium, forming a ring. The wiring has no terminated ends because it forms a complete circle. Each node on the cabling acts as a repeater, boosting the signal between workstations. Data travels around the ring in only one direction and passes through each node as it does (see Figure 15.2).

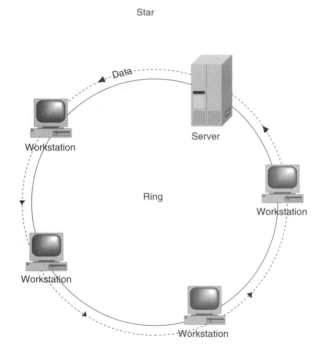

FIGURE 15.2 In a ring topology, data travels around the ring in only one direction and passes through each workstation.

One of the advantages of the ring topology is that less cable is needed, reducing costs. There also is no central hub, concentrator, or wiring center because this function is provided by the nodes.

On the down side, since the data is passed through each node, the failure of one node will bring down the entire network. Diagnostics are also harder to perform on a ring topology, and modifications are more difficult because the entire network must be brought down.

The Linear Bus Topology

The linear bus network consists of several nodes attached to a common cable. This cable is also known as a *trunk line*, *bus*, or *network segment*. The signal on the cable travels in both directions from the workstations. Each end of the cable is terminated, so when network traffic reaches the end of the cable it is removed from the network and does not bounce back. Unlike the ring topology, data in a linear bus network travels past the nodes rather than through them (Figure 15.3).

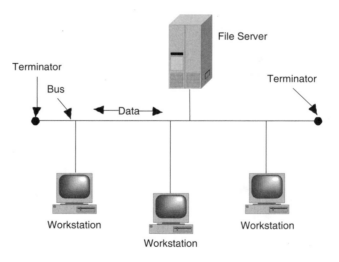

FIGURE 15.3 In a linear bus, the data can flow in either direction.
Both ends of the bus must be terminated.

The bus topology has certain advantages. Obvious ones are short cable length and a simple wiring layout. The workstations on the cable act as concentrators, or hubs. However, if one node goes down it doesn't affect the entire network, making it easier to expand the network by adding nodes.

The biggest disadvantage of the bus topology is that, because there are few points of concentration, fault diagnosis and isolation are difficult.

Hybrid Topologies

Modifying and combining some of the characteristics of these pure network topologies result in hybrid topologies, which often provide greater network efficiency. The hybrid topologies that currently dominate network design are the *star-wired ring*, and *tree*.

The Star-Wired Ring

As its name suggests, the star-wired ring combines the attributes of both the star and ring topologies. The hub of this topology, referred to as a *wiring center*, constitutes a ring. This wiring center can be in one location or several locations throughout the network and must form a complete physical connection. If the ring of the wiring center is broken, the network fails.

Workstations are attached to the ring, radiating outward from the wiring center. The workstations constitute the star section of this star-wired topology (see Figure 15.4). One important advantage of this topology is that if one or more workstations become inoperable, the network won't fail. The hardware and software in this topology bypass an inoperative workstation so the network can function without interruption. In this way, the benefits of the star are incorporated into a ringlike topology to produce the hybrid star-wired topology. This topology is rapidly gaining popularity, not only in the LAN community but also among users in the broader telecommunications arena. It has become so popular that many no longer consider it a hybrid topology.

The Tree

The tree topology, also referred to as a *distributed star*, consists of several linear buses daisy-chained together. One linear bus may initially be connected to a hub, splitting that bus into two or more linear buses. This splitting continues, creating additional linear buses from those split from the original bus, giving this topology the attributes of a star (see Figure 15.5).

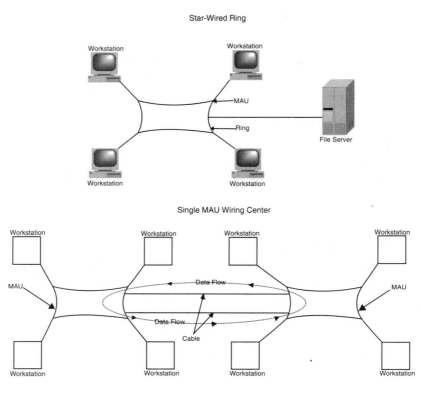

Star-Wired Ring

Workstation Workstation

MAU

Ring

File Server

Single MAU Wiring Center

Workstation Workstation Workstation Workstation

MAU MAU

Data Flow

Data Flow

Cable

Workstation Workstation Workstation Workstation

Two MAU Wiring Center

FIGURE 15.4 The workstations make up the star section of a star-wired topology.

A more specific illustration of the tree topology will help explain how it becomes a distributed star. If a linear bus is split to become three linear buses and each of those is then split into three buses, a total of 13 linear buses have been created. This topology is called a tree because it keeps branching out as it expands. The number of levels or branches that can be created is limited, however.

The advantages of a tree network are that it is easy to extend and it simplifies fault isolation. The disadvantage is that the structure depends on the root—if the primary bus fails, the network fails.

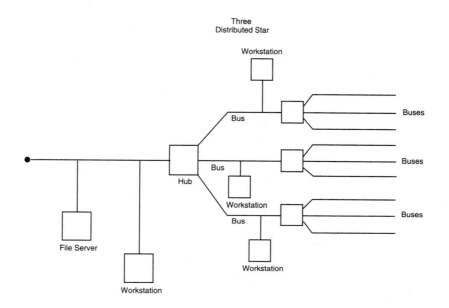

FIGURE 15.5 The tree or distributed star topology.

Protocols

Now that topologies have been explained, we return to the definition of architecture. Another characteristic of a network architecture is that it can be broken into *layers*, with each layer responsible for a certain task. When these tasks are combined, the result is a service performed by the network.

Each layer can communicate with the layer above and the layer below it. (Protocols define how this communication between layers occurs.) As each layer completes its function, it passes data and control of the service to the layer immediately above or below it.

The layering of protocols to create network architectures is a basic principle of *standards-based networking*. At this point, you don't need to understand each protocol and what each layer does. However, all networks are built on layers of protocols, and these layers are the building blocks used by standards organizations to create network architectures.

This brings up a problem: Which architectures or standards should be adopted as the model for all computer companies to follow?

Many diverse protocols already exist that are incompatible with other protocols, largely because major computer companies have their own established communications or networking standards. If each manufacturer has its own layered network architecture, its products can communicate with all other products in that product line. But what happens when two different manufacturers' machines must communicate with each other? This problem has created a demand for a manufacturer-independent standard for all layered network architectures. This result is the OSI model, discussed later in this chapter. Other standards organizations are also actively addressing this problem.

Standards Organizations

A handful of recognized organizations and committees are recommending certain standards: the Consultative Committee on International Telegraphy and Telephony (CCITT), the International Standards Organization (ISO), and the Institute of Electrical and Electronics Engineers (IEEE).

The *CCITT* is an international standards organization headquartered in Geneva, Switzerland. It has developed standards for various aspects of telephone transmission and data communications. The data communications standards are described in recommendations with names such as X.25, X.400, X.500, and X.29. These standards have more impact on wide-area networks than local ones. They can, however, have an impact on a LAN when it has to be connected to a wide-area network.

The ISO, also based in Geneva, has developed a reference model for computer networking known as *OSI* (Open Systems Interconnect). Many of the standards being perfected today and planned for the future are based on this reference model.

The *IEEE* is a U.S. standards-making organization that has been working extensively with standards for LANs. It has developed a set of standards followed by many computer manufacturers for use in LANs. This work was spearheaded by the IEEE Computer Society Local Network Committee's Project 802.

The work of the ISO and CCITT provide the foundation for evolving computer networking standards, particularly since the CCITT has adopted the OSI model. IEEE Project 802 is more specialized than the ISO and

CCITT and is responsible for many of the standards and architectures that exist today.

The OSI Model

Originally released in 1978, the OSI model describes a network architecture that connects dissimilar devices. The original document applied to *open systems*, those that are open to each other because they use the same communications protocols or standards. OSI is concerned with the interconnection between systems—the way they exchange information—rather than with the internal functions of particular systems. In 1984, a revised version of this document was released, and it has become an international standard, with many computer manufacturers modifying their layered network architectures to comply with the layers of the OSI model.

The OSI model has a protocol-layered structure with seven functional levels (see Figure 15.6):

- The *physical layer* transmits bit streams across a particular physical transmission medium (the cable). It involves a connection between two or more machines that exchange electrical signals.

- The *data link layer* provides reliable data transmission from one node to another and shields the higher layers from concern for the physical transmission medium. It is responsible for the error-free transmission of frames of data. This layer is divided into two sublayers: the *media access control* (MAC) and the *logical link control* (LLC). These sublayers will be explained later.

- The *network layer* routes data from one network node to another. It establishes, maintains, and terminates the network connection between two users and transfers data along that connection. It also does fragmentation and reassembly.

- The *transport layer* provides data transfer between two users at an agreed-upon level of quality. When a connection is established between two nodes, this layer selects a particular *class* of service. That class monitors transmissions to ensure that the appropriate level of quality is maintained and notifies users when transmission quality falls below that level.

- The *session layer* provides the services necessary to organize and synchronize the dialog that occurs between users and to manage the data exchange. This layer is primarily concerned with controlling when users can send and receive data—based on whether they can send or receive concurrently or alternately.

- The *presentation layer* is responsible for presenting information to network users in a meaningful way. This may include character-code translation, data conversion, or data compression and expansion.

- The *application layer* lets application processes access the system interconnection facilities to exchange information, including services used to establish and terminate connections between users. It is also used to monitor and manage the interconnected systems and the various resources they use.

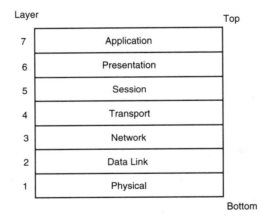

FIGURE 15.6 ISO's OSI model.

The development of the OSI model is ongoing. For some layers, specific standards have been defined to support the model, while standards for others are yet to be developed. The OSI model has had and is still having a great impact in the field of data communications—especially in the area of LANs. Many of the standards for LANs come from the OSI model. The first two layers of the model (physical and data link), for example, have greatly affected the development and definition of LAN standards. This was largely the result of Project 802, which focused on those layers of the OSI model (see Figure 15.7), while the functions of a LAN's upper layers were left to the LAN implementers.

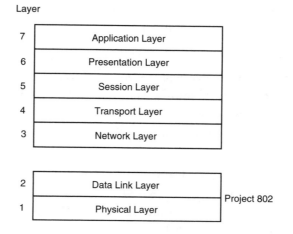

Layer

FIGURE 15.7 Project 802 specifically dealt with the bottom two layers of the OSI model: the physical and data link layers.

IEEE Project 802

In February 1980, the IEEE formed a standards committee to work within the scope of the OSI reference model. Project 802 made one change: It divided the data link layer into two subgroups. The lower sublayer became the *MAC* (media access control layer, which provides shared access to the physical layer of the network. The upper sublayer became the *LLC* (logical link control) layer, which provides a data-link service to higher levels of the OSI stack (see Figure 15.8).

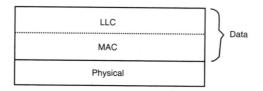

FIGURE 15.8 Project 802 divided the data link layer into two sublayers. The bottom subgroup is known as the media access control (MAC) layer, and the top subgroup is known as the logical link control (LLC) layer.

The 802 committee was divided into six working groups and two associated technical advisory groups (TAGs). These groups produced a series of documents including:

- 802.1—An overview of the work of the project defining the LAN reference model. It also addresses such issues as formats, network management, and internetworking.
- 802.2—Describes the LLC services and primitives to be used in all IEEE-specified LANs.
- 802.3—Defines standards for the MAC and physical layers for a CSMA/CD-based bus network.
- 802.4—Defines standards for the MAC and physical layers for a token-passing bus network.
- 802.5—Defines standards for the MAC and physical layers for a baseband token-passing ring network.
- 802.7—A TAG concerned with broadband networks. It advises the other groups on issues related to broadband transmission.
- 802.8—A TAG concerned with fiber optics exploring ways in which fiber-optic technology can contribute to the other groups.

Project 802 established many of the standards being implemented today. Of these groups and their work, two are of primary concern for today's LANs: 802.3 and 802.5.

The 802.3 group is interesting because it clarifies the relationship with CSMA/CD (discussed later in this chapter) as one of the primary access methods. This group also standardizes a baseband bus. The specification created by the 802.3 group is very similar to *Ethernet*, one of the principal network architectures used today.

The 802.5 group is also important because of its definition of token passing on a ring (discussed later in this chapter). The network architecture using it today is Token Ring.

As you can see, both Ethernet and Token Ring—two of the most widely accepted network architectures—have their roots in Project 802.

ARCnet

One network architecture not specified in Project 802 is *ARCnet*. This architecture has been in existence for some time; in fact, it was used extensively even before the Project 802 committee was formed. ARCnet can take the form of a bus, a tree, or a star. It uses a form of token passing different from that defined under 802.5. A tried-and-true architecture, however, its specifications are stable.

Most products manufactured for ARCnet are highly compatible because it has developed its own standards that many vendors follow, despite the lack of a formal layered network architecture. However, ARCnet does use the token passing on a bus, which is defined by the IEEE 802.4 specification. (ARCnet is discussed in more detail in Chapter 18.)

Access Methods

As you've already seen, a LAN with multiple workstations can be installed using several different topologies. The cabling and physical layout of the LAN may differ with each topology, and there is always the question of how the workstations will access the cabling to transmit and receive data. Nodes access the LAN using a *media access method*, a set of predefined rules or protocols.

Using a highway as an analogy may make this concept easier to understand. If you consider the cable a highway, the workstations and file server are the starting points and destinations. The workstation communicates with the file server by sending it a request, which must travel over the cable (the highway). Certain rules must be followed when entering and exiting the highway—on-ramps are designed to let you accelerate and match the flow of traffic, while an exit ramps allows you to slow down after leaving the mainstream of high-speed traffic.

Media access methods regulate how workstation data enters and exits the cabling. Of the three access methods, only two—CSMA/CD and token passing—are widely used.

CSMA/CD

CSMA/CD is an acronym for *Carrier Sense Multiple Access with Collision Detection*. Essentially, every node on the network listens to the network traffic and can transmit its data when it senses a lull, contending with the other nodes on the network for access.

CSMA/CD can best be described as an old-fashioned telephone party line. Before households had separate communication channels, they shared phone lines. If you wanted to place a call, you had to listen to be sure no one else was using the line. You could just pick up the phone and talk while someone else was using the line, but the voices on the line would collide and conversations would become garbled. Assuming everyone using the party line was friendly, they could establish a set of procedures (protocols) for dealing with such incidents.

This is how CSMA/CD operates. With protocols established, the nodes of the network can send their data accordingly.

Token Passing

Token passing is a deterministic access method because a node can only transmit on the network when it has the token. A token travels throughout the network, stopping at each node to see if it has anything to send. If not, the token travels to the next node and queries it in the same way. This continues until one of the nodes wants to transmit on the network (see Figure 15.9).

Let's say node 1 needs to communicate with node 3. When queried by the token, node 1 marks it as busy, includes data and destination information, and passes it on. The token continues to travel around the network, finally stopping at the destination (node 3). It then returns to node 1, which reactivates the token and sends it on to query other nodes on the network.

Polling

Polling is used primarily in mainframe and minicomputer networks. Protocols for polling require an intelligent central device. This central device communicates with each workstation in a predefined sequence. If the workstation has a request for the file server, the request is transmitted when that workstation is polled. If the workstation has no request, the central device moves on to the next workstation. The only time a workstation can access the network is when it is being polled or queried (see Figure 15.10). This access method is not as popular today as CSMA/CD or token passing, but it is still used extensively for mainframe or host-based networks.

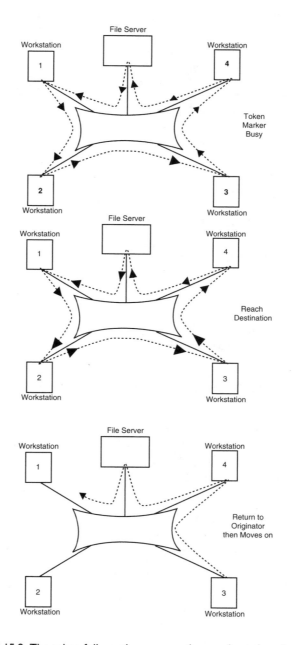

FIGURE 15.9 The token follows the arrow path to each workstation.
When workstation 2 wants to transmit, it must wait for the token to arrive.

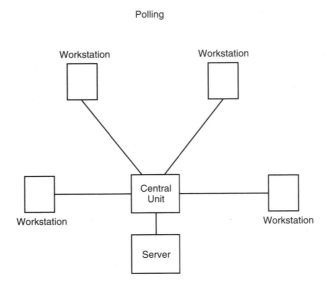

Polling

FIGURE 15.10 Polling requires an intelligent central device. Workstations can only communicate with the server when polled by the central unit.

Communications and Routing Protocols

Protocols regulate how data packets are transmitted through a network or internetwork. IBM's communications protocol set is NETBIOS, while Novell uses a version of XNS (Xerox Network Systems). Many UNIX-based computing systems use TCP/IP (Transmission Control Protocol/Internet Protocol) or NFS. Sun Microsystems uses a protocol set known as TOPS.

These protocols operate at the network and transport layers, and sometimes at the session layer, of the OSI model. They also provide for addressing nodes on interconnected LANs. (All interconnected networks must use either the same protocol or a conversion mechanism that translates to that protocol. NETBIOS does not provide for routing on internetworks other than Token Ring.)

Novell uses a version of XNS, which Xerox created to allow communications between their products. This involves interconnecting Ethernet LANs with each other or with public data networks. XNS actually comprises many protocols, but the two used most frequently are *IPX* (Internet Packet Exchange) and *SPX* (Sequence Packet Exchange).

SPX is used when a message or request is guaranteed to arrive. This protocol establishes a connection, or virtual circuit, between the sender and receiver. Messages that flow across the connection are assigned sequence numbers that the receiver uses to check for missing, out-of-sequence, or duplicate messages. The receiver returns an acknowledgment; if a message is not acknowledged, it is retransmitted.

IPX is a simpler protocol that doesn't involve sequence numbers. If a response isn't received, the message is retransmitted. While IPX lacks the reliability of SPX, it doesn't have the overhead. Simple networks tend to use this protocol.

Another widely used set of routing protocols is *TCP/IP*. It was developed by the Department of Defense as part of the work done on ARPANET, an early packet-switching network. IP is designed to allow data packets to be sent and received across networks, though the data transfer can't be considered reliable. TCP provides reliable connection-oriented data transfer using the underlying IP.

CHAPTER 16

ETHERNET

This chapter explores the baseband LAN architecture known as *Ethernet*. After taking a quick look at its history, we'll turn to Ethernet architecture and associated components. Ethernet tends to be fairly intimidating, so many of the highly technical aspects—those that aren't prerequisites to understanding this architecture—won't be discussed in detail.

The History of Ethernet

Many of the underlying concepts of Ethernet come from a wide-area network implemented at the University of Hawaii in the late 1960s. The university developed Ethernet's basic functionality—or, more specifically, the CSMA/CD access method—that was first used in the ALOHA wide-area network, laying the foundation for today's Ethernet. In 1972, Ethernet underwent further development at Xerox, where it was known as Experimental Ethernet. The design was very successful, and Ethernet grew in popularity. Xerox's work also advanced the progress of the Institute of Electrical and Electronics Engineers Project 802, particularly in helping the group define IEEE 802.3 specifications.

In the early 1980s, Digital Equipment Corporation, Intel, and Xerox issued a joint vendor standard for Ethernet. The three corporations continued their effort in the years following, and in 1982 issued Ethernet version 2.0.

This specification is somewhat compatible with the IEEE 802.3 standard and in fact, as defined today, Ethernet still follows the specifications of IEEE 802.3; however, older installations may not be entirely 802.3-compliant because they're based on Ethernet version 2.0.

Ethernet Architecture

Now that Ethernet follows the IEEE 802.3 standard, it uses the CSMA/CD method of network access and functions at a transfer speed of 10 Mbits/sec (10 million bits, or 10 megabits, per second). Combining this transfer speed with the CSMA/CD access method makes Ethernet an excellent choice for networks that have occasional bursts of heavy traffic. However, Ethernet is not as efficient as other LAN architectures when a constant moderate-to-heavy network load must be maintained.

Another advantage Ethernet offers is its ability to use other communication protocols—specifically, TCP/IP (primarily used in UNIX and DEC VAX workstations). This makes it easier for Ethernet to access minicomputers and high-powered workstations. It is also an excellent choice for networking in an engineering environment because the nodes are often high-end, UNIX-based workstations.

Although Ethernet's primary topology is a linear bus, with certain components it can appear as a star; see Figure 16.1.

Cabling

Ethernet can operate on three cable types—thick, thin, and unshielded twisted pair (UTP)—each with its own limitations, requirements, and specialized components. (Thick and thin cables are also known as *thicknet* and *thinnet*; thinnet is sometimes referred to as *cheapernet*.)

Thicknet is a large coaxial cable, 0.4 inch in diameter, with properties that make it exceptional for transmitting data over long distances. Thinnet is an RG-58, A/U coaxial cable with a diameter of only 0.2 inch. Since thinnet is so much smaller and more flexible than thicknet, it is useful for cable installations that require many twists and turns. Both cable types have an impedance of 50 ohms.

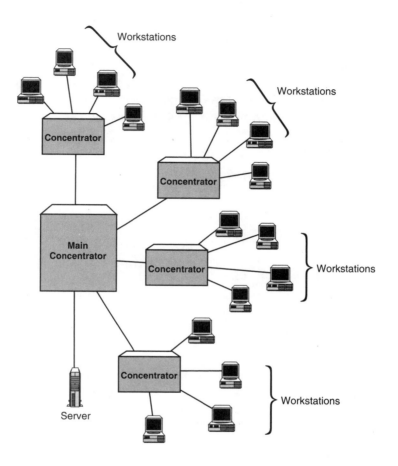

FIGURE 16.1 Distributed star or tree topology of 10BASE-T network.

The IEEE 802.3 and Ethernet standards contain three references specifying the type of cable used in an Ethernet network:

- *10BASE2* refers to Ethernet LANs that use thinnet cabling. The thinnet coaxial cable can carry a signal for approximately 185 meters. Beyond this distance the signal must be regenerated by a device known as a *repeater*.

- *10BASE5* refers to Ethernet LANs that use thicknet cabling, which can carry a signal for approximately 500 meters before a repeater is required.

- *10BASE-T* refers to Ethernet LANs that use UTP cabling, which can carry a signal for 100 meters before a repeater is needed.

Thicknet and thinnet are discussed in more detail later in this chapter.

Trunk Segments

An Ethernet network consists of nodes attached at different intervals to its bus, which is actually the main network cable. This setup is known as a trunk segment (see Figure 16.2).

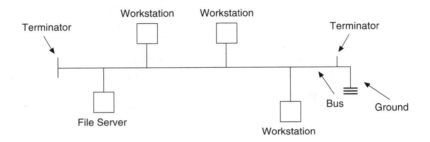

FIGURE 16.2 An Ethernet trunk segment.

Few Ethernet networks implement one long, continuous cable; rather, the trunk segment is divided into a series of cables that are connected via repeaters, bridges, or routers (see Figure 16.3).

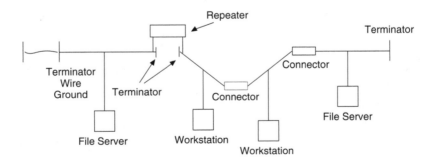

FIGURE 16.3 The trunk segment can be divided into smaller units using connectors.

By following the 10BASE2 or 10BASE5 specification, the distance the trunk segment cable can transmit a signal can be limited. The number of nodes attached to the cable is also limited (see Figure 16.4). The network can overcome the limitations of having just one trunk segment by connecting two or more cables. All of the trunk segment cables of an Ethernet network combine to form the network trunk cable. Unlike a ring or star topology Ethernet does not have a separate hub or concentrator because each trunk segment has nodes directly attached to it.

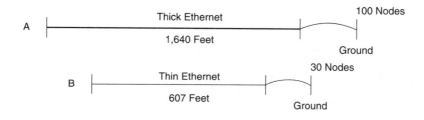

FIGURE 16.4 Number of nodes in thick versus thin Ethernet.

Thick versus Thin Ethernet

An Ethernet network can also combine thinnet and thicknet cables into one network, though each cabling type has its own specifications and the network installation must adhere to the specifications of both types (see Figure 16.4)

To clarify these implementations we'll discuss a thinnet Ethernet network, then a thicknet network, and finally a combined thinnet/thicknet network.

Thinnet Ethernet

In addition to the thinnet cable and the traditional repeater, a basic thinnet Ethernet LAN has the following components:

- *BNC connectors*—These male and female connectors link the Ethernet cable to T-connectors and terminators (see Figure 16.5).
- A *BNC barrel connector*—This female-to-female connector joins two lengths of thinnet cable, each ending in a male BNC connector. It

extends a length of cable or repairs a break in a damaged section of cable (see Figure 16.6).

- A *BNC T-connector*—This connector is in the shape of a T and resembles the mating of a BNC connector to a barrel connector (see Figure 16.7). The T-connector's two female ends connect and maintain the continuity of the segment they're on. The male connector is used to attach an NIC, bridge, router, or some other network device, allowing it to tap into the signals coming from the network (see Figure 16.8).

- A *BNC terminator*—Since both ends of an Ethernet segment must be terminated, a BNC terminator is used to stop a length of thinnet cable. Its function is to block electrical interference on the Ethernet network (see Figure 16.9). One end of each trunk must be grounded, so some BNC terminators have a ground cable as well (see Figure 16.10).

Thin Coaxial Connectors

BNC Connector

FIGURE 16.5 The BNC connector attaches to the end of the thin coaxial cable.

BNC Barrel Connector

FIGURE 16.6 The BNC barrel connector links two segments of thin coaxial cable.

BNC T-Connector

FIGURE 16.7 The BNC connector attaches a network node to the trunk segment.

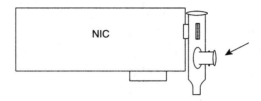

NIC

FIGURE 16.8 The BNC connector jack on an NIC links the node
to the trunk via a T-connector.

FIGURE 16.9 The BNC terminator is used at the end of a segment of thin coaxial cable.

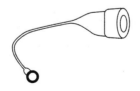

FIGURE 16.10 One end of each thinnet cable segment must be grounded
using a grounded BNC connector.

The Ethernet design using thinnet cabling follows the 10BASE2 and Ethernet
2.0 specifications. Most manufacturers of thinnet Ethernet products conform to
these standards as well. Although the variant standards introduced by vendors

tend to have different NICs and associated driver software, the differences are sometimes merely related to cable distances.

As explained earlier, the 10BASE2 specification states that a trunk segment cable can be 185 meters (610 feet) long. Some manufacturers' NICs exceed this limit and support cable distances of up to 300 meters (990 feet). The maximum distance of an Ethernet thinnet trunk segment cable is 185 meters, with a maximum of five trunk segments in the LAN (see Figure 16.11). This means the network is made up of five trunk segment cables with repeaters connecting them, and the network trunk cable consists of five connected trunk segments. Another requirement of Ethernet, according to 10BASE2 specifications, is that only three of the five trunk segments can be populated with workstations. A trunk segment cable that is divided into smaller sections of cable and remains smaller than 200 meters in total length is still considered one trunk segment.

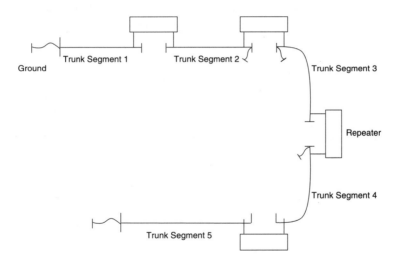

FIGURE 16.11 As many as five trunk segments can be aligned into a single Ethernet network.

Although an Ethernet network may have 20 to 30 cable connections, it is still limited to five trunk segments. An Ethernet network that uses all five trunk segments with the maximum distance between each segment has a total network trunk cable length of 925 meters (3,035 feet).

Other rules affect the trunk segments themselves. One is that each end of a trunk segment must be terminated; another is that one of the two terminated ends must be grounded. Each trunk segment on a thinnet Ethernet network can support no more than 30 attachments (nodes), and the nodes on a trunk segment must have at least 0.5 meter between T-connectors. A repeater that connects trunk segments counts as one node on each of the trunk segments it joins (see Figure 16.12).

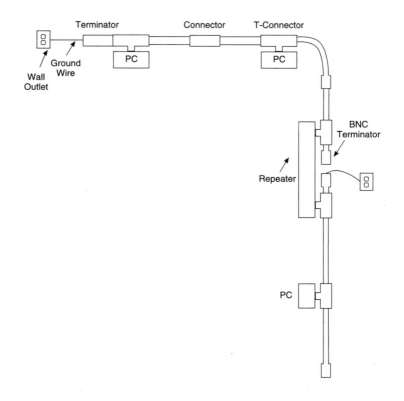

FIGURE 16.12 Trunk segments are linked using repeaters, and each repeater counts as one node on that segment.

Thicknet Ethernet

Ethernet networks that use thicknet cable must follow the 10BASE5 specifications. As with thinnet, specifications may vary from manufacturer to manufacturer.

However, because most manufacturers' products are close to the specification, compatibility problems are rare.

In addition to the cable and repeaters, a thicknet Ethernet network comprises a number of other components:

- *Transceiver*—This external device allows the node to communicate with the main network cable. The transceiver attaches to the trunk segment cable.

- *Transceiver cable*—This cable attaches the external transceiver to the node's NIC (see Figure 16.13).

- *DIX connector*—The DIX connector, which stands for Digital, Intel, Xerox connector—after the companies that pioneered Ethernet—has two configurations, male and female. The male connector has several small pins extended from it. Both the male and female DIX connectors are attached to either end of a transceiver cable. The male connector attaches to the NIC in the node, while the female connector attaches to the transceiver (see Figure 16.14).

- *N-series male connectors*—These connectors are installed on both ends of a thicknet cable (see Figure 16.15).

- *N-series barrel connectors*—Like the BNC barrel connectors for thinnet, these are used to connect two lengths of thicknet cable. One end of each cable attaches to one end of the connector (see Figure 16.16).

- *N-series terminators*—When no other nodes are connected to the cable, the end of the cable must be capped or terminated. The N-series terminator attaches to the N-series male connector on the thicknet cable to block electrical interference on the network. The terminator may be grounded or ungrounded; a thicknet Ethernet network must have both types (see Figure 16.17).

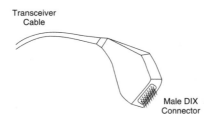

FIGURE 16.13 The transceiver cable is terminated by a male DIX connector.

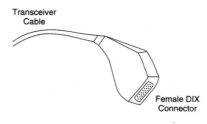

FIGURE 16.14 The female DIX connector provides the network connection for the NIC.

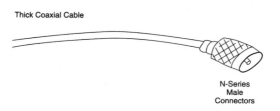

FIGURE 16.15 The thick coaxial cable can be connected using N-series male connectors.

FIGURE 16.16 The N-series barrel connectors link thick coaxial cable segments.

FIGURE 16.17 N-series terminators are used to terminate thick coaxial trunk segments.

The design of a thicknet Ethernet network is similar to a thinnet Ethernet network. The thicknet trunk segment can extend 500 meters (1,650 feet). Several lengths of thicknet cable may be connected using the N-series barrel connectors. If the cable is less than 500 meters long, it is considered one trunk segment. Multiple trunk segments must be connected by a repeater.

One thicknet Ethernet network can have five trunk segments, for a total of 2,500 meters (8,250 feet). Only three of the five segments can be populated with workstations and no more than 100 nodes can be attached to a trunk segment; a repeater again counts as one node on each of the trunk segment cables it joins.

The transceivers must be at least 2.5 meters (8 feet) apart. (This limit applies only to transceivers; nodes may be closer) Transceiver cables are limited to a length of 50 meters (165 feet). Each end of a thicknet Ethernet cable must be terminated, and one of the two terminations must be grounded (see Figure 16.18).

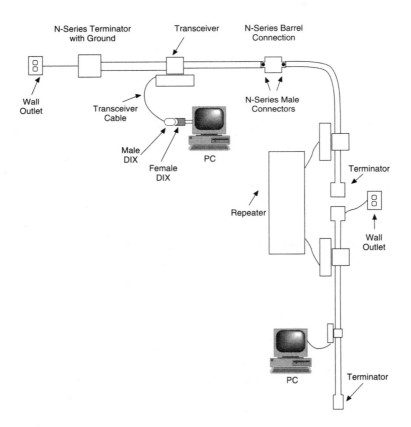

FIGURE 16.18 A typical thicknet Ethernet configuration.

Combined Thinnet/Thicknet Ethernet

An Ethernet network can be designed using both thinnet and thicknet cable. Combining the two types in one network has several advantages. One of these advantages is that thinnet can be used for an easier, less expensive installation, while thicknet can support long-distance cable lengths. The resulting network takes advantage of the best qualities of both cable types (see Figure 16.19).

A combination thinnet/thicknet network can be created in two ways— either by joining a thinnet trunk segment with a thicknet trunk segment or by joining thinnet and thicknet cabling within the same trunk segment.

The first method, which involves joining dissimilar trunk segments, is actually the is the simpler way to design a thin/thick Ethernet network. Each trunk segment is designed following the rules and limitations of that particular type of cabling, so a thinnet trunk segment is designed as if it were to be an entirely thinnet network and a thicknet trunk segment as if it were to be an entirely thicknet network. These separate segments are then joined by a repeater (see Figure 16.20).

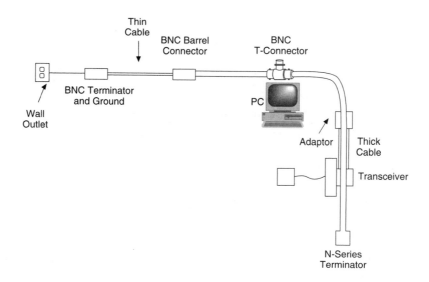

FIGURE 16.19 Two dissimilar cable segments can be joined within the same trunk using an adapter.

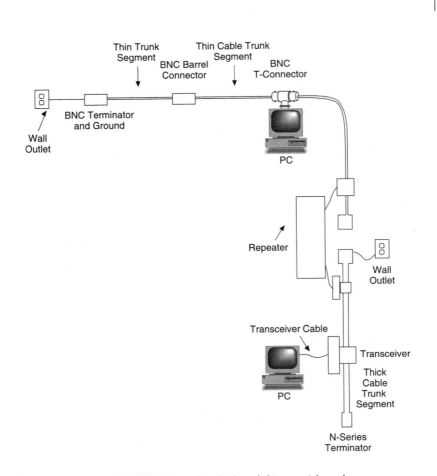

FIGURE 16.20 Up to five thick and thin coaxial trunks
can be linked together using repeaters.

Since one segment may be a thinnet trunk, the overall length of the network
trunk cable is limited. The number of allowable trunk segments remains the
same, so five trunk segments can be linked in a combination cabling network;
this is the same number of segments allowed in either a thinnet or thicknet
Ethernet network.

The second method uses both types of cable on the same trunk segment.
The components are the same as those used in thinnet and thicknet Ethernet
networks. Joining the two cables in the same trunk segments requires a BNC
female to N-series female adapter (see Figure 16.21) and a BNC male to N-series
male adapter (see Figure 16.22).

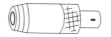

FIGURE 16.21 A BNC female to N-series female adapter.

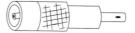

FIGURE 16.22 A BNC male to N-series male adapter.

These connectors have the same function as a BNC barrel connector for thinnet and an N-series barrel connector for thicknet, but in this case the connectors join lengths of dissimilar cable.

The maximum length of a trunk segment using thicknet alone is 1,640 feet. The maximum length of a thinnet trunk segment is 607 feet. With these figures in mind, let's consider some cabling options. Most trunk segments are between

607 feet and 1,640 feet long. If the trunk segment is shorter than 607 feet, thinnet alone can be used. If the trunk segment is 1,640 feet long, thicknet alone can be used. When the two cable types are combined, the length of thinnet cable must be subtracted from the length of thicknet. Thus, if the maximum of 607 feet of thinnet cable is used, only 933 feet of thicknet can be used.

The following formula is used to determine how much cable of each type can be used:

```
(1,640 feet-L)/3.28=t
```

where L is the length of the trunk segment (up to 1,640) and t is the amount of thinnet cable to be used.

To illustrate, let's apply the formula in the following example: A network trunk segment is 1,000 feet long, and the maximum amount of thinnet cable is needed. Subtract 1,000 from 1,640, then divide the result (640) by 3.28. The result is 195 feet—the maximum length of thinnet cable we can use.

When installing any cable or cable combination for Ethernet, you must follow several rules. The cable cannot loop back on itself, and there can be no closed loop or ring. Each segment must be terminated at both ends, with one terminator being grounded.

Now that we've covered Ethernet on coaxial cable, 10BASE2, and 10BASE5, we can move on to Ethernet on UTP 10BASE-T.

10BASE-T

10BASE-T varies somewhat from the other forms of Ethernet described so far. Some of the differences are found in the following areas:

- *Cabling*—Unlike the other cabling methods, 10BASE-T uses untwisted pair cabling (UTP), also known as telephone wire. (10BASE-T can also operate on shielded twisted pair without changing any of its characteristics.)
- *Topology*—10BASE-T uses a star topology rather than a bus topology (see Figure 16.23).
- *Concentrator*—Unlike the other two specifications for Ethernet, a hub or concentrator is required (see Figure 16.24).

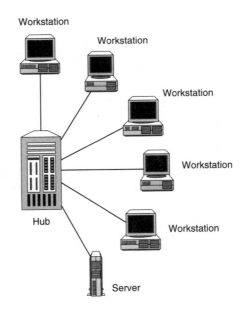

FIGURE 16.23 Star topology of 10BASE-T network.

- *Segment length*—The UTP segment cable has a maximum length of 100 meters (328 feet). To extend the segment beyond that, a repeater is needed (see Figure 16.25).

- *Number of nodes*—The maximum number of nodes on a 10BASE-T segment is 1,024. This is the same number of nodes that can exist on an entire network based on 10BASE-T, therefore, one segment can form an entire network (see Figure 16.26).

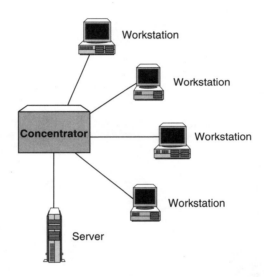

FIGURE 16.24 Nodes are attached to the 10BASE-T network using a concentrator.

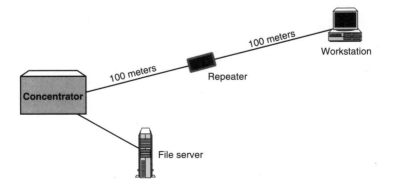

FIGURE 16.25 A repeater is needed for any cabling distance greater than 100 meters.

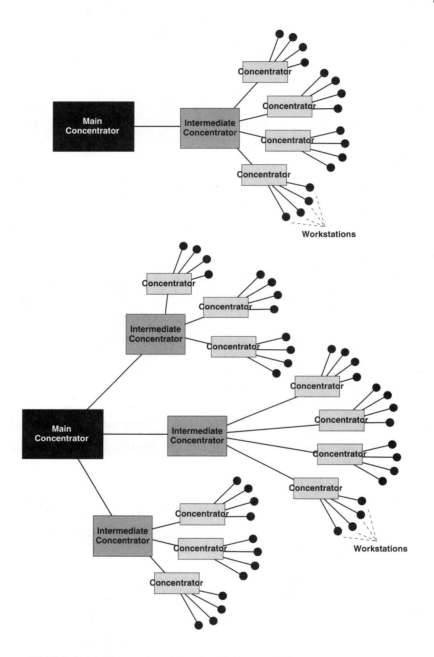

FIGURE 16.26 The total number of nodes on a 10BASE-T network is 1,024. They can all be assigned to one segment or divided among several segments.

10BASE-T still follows the four-repeater rule of Ethernet. This rule specifies that an Ethernet signal can pass through only four repeaters (see Figure 16.27). If more than four repeaters are necessary, the segments must be bridged. Unlike 10BASE2 and 10BASE5, more than five segments are possible with 10BASE-T because of the difference in topology (see Figure 16.28).

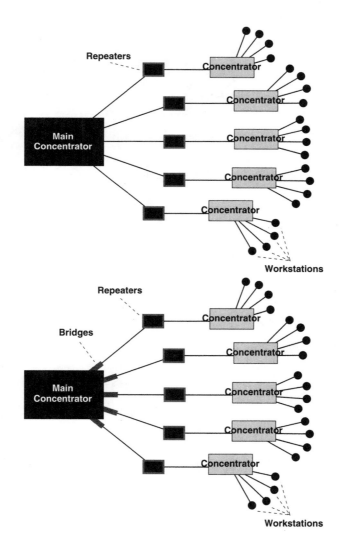

FIGURE 16.27 An Ethernet signal can only pass through four repeaters.

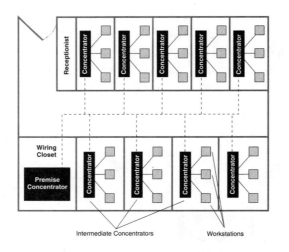

FIGURE 16.28 There can be more than five segments in a 10BASE-T network.

CHAPTER 17

TOKEN RING

Token Ring is another popular approach to local area networking. While these networks have become synonymous with IBM, the driving force behind their development, a number of independent vendors have developed products that support Token Ring.

This chapter begins with a brief history of Token Ring, then turns to the actual architecture and components of a Token Ring network.

The History of Token Ring

IBM was a relatively late entrant in the LAN arena. introducing two other LANs before the advent of its Token Ring network. IBM's first baseband LAN offering was *PC Cluster*, a slow linear bus network. This was followed by *PC Network*, a broadband tree network that is still in use today.

When PC Network was introduced, IBM made it clear that the product was for personal computers only; any other communications within the IBM product line would follow the established System Network Architecture (SNA). With the communications that existed at that time, personal computers could not be integrated into the larger SNA networks. IBM later hinted that an up-and-coming local network could be used with the majority of its computing products and would allow personal computers access to SNA networks. To help customers prepare for this network breakthrough, IBM devised a cabling system allowed computer companies and building contractors to develop a wiring strategy for new buildings, forming the basis of a completely IBM-compatible corporate network.

In 1985, IBM unveiled Token Ring network, its most advanced high-speed network to date. Token Ring was based on the Zurich Ring, which was developed at IBM research facilities in Switzerland, and was released in early 1986.

Token Ring Architecture

Token Ring architecture follows the standards set by Project 802—the same standards created by IEEE's 802.5 subcommittee.

The Token Ring network includes:

- Star-wired ring topology
- Token passing for access method
- Shielded and unshielded twisted pair wiring
- Transfer rates of 4 Mbps and 16 Mbps
- Baseband transmission
- 802.5 specifications

The topology is a star-wired ring, with the ring formed by the hub. The star is formed by the nodes attached to the hub. As discussed in Chapter 15, the Token Ring network takes a determined approach to cable access. The token, a predetermined formation of bits, permits a node to access the cable. The token is passed from node to node until a request to transmit data is made. Token passing on a ring uses IEEE's 802.5 specifications for its cable access. (Token passing is discussed later in this chapter.)

One point to remember is that a ring for the token to follow must be provided at all times; no matter how convoluted the ring becomes, it must remain a ring. Data flows on the ring in only one direction.

The two major versions of Token Ring have transfer rates of 4 and 16 Mbit/sec respectively, and both use baseband transmission. Compatibility problems may arise when both approaches are used in the same network, making it impossible to mix the two. Plans being formulated by IBM and others will determine the future of 4- and 16-Mbit/sec Token Rings. For now the dominant version is the 16-Mbit/sec token ring.

Both versions can use either shielded or unshielded twisted pair (UTP) wiring, though the latter gives greater signal reliability and extends the signal distance. Most Token Ring networks are currently wired with UTP.

Token Ring Components

There are four basic components in a Token Ring network:

- Network interface card (NIC)
- Multistation access unit (MAU)
- Cabling system
- Network connectors

Although IBM developed the Token Ring network system, it is not the only manufacturer of IEEE 802.5 Token Ring products; the components discussed in this section are available from a variety of sources.

The Network Interface Card

The NIC for Token Ring has the same function as the NIC for Ethernet: It allows the node to communicate with the network's cabling. The two types of NICs are PC Adaptor, which is designed for use in any computer that has the Industry Standard Architecture bus and the TRN/A Adaptor card. The TRN/A Adaptor card is designed specifically for computers using an IBM Micro Channel architecture bus (specifically, PS/2 models).

The Multistation Access Unit

The MAU (or SMAU, for smart multistation access unit) is also referred to by a number, usually 8228. It is important to remember this number because other manufacturers make MAUs that meet IBM's 8228 specifications.

The MAU is the hub of the network and can connect as many as eight nodes (see Figure 17.1). When more nodes are required, more MAUs are added (see Figure 17.2). The MAUs installed in one network can accommodate up to 72 nodes when IBM Type 3 cable is used (see Figure 17.3). When IBM Type 1 or Type 2 cable is used, a network can accommodate up to 260 nodes. The MAUs form the ring portion of the network, and the nodes create a star (see Figure 17.4).

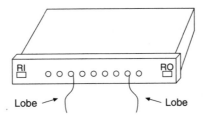

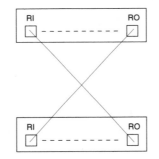

FIGURE 17.1 Each multistation access unit has an internal ring and can support up to eight nodes.

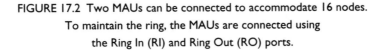

FIGURE 17.2 Two MAUs can be connected to accommodate 16 nodes. To maintain the ring, the MAUs are connected using the Ring In (RI) and Ring Out (RO) ports.

An 8228 setup aid, supplied with each MAU, is used to reset the 8228 before it is installed. An 8228 MAU has 10 ports: eight for connecting the network nodes, and two—the Ring In and Ring Out ports—to maintain the integrity of the ring when connecting a series of MAUs. The Ring In is a signal input port while the Ring Out is essentially a signal output port. In a network with only one MAU, these ports must be left untouched.

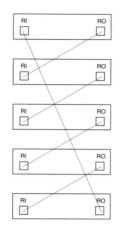

FIGURE 17.3 Up to nine MAUs can be added for IBM Type 3–cabled networks, supporting a total of 72 nodes. Note that the ring remains intact.

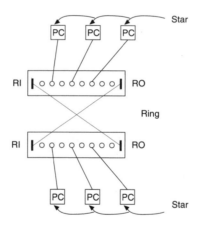

FIGURE 17.4 The MAUs are wired to form a ring. The nodes are connected to the MAUs to form the star portion of the network.

The Cabling System

Today many Token Ring networks use IBM Type 3 UTP cable. One reason is the ease with which a new building can be wired with UTP. It is also possible to use some of the building's existing UTP wiring, such as unused telephone cabling. (When using preexisting telephone wire, check it thoroughly for cable breaks and dead-end lines.) In most new buildings, extra telephone line is installed in anticipation of a data network, but using preexisting cable is not always advisable. The anticipated convenience may disappoint when problems arise in the wiring system at a later time. It may be better to begin by installing a new cabling system.

IBM Type 3 cable is also widely used as adapter cable, eliminating the need for Type 6 adapter cables. In addition to IBM Type 1, Type 2, and Type 3 cable, several other cable types can be used with Token Ring, including IBM Type 6 and Type 9. IBM Type 6 is a shielded adapter cable. One end has a 9-pin D-shell or a 25-pin serial connector that attaches to the NIC; the other has an IBM data connector that attaches to either a face-plate jack or an IBM 8228 MAU (see Figure 17.5).

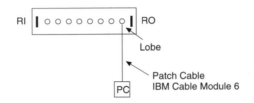

FIGURE 17.5 IBM Type 6 shielded cable can be used as an adapter cable
to connect a workstation to a MAU.

Type 6 can also function as a patch cable (see Figure 17.6). It comes in varying lengths, from 8 to 150 feet, with an IBM data connector at each end. As a patch cable, Type 6 can be connected to other patch cables, adapter cables, or IBM 8228 MAUs. For example, an IBM Type 6 patch cable can be used to attach a node to an MAU. If the adapter cable is shorter than the distance to the MAU, a patch cable can be used to make up the difference, connecting the adapter cable on one end and the MAU on the other.

IBM Type 9 cable is used primarily when plenum is required. *Plenum* is a type of cable that can be laid in ceilings to meet building codes. It has a special outside covering and may be used in place of IBM Type 1 and Type 2 cables.

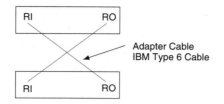

FIGURE 17.6 IBM Type 6 cable can be used as a patch cable to connect two MAUs.

Network Connectors

Token Ring networks can be cabled with the following connectors:

- Data connectors for Type 1 and Type 2 cables
- RJ-45 telephone connectors (eight-pin) for Type 3 cable
- RJ-11 telephone connectors (four-pin) for Type 3 cable

When IBM Type 3 cable is connected to the MAU, a Type 3 media filter is needed (see Figure 17.7). This filter often attaches directly to a data connector for IBM Type 1 and Type 2 cable. One end of the media filter connects to the data connector, while the other has an outlet that allows the RJ-11 connector to be attached. Of the two RJ connectors, RJ-11 is more widely used.

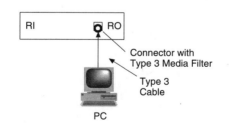

FIGURE 17.7 IBM Type 3 cable can be used to connect a node,
but a media filter is required for UTP cable.

Token Ring Network Specifications

For the purposes of this section assume that the Token Ring networks presented here use IBM Type 3 cabling. Token Ring networks wired with Type 1 and Type 2 cable are more expensive, and the extra diameter and inflexibility of these cables makes it hard to expand, relocate, or add new nodes to the network. IBM considers Types 1 and 2 to be almost entirely different cabling schemes from Type 3 for an IBM Token Ring network. Types 1 and 2 refer to a large, nonmovable cabling system, but networks that use these cables allow as many as 260 nodes on the ring and permit longer cable runs.

When the maximum number of nodes on a Token Ring network has been reached, another network ring must be established. The MAUs may either be in the same physical area or separated, but in either case they must be connected in the form a ring. IBM states that the maximum cable distance from the MAU to a node or file server using Type 3 cable is 150 feet; other companies say cable lengths of 350 to 500 feet are acceptable. The distance from a node to the MAU is referred to as the *lobe length*. A lobe length of 300 feet should be acceptable.

The distance between the hubs, where the MAUs are housed, is subject to other limitations. The maximum distance between hubs is normally 400 to 500 feet. Distances can be increased using repeaters, similar to those mentioned in Chapter 16. Repeaters regenerate the signal on the cable. The two types of repeaters for Token Ring—the Token Ring repeater and the lobe repeater—are discussed in more detail in Chapter 24.

Token Passing

The 802.5 specifications regulate how the token is passed on a ring. Token passing was discussed in Chapter 15 and is illustrated in Figure 17.8.

The high-speed fiber-optic networks being developed also use token passing, which is generally acknowledged to be more efficient than the CSMA/CD access method Ethernet uses.

Supplemental Software

Depending on the age of the components used in the network, personal computers on an IBM Token Ring network may require supplemental software to connect to the MAUs. This software, collectively known as the *IBM Local Area Network Support Program*, consists of device-driver files with .SYS file name extensions (indicating that they are system files). These file names are included in the PCs CONFIG.SYS file.

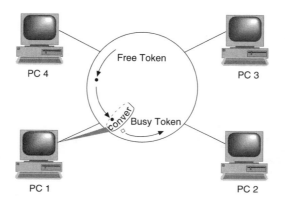

FIGURE 17.8 In token passing, a free token is routed around the ring, polling nodes to see if they want to transmit. If PC 1 chooses to transmit, it converts the nonbusy token to a busy token. The data is then sent around the ring and delivered to the appropriate workstation. The token returns to PC 1, which acknowledges the transmission and releases the token.

Summary

Token Ring networks can be simple, but at times they can also be very complex and sophisticated. As network designers and installers gain experience and become more knowledgeable about Token Ring, they will be able to add to the network's sophistication.

CHAPTER 18

ARCNET

The Attached Resource Computer network (ARCnet) was developed by Datapoint Corporation and has been a popular reliable LAN for years. Because of its popularity, standards existed for ARCnet even before IEEE Project 802 was established. The IEEE 802.4 specification, which defines token passing on a bus using broadband technology, is the standard most similar to ARCnet. However, because ARCnet is a baseband network, it is very inexpensive and easy to install, making it more appealing to some network developers.

ARCnet Architecture

ARCnet uses token passing on a bus, which is very similar to token passing on a ring. It has a transfer rate of 2.5 Mbits/sec and normally uses RG-62 93-ohm coaxial cable, though it can use twisted-pair cable. In 1993 a version of ARCnet was released that attained transfer rates of 20 Mbits/sec.

ARCnet can have a star or bus topology. Often, however, it is considered to have a distributed star or tree topology. Manufacturers consistently follow ARCnet standards, and the products released for ARCnet networks are usually compatible with equipment from other vendors.

Because it uses both active and passive hubs, ARCnet is excellent for elaborate wiring configurations. For our purposes, we will consider only ARCnet networks designed with coaxial cable.

ARCnet Components

ARCnet uses many of the same BNC connectors discussed earlier for thinnet Ethernet networks. In addition to these connectors, it uses a high- or low-impedance NIC, an active hub, a passive hub, and active links.

Each ARCnet NIC has a built-in transceiver and the majority of the NICs found in ARCnet networks use low-impedance transceivers. The type of transceiver on the card creates different characteristics for the network and can require different wiring options. For more information on these characteristics, refer to the vendor specifications. Low-impedance NICs usually support a distributed star or tree topology. Since characteristics of both a bus and a star are present, the high-impedance NICs use a bus topology.

Active hubs relay network messages and repeat the signal. An active hub usually has eight ports, but they can have as many as 64. Similar to the configuration of a star topology, cables branch from the active hub. Terminating unused ports on active hubs is recommended but not necessary. The active hub may also serve as a repeater (see Figure 18.1).

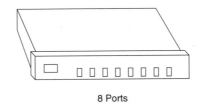

8 Ports

FIGURE 18.1 An active hub can support from 8 to 64 ports.

Passive hubs have four ports that can accommodate cables for relaying network signals. These devices usually form the tree structure of the topology. Any unused port on a passive hub must be terminated with a 93-ohm terminator. The passive hub does not amplify the signal (see Figure 18.2).

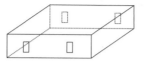

FIGURE 18.2 An ARCnet passive hub has four ports, two on either side.

Active links can be used to connect two cables when both include a string of stations containing high-impedance NICs (see Figure 18.3).

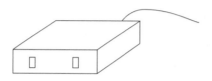

FIGURE 18.3 An active link has two ports, one for each cable or the bus it connects.

Network Specifications

Low-Impedance Network Design

A low-impedance ARCnet LAN must follow certain rules and is subject to certain limitations. The following are the distance limitations for low-impedance ARCnet networks:

- The total length of the network cable between workstations can't exceed 20,000 feet. The maximum distance between active hubs is 2,000 feet.

- The maximum distance between an active hub and a node is 2,000 feet (see Figure 18.4).

- The maximum distance between an active hub and a passive hub is 100 feet.

- The maximum distance between a passive hub and a node is 100 feet.

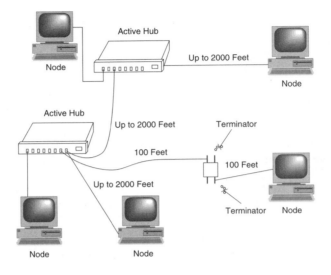

FIGURE 18.4 With low-impedance wiring, the maximum distance between active hubs and between an active hub and a node is 2,000 feet.

The following rules apply to low-impedance ARCnet networks:

- Active hubs can be connected to other active hubs, passive hubs, and nodes (see Figure 18.5).

- Passive hubs can be used only as intermediate connections between active hubs and nodes and can't be connected in a series (see Figure 18.5).

- All nodes (personal computers, file servers, and bridges) can be connected at any place in the network.

- ARCnet cabling can't loop back on itself.

High-Impedance Network Design

A high-impedance ARCnet network must also adhere to certain rules and limitations. The following are the distance limitations:

- The maximum cable length distance between workstations for the network is 20,000 feet.

- A maximum of eight nodes can be connected in a series.

- The minimum distance between T-connectors is 3 feet.
- One length of cable, or bus, can be no more than 1,000 feet long (see Figure 18.6).
- The maximum distance between two active hubs with no intervening nodes is 2,000 feet (see Figure 18.6).

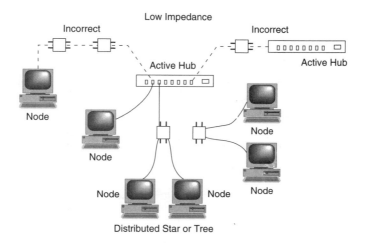

FIGURE 18.5 Passive hubs can be used between active hubs and nodes and can't be connected in a series.

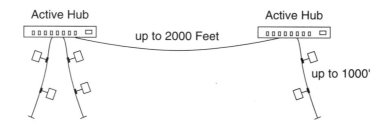

FIGURE 18.6 The maximum length of any one cable in a high-impedance ARCnet network is 1,000 feet. High-impedance ARCnet can support up to 2,000 feet between active hubs.

The following rules must be followed when using high-impedance NICs:

- The use of passive hubs is prohibited.
- Nodes must be attached to the cable with T-connectors.
- A cable cannot be used between the T-connector and the node.
- Both ends of a length of cable must be terminated with either an active hub or a BNC terminator.
- The cabling cannot loop back on itself.

Figure 18.7 demonstrates the various wiring configurations possible with a high-impedance ARCnet network.

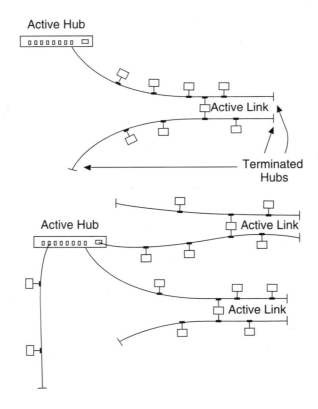

FIGURE 18.7 Two sample high-impedance ARCnet configurations.

Combined-Impedance Network Design

Both low- and high-impedance NICs can be used in the same network. The rules for high-impedance NICs still apply, as do the rules for low-impedance NICs. For example, a high-impedance NIC can be used in place of a low-impedance NIC on a low-impedance designed ARCnet network. However, a low-impedance NIC cannot be used in place of a high-impedance NIC in a high-impedance designed ARCnet network.

Figure 18.8 demonstrates the wiring configurations for a mixed-impedance ARCnet network.

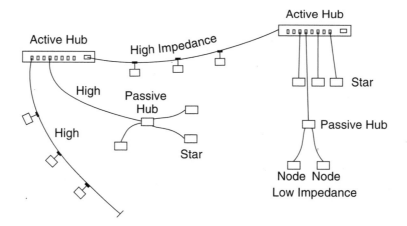

FIGURE 18.8 A combined high-impedance/low-impedance environment.

The degree of complexity of the network depends on the expertise of the developer. As the developer gains experience, it becomes easier to create more complex networks using ARCnet.

An ARCnet network has a limit of 255 stations, due to the fact that the user or installer must set the node ID using an 8-position dip switch on the card. By using this dip switch the combinations available are limited to 255 different, unique node IDs (address 0 is invalid). The PS/2 ARCnet cards need to have their address set via the reference disk configuration program.

CHAPTER 19

FDDI: FIBER DISTRIBUTED DATA INTERFACE

Fiber Distributed Data Interface was designed to meet the requirements of high-speed individual networks and high-speed connections between individual networks.

The FDDI standard was developed by the accredited standards committee X3T9.5 and is recognized by the American National Standards Institute. The standard is based on fiber-optic media or cable, has a speed of 100 Mbps, and uses the token-passing access method. The main reasons for choosing FDDI are distance, security, and speed.

The FDDI standard was developed primarily to handle the requirements of three types of networks: back-end local networks, high-speed office networks, and backbone local networks.

Back-End Local Networks

Back-end local networks are used to interconnect mainframe computers and large data-storage devices that require high data-transfer rates. A back-end local network normally has few devices to connect, and these devices are usually close together.

Typical characteristics of a back-end local network include:

- *High data rate*—To keep up with the demand for high volume, the network needs data rates of 50 to 100 Mbps.

- *High-speed interface*—File-transfer operations are typically performed through high-speed parallel I/O (input/output) interfaces rather than slower communication interfaces. Thus, the physical link between station and network must be high-speed.

- *Distributed access*—For reliability and efficiency, a distributed MAC (media access control) technique is used.

- *Limited distance*—A back-end local network is generally used in a computer room or a small number of rooms.

- *Limited number of devices*—The computer room generally contains many expensive mainframes and mass-storage devices.

The FDDI network in a back-end application has a preponderance of dual-ring stations and relatively few single-ring stations (dual- and single-ring stations are explained later in this chapter). The back-end network introduces one new performance requirement related to the type of traffic handled: It is more likely to see the file-transfer application than interactive use. For efficient operation, the MAC protocol should allow sustained use of the medium, either by permitting transmissions of unbounded length or by letting a pair of devices seize the channel for an indefinite period.

In the latter case, MAC permits multiframe dialog between two devices, with no other data allowed on the medium for the duration of the dialog. This allows a long sequence of data frames and acknowledgments to be interchanged. An example of this feature's utility is its ability to read from or write to high-performance disks. Without the ability to seize the bus temporarily, only one sector of the disk can be accessed with each revolution of the token (such performance would be unacceptable). The restricted-token feature of the FDDI MAC protocol (discussed later in this chapter) supports the multiframe dialog.

High-Speed Office Networks

The advent of image and graphics processing in the workplace gives rise to the need for high-speed office networks because of the burden imaging and graphics place on the network. For example, a typical data transaction may involve 500 bits, while a document page image may require the transmission of 500,000 bits or more. Additionally, optical disks are becoming more popular with the advent of multimedia and are being developed with realistic desktop capacities exceeding 1 Gbyte. These new demands require high-speed networks that can support the larger numbers and greater geographic extent of office systems. Unlike a back-end application, the FDDI network in this environment is likely to have a preponderance of single-ring stations and relatively few dual-ring stations to minimize the cost of connection.

Backbone Local Networks

A high-capacity network, backbone local networks are used to interconnect lower-capacity LANs. The increasing use of distributed processing applications and personal computers has led to a need for a flexible strategy for local networking. Support of premises' wiring data communications requires a networking and communications service capable of spanning the distances involved and interconnecting equipment in a single (perhaps large) building or cluster of buildings. Although it is possible to develop a single local network to interconnect all the data-processing equipment on the premises, this is probably not a practical alternative in most cases for the following reasons:

- *Reliability*—With a single local network, even a brief interruption in service could result in major disruption for users.
- *Capacity*—A single local network can become saturated as the number of devices attached to it grows. Although studies have shown that intradepartmental and intrabuilding communications greatly exceed interdepartmental and interbuilding communications, the backbone local network in a large, distributed-processing environment will most likely have to sustain high peak loads and ever-increasing sustained loads. Thus, a major advantage of the backbone is its large capacity.
- *Cost*—It may not be cost-effective to use a single large network. A more practical approach is to use lower-cost, lower-capacity local networks within buildings or departments and link these networks with a higher-capacity, higher-cost local network (a backbone local network).

Access Method

FDDI's access method is token passing on a ring. FDDI standards are similar to the IEEE 802.5 Token Ring protocol, although FDDI differs in its mechanisms for token handling, access allocation, and fault management.

Token Handling

A *frame* with a specific format (the token) is passed from one station to the next around the ring. When a station receives the token, it is allowed to transmit. The station can send as many *frames* (data) as desired until a predetermined time is reached. When the station either has no more frames to transmit or reaches the time limit, it transmits the token. Each station on the network retransmits the frames it receives and copies those frames that are addressed to it. When a frame returns to the sending station, that station is responsible for removing the frame from the ring.

As stations copy frames, they can set status bits in them to indicate whether or not errors were detected, addresses recognized, or frames copied for processing. Based on these status bits, a sending station can determine whether a frame was successfully received. Error-recovery processing and retransmission are not part of the first two layers of the Open System Interconnection Protocol Suite (OSI) but are left to the higher layers.

Since the token is passed on as soon as a station has finished transmitting frames, a station might transmit new frames while frames it transmitted earlier are still circulating on the ring. Thus, multiple frames from multiple stations could conceivably be on the network at the same time.

Access Allocation

FDDI doesn't use the priority mechanism documented in the IEEE 802.5 Token Ring standard. Instead, it uses a capacity allocation scheme based on the time it takes for the token to return. This scheme is designed to support a mixture of stream and burst transmissions and transmissions that involve dialogs between pairs of stations.

There are two types of frames defined: *synchronous* and *asynchronous*.

Each station may be allocated a certain length of time to transmit synchronous frames. This interval is called its *synchronous allocation*. A *target token rotation time* (TTRT) is also defined for the network. The TTRT must be large enough to accommodate the sum of all the station synchronous transmission times plus the time it takes the largest possible frame to travel around the ring. Each station keeps track of the time that has elapsed since it last received the token. When it next receives the token, it records the time elapsed and is then allowed to transmit synchronous frames for its synchronous allocation time. If the elapsed time as recorded when the token was received is less than the TTRT, the station can send asynchronous frames for a period equal to that time difference. Thus, stations that have a synchronous allocation are guaranteed an opportunity to transmit synchronous frames but they can transmit asynchronous frames only if time permits. Asynchronous frames can optionally be subdivided using levels of priority, which are then used to prioritize the sending of asynchronous traffic.

FDDI also provides for multiframe dialogs. When a station needs to enter into a dialog with another station, it can do so using the asynchronous transmission capacity. After the station transmits the first frame in the dialog, it transmits a restricted token. Only the station that receives the first frame can use the restricted token to transmit asynchronous frames. The two stations can then exchange data frames and restricted tokens for the duration of the dialog. During this time, other stations can send synchronous frames only.

Fault Management

FDDI specifies general fault-management techniques for handling token-related problems. All stations on the network are responsible for monitoring the token-passing protocol and initializing the ring if an invalid condition occurs. An invalid condition can include an extended period of inactivity on the ring (indicating a lost token) or an extended period of data transmission without a token (indicating a persistent frame).

When a station detects either condition, it begins ring initialization with the *claim-token procedure*. The station issues a continuous stream of control frames, called *claim frames*. Each frame contains a suggested TTRT value. If a station sending claim frames receives one from another station, it compares their TTRT values. If its own TTRT value is lower, it continues to transmit claim frames. If the other station's value is lower, it transmits that station's frames. If the values are the same, the station addresses are used to determine which station takes precedence. Eventually, the claim frame with the lowest

TTRT value is passed on by other stations and returns to the sending station. At this point, the sending station recognizes itself as the winner in the claim-token procedure.

The actual ring initialization then begins. The winner in the claim-token procedure sends out a token containing its TTRT value. The other stations recognize that the ring is now being initialized because they previously received claim frames rather than tokens. Each station saves the TTRT value, performs initialization processing, and passes the token on to the next station. No frames are transmitted until the token has passed once around the ring.

When a serious failure occurs, such as a break in the ring, a *beacon process* is used. When a station that has been sending claim frames recognizes that a specified period has elapsed without resolution of the claim-token process, it begins the beacon process by transmitting a continuous stream of beacon frames. If a station receives a beacon frame from another station, it stops sending its beacon frames and passes on the beacon frames it has received. Beacon frames from the station immediately following the break will eventually be propagated through the network, allowing the network to be reconfigured. If a station receives its own beacon frames, it assumes that the ring is restored and initiates the claim-token procedure.

Reliability

In addition to a high-speed transmission rate, FDDI is designed to provide highly reliable communication. Certain reliability-enhancing techniques have been incorporated into the design of FDDI; these include the use of wiring concentrators and automatic optical bypass switches, which makes it easier to locate faults and to bypass nonfunctioning stations.

FDDI also allows a dual-ring configuration, in which two rings are used to interconnect stations with data flowing in opposite directions on the rings. One of the rings is designated as the primary ring and the other as the secondary ring (see Figure 19.1). If a link failure occurs, the stations on either side of the link reconfigure the secondary ring (see Figure 19.2). This restores the ring and allows transmission to continue. If a station fails, a similar reconfiguration takes place (see Figure 19.3).

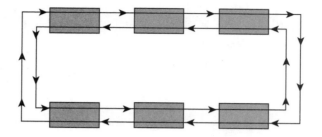

FIGURE 19.1 Dual FDDI ring. Primary and secondary rings in normal operation.

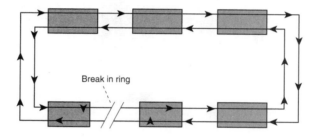

FIGURE 19.2 When a cable breaks in a dual-ring network, the ring will reconfigure itself.

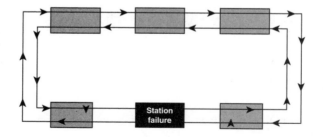

Figure 19.3 When a station fails in a dual-ring FDDI network,
the network reconfigures itself.

FDDI defines two classes of stations. *Class A* stations connect to both the primary and secondary rings and can reconfigure a network if a failure occurs. *Class B* stations connect only to the primary ring.

If a failure occurs and the network is reconfigured, a Class B station can become isolated. However, the single connection required for a Class B station typically makes it less expensive to attach to the network.

Another feature of FDDI is the use of wiring concentrators. These can be used in a star-wiring strategy. Figure 19.4 illustrates FDDI ring architecture.

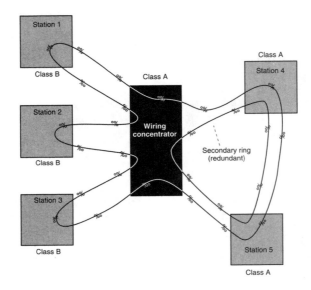

Figure 19.4 FDDI ring architecture.

FDDI and 802.5

Although FDDI follows 802.5 specifications for token passing on a ring, the two differ in the way a workstation seizes the token. With 802.5, a bit is flipped; with FDDI, the token is seized and held until the node transmits and releases the token. The bit flipping isn't useful at FDDI's high speeds. Another difference is that FDDI releases a token as frame transmission is completed, even if it has not received its own transmission. The high data rate makes this technique necessary. Figure 19.5 illustrates token passing on an FDDI network.

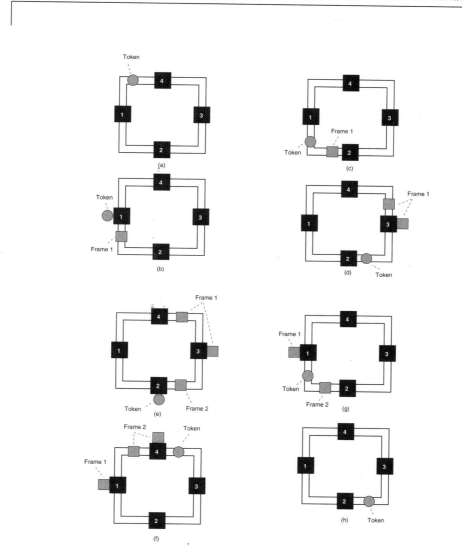

FIGURE 19.5 (a) Station 1 waits for the token to arrive. (b) Station 1 removes the token from the ring and begins transmitting Frame 1. (c) Station 1 adds the token to the end of Frame 1. (d) Frame 1 is addressed to Station 3, so Station 3 copies Frame 1 from the ring. (e) While Station 3 continues copying Frame 1 and Frame 1 proceeds around the ring, Station 2 removes the token from the ring and begins transmitting Frame 2. (f) Station 2 transmits the token after Frame 2 (which is addressed to it), and Station 1 removes Frame 1 from the ring. (g) Station 1 removes Frame 1 from the ring, but lets Frame 2 and the token pass. (h) Station 2 lets the token pass.

CHAPTER 20

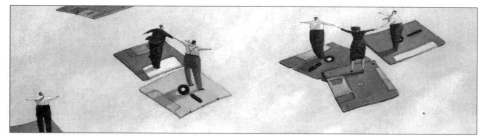

APPLETALK

The popularity of Macintosh has given rise to Apple's networking protocol, *AppleTalk*. *LocalTalk* is Apple's networking hardware, and *AppleShare* is the company's network software. Generally, a Macintosh network is referred to as AppleTalk.

Like the Macintosh, the AppleTalk network is easy to use. Because AppleTalk protocols are included in the Macintosh hardware and its operating system, basic networking capability is built into every computer. The protocols are also built into other devices, such as Apple's laser printers. This means you can build a Macintosh network with a shared-printer capability simply by connecting the devices with the appropriate cables. AppleShare allows a Macintosh to function as a file server on the network.

The basic AppleTalk network provides simple device-to-device communication and printer sharing. Network installation and reconfiguration are easy and inexpensive; no special hardware, software, or administration is necessary. The basic AppleTalk network does, however, have limited functionality and physical limitations. These will be discussed later.

Many third-party developers' products extend the capabilities of AppleTalk-based networks to include non-Apple devices, such as IBM-compatible computers and UNIX-based computers. Third-party products also extend the range of AppleTalk functions, providing such facilities as file sharing, electronic mail, communication servers, and printer spooling. Gateways provide dial-up access to AppleTalk networks and interconnection with Ethernet networks.

AppleTalk Basics

The AppleTalk network uses a bus or tree topology, usually with shielded twisted-pair cabling, although optical fiber and UTP can also be used—many AppleTalk networks are using unshielded twisted-pair cabling known as *phone net*. AppleTalk uses the CSMA/CA access method, and while the maximum number of devices on one network is 32, networks can be interconnected using bridges and routers. The maximum cable length is 300 meters, and the data rate is 230 Kbps.

The protocols defined by AppleTalk reflect the OSI layered model. However, they don't follow published specifications (such as IEEE's 802 specifications). Apple is trying to be OSI-compatible to ensure that Apples and IBMs can communicate on the same network.

AppleTalk and the OSI Model

The following descriptions of each layer of the OSI model, along with the accompanying features of AppleTalk, illustrate Apple's attempt to be compatible in today's networking environment. (Note that these protocols also support Ethernet and Token Ring architectures when the appropriate cabling and NICs are used.)

Physical Layer

This is the lowest layer and includes the interface for the LocalTalk hardware. If Ethernet or Token Ring is used, the interface is for the respective architecture's hardware.

Data Link Layer

At the data link layer, Apple uses the *AppleTalk Link Access Protocol* (ALAP). This protocol allows devices on the network to transmit and receive frames. It includes specifications for media access management, addressing, data encapsulation/decapsulation, and frame transmission dialogs.

Network Layer

Apple uses the *Datagram Delivery Protocol* (DDP) at the network level. This protocol provides for the delivery of *datagrams* (packets of data), either within a network or across networks. Delivery is on a best-effort basis, with error recovery left to higher layers. Without this protocol, AppleTalk could not interconnect multiple networks with bridges or routers to create an internet.

AppleTalk allows multiple communicating processes, known as *socket clients*, within a single node. A socket client uses a logical entity—a *socket*—to send and receive datagrams on the Internet. Each socket is identified by an eight-bit socket number. Each network in an internet has a 16-bit number that identifies it uniquely. A complete Internet address consists of a network number, a node ID, and a socket number. It identifies both the node and the process within the node (socket) that is communicating.

A key function of the DDP is routing datagrams within the Internet. If a datagram is sent to a destination on the same network as the source node, it is transmitted directly using ALAP from the data link layer. If the transmission is sent to a node on a network other than the source node, it is transmitted to a router node on the local network. This router checks its tables and determines where the datagram should be sent next, either to another router on another network or to the destination node. This continues until the datagram reaches the destination node. The DDP has access to the *Routing Table Management Protocol* (RTMP), which creates and maintains routing tables. (The RTMP is actually in the transport layer.)

Transport Layer

This layer has three protocols: RTMP, Name Binding Protocol (NBP), and AppleTalk Transaction Protocol (ATP).

The *RTMP* creates and maintains the routing tables used by the DDP. Each router on the Internet maintains a complete routing table. For each destination network number, the routing table indicates where the packet should be transmitted next and how many 'hops' are needed to reach the destination network. Routers periodically exchange their routing tables, allowing changes to be propagated throughout the Internet.

NBP is AppleTalk's naming service. Names are assigned to network-visible entities, such as socket clients and services available over the network. The NBP is responsible for matching names with Internet addresses.

The *ATP* provides reliable guaranteed delivery of packets from a source socket to a destination socket. It is based on the idea of a *transaction*, which consists of a request and its corresponding response. Each request is assigned a 16-bit transaction ID, which is also included in the response. If a response is not received within a specified time, the request is retransmitted. This mechanism ensures that the request is received and processed.

Session Layer

The *session layer* is designed to establish a communications session. In an AppleTalk network, four protocols are used in the session layer.

The *Data Stream Protocol* establishes a communication session between nodes. It can establish full-duplex communications, detect and eliminate duplicate datagrams, and request retransmissions to ensure error-free service.

The *Zone Information Protocol* helps subdivide the network into zones and helps manage the zone names. Zone names help the NBP determine which networks are found in what zone. This information also allows bridges and routers to establish a delivery path for packets.

The *Session Protocol* is concerned with the correct sequencing of datagrams when they arrive out of order. The SP also packages data into datagrams of the correct size and establishes breakpoints during conversation sessions to ensure efficient communication.

The *Printer Access Protocol* is concerned primarily with streamlike service for devices such as printers, or streaming tape backup systems when a network wants to communicate with such a device.

Presentation Layer

In an OSI-compatible network, this layer is concerned with the way data is presented and the type of syntax used. AppleTalk uses two protocols in this layer.

The *AppleTalk Filing Protocol* (AFP) provides a crucial interface for file-server software, particularly with two network operating systems: Apple's AppleShare and Novell's NetWare.

The AFP is concerned primarily with file structure, providing the foundation for a network's hierarchical structure of volumes, folders, and files. It also entails the appropriate log-in techniques. AppleTalk workstations can access both local and remote file servers using AFP, which contains a program that translates the native AppleTalk file-system calls into whatever format is needed by the file server being accessed.

The *PostScript Protocol* provides an interface that ensures effective communication between network workstations and PostScript devices, such as Apple's LaserWriter.

Zones

An internet can be divided into *zones*, which are defined at the transaction layer. Each network belongs to only one zone, but each zone can contain more than one network. This is a way to segment the network into work groups, which are set up arbitrarily by the network administrator.

One last point: Phase 2 AppleTalk allowed 256 zones per network, providing support for as many as 16 million AppleTalk devices and routing support for as many as 1,024 interconnected AppleTalk networks. This is a vast improvement over previous versions of AppleTalk. In real-world environments, internetworks probably would not meet these maximums, however, this routing support does make connectivity simpler for companies that have several small networks.

CHAPTER 21

OTHER ARCHITECTURES

There may only be one certain thing in the computer industry—nothing remains the same. New products are constantly being developed and released into the market place; new technologies are researched, created, and developed; and existing products and services are continually enhanced or modified. All this change can leave a person a little confused, or even unaware, that there was a change in a technology or that a new technology had emerged. It is also confusing to figure out what these technologies really do, and what impact these changes and new technologies will have—now and in the future.

It can take many hours of research to stay abreast of these new and changing technologies. No matter how much time is spent, it is important to ask yourself the following questions:

- Is the change right for me? If so why?
- Do I really need the change or new technology? If so why?
- What is the financial impact of the change? Is it worth it?
- How will the change or new technology affect my long-range planning?
- Which technology should I select?
- Do the technologies really live up to their claims?
- When is it right to make the change or implement the new technology?
- Should I go with the change or go with the new technology?

This chapter serves to update you on the changes within the existing architectures. It also serves to inform you of the new architectures that are being standardized. Finally, you should be able to glean from this chapter what these changes and new architectures mean for you now and in the future.

Enhancements

Switched Ethernet

When a 10Base-T network performance needs a substantial boost, the answer may be to use switches. Switches can alleviate network congestion, lessen throughput, and lower collision rates.

A *switch* is essentially a multiport bridge. It operates on OSI level 2.—the *media access control* (MAC) level. The switch filters (as explained in Chapter 24) between the port addresses of the switch. (See Figures 21.1 and 21.2.) Each port on a switch is the entrance to a segment on the network, and each segment has the address of its associated port on the switch. It is basically a more sophisticated method of bridging a network. However, these switches offer other advantages. They are much faster. They usually have a high-speed backplane that can support a very high rate of throughput—usually it is the number of paths through the switch multiplied by the throughput of each path, i.e., if there are 8 paths through the switch the backplane of the switch can accommodate 80 Mbps of throughput.

The correct placement of switches in a network results in what is known as aggregate total throughput. The whole is equal to the sum of the parts. Each switch can add to the total performance of a network (see Figures 21.3, 21.4, and 21.5).

There are other more technical features that have been added to these switches to differentiate them from the earlier bridges. One of the main features is the availability of *cut-through technology*. This technology increases the speed at which data passes through the switch. This cut-through technology is an alternative to *store-and forward technology*, as discussed in Chapter 24.

There are switches available where the port gives a node a dedicated collision-free line. The device attached to this port does not share an address with any other device for this port—it is a dedicated port to that device.

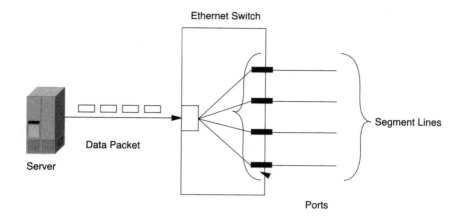

FIGURE 21.1 The Ethernet switch is a packet-switched device that routes
the packet to the correct out port. When the packet comes into
the switch, it activates the mechanism and the packet is routed (switched)
to the correct port going out to the other network segments.

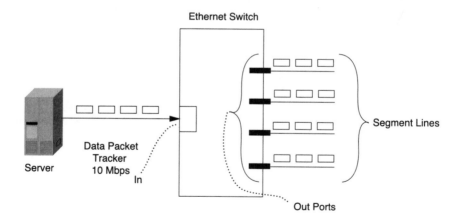

FIGURE 21.2 Note that the switching allows each segment to enter
the full bandwidth. Segments do not have to share the bandwidth.

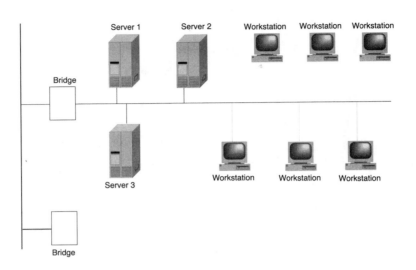

FIGURE 21.3 All workstations must share the band with between the three servers.

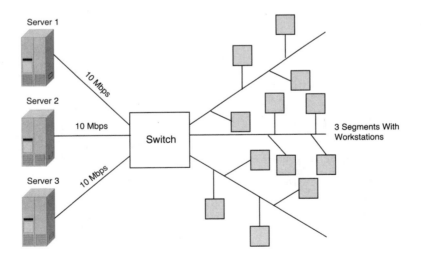

FIGURE 21.4 With the switch, the network is segmented
and each server has full bandwidth to the network.

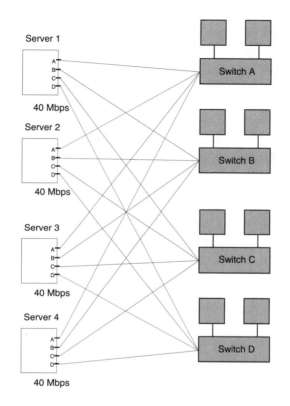

FIGURE 21.5 Four servers, each having four NICs. The total throughput for each server is 40 Mbps (10 Mbps/server x 4 servers). Any workgroup has full access to any server at any time. The total aggregate network throughput is 160 Mbps (40 Mbps/server x 4 servers).

Full Duplex Ethernet

As stated in Chapter 16, Ethernet has a throughput of 10 Mbps. An enhancement to Ethernet has been developed that can essentially double this throughput. This enhancement must be implemented on Ethernet 10Base-T architecture, and a switch, as described above, must be used in the network architecture. Doubling throughput is accomplished by using a communication method known as *full duplex* (which will be discussed later in this chapter). A simple discussion of communication methods is now in order. Essentially there are three methods of communicating a signal:

1. Simplex
2. Half duplex
3. Full duplex

Simplex allows the signal to be transmitted in one direction only—from point A to point B (see Figure 21.6). An example is a cable television system. The cable originates at a central office, point A. The cable radiates out from this one point to your house, point B. The television programs, or signal, can only go from point A to point B. As of this writing—before interactive TV arrives—a transmission signal cannot be transmitted back from point B to point A (from house to TV studio).

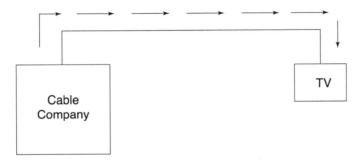

FIGURE 21.6 Simplex communication allows the signal to travel in one direction only. Here the television signal is transmitted from the cable communication company to the house.

With *half duplex* the signal travels from point A to point B, but can also be transmitted from point B to point A. This process is two way-communication. However, the signal can only go in one direction at a time. The signal must stop transmitting from point A to point B before transmission from point B to point A can begin. It is like a citizens band radio (CB). The person speaking on the CB radio, point A, is transmitting a signal out to point B. The person at point A must stop transmitting before the CB radio can receive a signal from point B—There is two way communication but, only one signal at a time (see Figure 21.7).

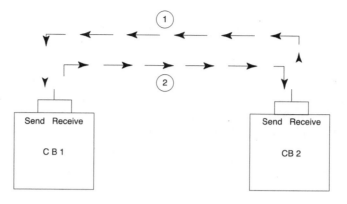

FIGURE 21.7 Half-duplex communication allows the signal to flow in both directions, CB 1 to CB 2 and CB 2 to CB 1. However, the signal can only be going in one direction at a time. Either signal 1 is transmitting or signal 2 is transmitting, never both at the same time.

With *full duplex* the signal travels from point A to point B, and a signal can go from point B to point A simultaneously. A signal can be transmitted from point A to point B while a signal is also being transmitted from point B to point A. This is like using a telephone. The person speaking on a telephone at point A, can also hear the person speaking on the telephone at point B, and vice-versa (see Figure 21.8).

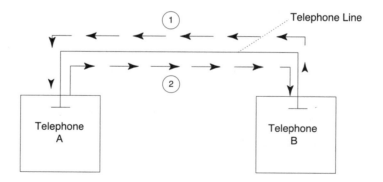

FIGURE 21.8 Full duplex communication allows the signal to flow in both directions from telephone A to telephone B and from telephone B to telephone A. Unlike the other methods, the signals, can flow at the same time.

Ethernet operates in the half duplex mode of communication. A workstation, point A, can transmit data to the server, point B, but the server must wait for the workstation to stop transmitting before it can transmit back to the workstation. By using full duplex, the process is changed. The workstation can now transmit data to the server and the server can transmit back to the workstation while the workstation is still transmitting. It is essentially the same thing as having two lines between the workstation and the server, resulting in a doubling of the throughput. The transmission rate is 10 Mbps in and 10 Mbps out. This happening at the same time gives a throughput of 20 Mbps (see Figure 21.9). With an additional server the transmission rate jumps to 60 Mbps (see Figure 21.10).

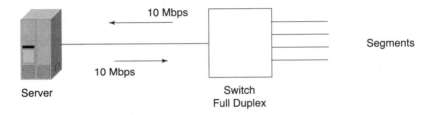

FIGURE 21.9 By using a full duplex switch the throughput is doubled between the server and the switch, increasing aggregate server throughput to 20 Mbps.

Full duplex cannot happen without the use of additional devices. First the NICs in the workstations and servers must be full duplex NICs. A regular half duplex NIC will not work. The workstation must be connected to a full duplex Ethernet switch.

Many times workstations themselves are not configured to be full duplex. Applications at this time don't require a desktop PC to need this much throughput. However, with the advent of video over the LAN this may change, and higher throughput will be necessary at the desktop.

Usually full duplex is incorporated in the switch to the server. The full duplexing feature is also implemented in switch-to-switch communication in a segmented network.

The use of full duplex has its advantages, some of which are:

- It gives a better price/performance ratio than 100-Mbps alternatives
- It supports existing 10Base-T cabling

- It takes full advantage of the server's performance due to the limitations of the PC, bus and CPU. It is estimated that a server has a deliverable bandwidth between 25 and 30 Mbps.

The one disadvantage of full duplex is if 100-Mbps transmission is truly needed, full duplexing will not deliver it.

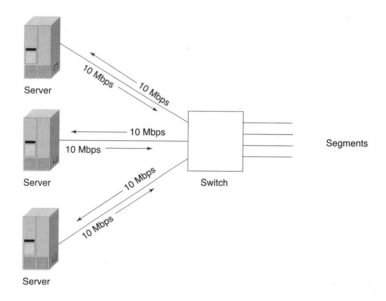

FIGURE 21.10 With a full duplex switch and three servers, the aggregate throughput is now 60 Mbps for the servers.

Token Ring

Switches and full duplexing are now being released for Token Ring,. It is expected that switching and full duplex will provide the same advantages for Token Ring as they now do for Ethernet.

ARCnet

Datapoint, the company responsible for the development of ARCnet, has produced a 20-Mbps version of the ARCnet protocol called *ARCnet Plus*.

ARCnet Plus uses the same coaxial cable as ARCnet and can accommodate both the 20-Mbps and 2.5-Mbps boards on the same cabling segment. The new ARCnet Plus hubs have the intelligence to automatically arbitrate the speed between the nodes with different speed NICs. The only networkwide requirement to step up the performance of your network with ARCnet Plus is the replacement of all active and passive ARCnet hubs with ARCnet Plus active hubs.

Another development concerning ARCnet deals with the *Thomas Conrad Network Solution* (TCNS). This is a 100-Mbps protocol that uses ARCnet's token-passing scheme with standard ARCnet and Enhanced ARCnet network drivers. TCNS supports three different cabling options:

- Coaxial
- IBM Type 1 shielded twisted pair
- Fiber optic

By using the coaxial cabling, you can maintain compatibility with the installed base of ARCnet StarBus systems.

New Architectures

Two new networks have arrived on the scene and are trying to become the 100-Mbps network of choice. They are actually variations of Ethernet. They are:

- Fast Ethernet
- 100VG-AnyLAN

Please don't think the two are the same. They are both Ethernet, but you may have problems should you refer to 100VG as an Ethernet network.

Fast Ethernet

Fast Ethernet has a throughput of 100 Mbps. It is very much like its slower and older Ethernet brother, complying with the IEEE 802.3 standards. It uses the same protocols and packets as Ethernet, and uses the CSMA/CD access method (see Figure 21.11).

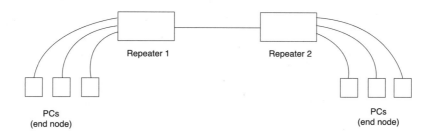

FIGURE 21.11 Ethernet permits only two repeaters between end nodes.

Unlike its Ethernet brother, the distance limitations are much more severe with Fast Ethernet. The limit between repeaters is 210 meters (see Figure 21.12). This is actually the distance between collision domains. Several segments can be connected, but each segment (usually its own collision domain) is limited to 210 meters (see Figure 21.13). The laws of physics dictates this due to the increased speed resulting in signal propagation. There can be only two repeaters between end nodes. At this point Fast Ethernet is more limited to the cabling it can use.

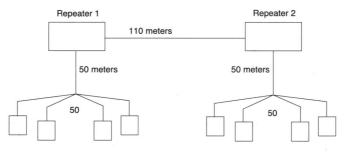

FIGURE 21.12 There can only be 210 meters between any two end nodes.

The 100BaseT standard defines three OSI physical-layer specifications that support different cabling types:

- 100BaseTX—two-pair Category 5 UTP
- 100BaseT4—four-pair Category 3, 4, or 5 UTP
- 100BaseFX—for fiber optic

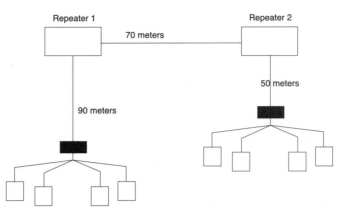

FIGURE 21.13 Total end node to end node is 210 meters maximum.

Of these cable types, most Fast Ethernet runs over 100BaseTX. At this time no products really exist for 100BaseT4.

Connecting a Fast Ethernet network is virtually the same as connecting a regular Ethernet network. There is a workstation (node) with a Fast Ethernet NIC. This NIC is connected to cabling going to a wall jack, and the wall jack is cabled to a concentrator. There may be cables that link concentrators, and punch blocks or patch panels may be used for more flexibility. Bridges can also be used to convert small Fast Ethernet networks into large Fast Ethernet networks.

The Fast Ethernet portion of a network must be segmented from the rest of the network. This can be done with bridges or switches.

100VG-AnyLAN

This is also a 100-Mbps throughput network. It does not have as much support as Fast Ethernet; its major champion is Hewlett-Packard. It was originally designed to serve as an upgrade from 16-Mbps Token Ring and Ethernet because it can carry both Token Ring and Ethernet packets.

What really sets this network aside from Fast Ethernet is the access method it uses. Unlike Ethernet it uses a deterministic access method, referred to as *demand priority*. The hub scans each port in succession to transmit data. This avoids many of the collisions inherent to CSMA/CD. 100VG-AnyLAN complies with the IEEE 802.12 specifications. A provision exists to implement *isochronism*—

the ability to send timing-data, such as video. It can operate over four-pair Category 3, 4, or 5 UTP cabling.

100VG-AnyLan has a star topology with up to five repeaters placed between two end nodes. There can be up to 100 meters between each device, giving 100VG-AnyLAN a greater operating distance than Fast Ethernet.

Repeaters can be cascaded to three levels. This indicates that 100VG-AnyLAN is built hierarchically (see Figure 21.14).

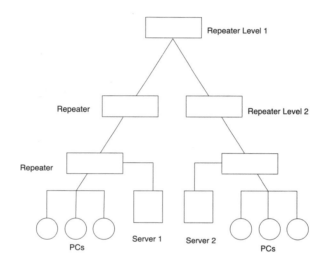

FIGURE 21.14 In a 100VG-AnyLAN, the repeaters can be cascaded only to three levels with a maximum of five repeaters between any two end nodes.

To build the network, one hub or repeater starts and becomes level 1. The network can then cascade down, a total of three levels. The drop can be 100 meters with Category 3 UTP and 150 meters with Category 5 cable. Using fiber-optic cable can extend the drop to 5000 meters.

The ports on the hubs function in two modes:

1. Normal—see only data sent to the connected workstation.
2. Monitor—see all data in the hub. This is good for diagnostics or decision support.

Each hub has at least one uplink port. Every other port can be used as a downlink port.

CHAPTER 22

ATM—Asynchronous Transfer Mode

Broadband networks are now popular due to the need for more throughput. It is clear that baseband-type transmission of LANs can't rival the transfer speeds attainable with broadband networks. One that is talked about often in the trade press is *Asynchronous Transfer Mode* (ATM). As of now, ATM is not widely implemented because it is still too new and has not been officially sanctioned.

In the near future, much more is going to be done with ATM, primarily because of the promise that it holds—it can connect LAN to LAN, be used for wide-area networks, and can be used as a backbone. It is very versatile and is being delivered in varying speeds.

ATM and ISDN

The original specifications for ATM came from the *International Telecommunications Union* (ITU), the organization whose standards address the worldwide telecommunication infrastructure. In the early 1980s the ITU defined *Integrated Services Digital Network* (ISDN), which is now called *N-ISDN* for narrowband ISDN. N-ISDN had two access interfaces, or transfer rates. The two rates are:

1. Basic—which operates at 144 kbps
2. Primary—which operates at 1.544 Mbps

AS ISDN's name implies these interfaces were designed to carry integrated services—digital voice, data, and control information—and are both digital.

In the late 1980s, the ITU further enhanced N-ISDN by bringing out the specifications for *B-ISDN*, or broadband ISDN. Unlike N-ISDN, B-ISDN offered much higher transmission rates, up to 622 Mbps. The signals generated by B-ISDN are carried by ATM.

How ATM Works

ATM transmits in what is known as a *cell stream*. A *cell* is a term defined for ATM broadband transmission—it can be thought of as a predefined data packet. The data packet, or cell, is 48 bytes long for data and has 5 bytes for a header (for addressing). Every cell that goes across an ATM circuit is a set 53 bytes long (see Figure 22.1).

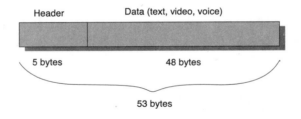

FIGURE 22.1 Each ATM cell, or data packet, is 53 bytes long.

ATM collects incoming signals from B-ISDN sources. It then formats these signals and places them into a 48-byte cell. (Remember a 5-byte header is also added to the cell.) The cells are then mixed or multiplexed with other cells. The multiplexed cells are then transmitted over the ATM cell steam. At the destination, the cells are broken apart and the signals are reassembled as they were before transmission (see Figure 22.2).

ATM is connection-oriented. It requires an established connection before it can transmit data (see Figure 22.3). The connection can take two forms. One form is a *permanent virtual circuit* (PVC). In a PVC network managers manually configure connection paths. The other form is a *switched virtual circuit* (SVC), where connections are made on the fly. As of this writing no ATM equipment exists for making SVCs.

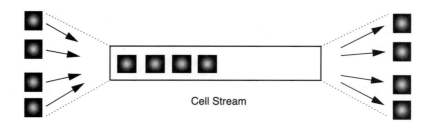

FIGURE 22.2 Cells are formed, or multiplexed, and they flow onto the cell stream, out the other side, and then are disassembled.

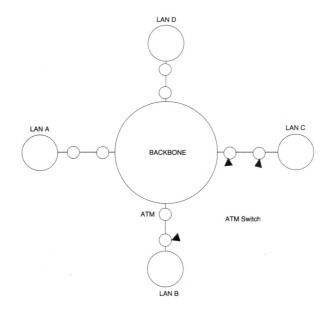

FIGURE 22.3 ATM can serve as a backbone for a network.

ATM's cell transmission is not fixed and timed. The cell delivery may be periodic, depending on traffic load. The fact that the cell transmission is periodic puts ATM in the asynchronous communication category.

An ATM line can carry frame relay packets. It is a technology whose time has not yet come. But when it does, watch out (see Figure 22.4 and 22.5).

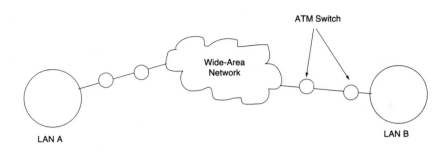

FIGURE 22.4 ATM can serve as a for wide-area networking.

ATM Switch

FIGURE 22.5 ATM can connect LANs.

CHAPTER 23

FRAME RELAY WIDE-AREA NETWORKING

Frame relay is used for broadband *wide-area network* (WAN) service. It is becoming very popular and is very effective. In many places the outdated protocol X.25 of the CCITT is being replaced by frame relay. If you are looking to create a wide-area network, you should consider frame relay (see Figure 23.1).

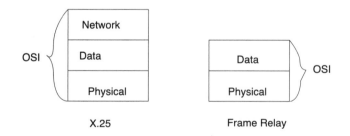

FIGURE 23.1 Frame relay is a protocol that defines how a data packet, or frame, is formed. It is shown compared to the outdated X.25 protocol of the CCITT. Frame relay is more effective and in many places replaces X.25 networks.

Frame relay is actually a combination of several different protocols, and instead of being the actual transmission line, it is the routing—how the data arrives where it should. Thus, routers and addressing bear heavily on frame relay.

Frame Relay and ISDN

Frame relay, as defined by ANSI, is an ISDN packet-mode bearer service (see Chapter 22) that transfers frames of information from the network side of one UNI to the network side of another user network interface (UNI), where the UNI is the separating point between the user and the transport facility, or network provider. The owner of a network of two LANs implements frame relay, when the services of a public or private data network are contracted. This public or private network uses frame relay for the connection of data transmissions from the two LANs.

Frame Relay to the Rescue

If we want three LANs communicating among themselves—LAN A is in New York City, LAN B in Dallas, and LAN C in San Francisco—these three LANs could be connected by *lease lines*, also known as *dial-up lines*. The first thing to be done is look at the amount of traffic and how much interconnectivity is required. If the traffic and the connectivity are light, a lease line may be a viable option. Assume that traffic is heavy and the three LANs need to be communicating constantly. Then lease or dial-up lines would not be economical or efficient. If ISDN was available, lease lines could be used for heavy and constant communication. However, ISDN is a dedicated service and many lines would be needed to mesh (interconnect all three LANs). Also, since ISDN charges by usage, it could get expensive. Enter the Frame relay network.

Frame relay, which usually charges a flat rate, with certain options only makes a connection when a request is made—a virtual circuit. No traffic, no circuit. When traffic starts, a circuit is made (see figure 23.2).

Each LAN may have an access loop into the frame relay network. This could be a private or public network such as AT&T or MCI. The access loop is connected to a router that interfaces with the LAN. This router is the UNI. Once a signal is placed on the frame relay network by this router it disappears into that magical WAN cloud that is always shown in diagrams of remote networks (see Figures 23.3 and 23.4). The WAN cloud which could be AT&T or MCI, contains a series of routers that forward the signal to its destination.

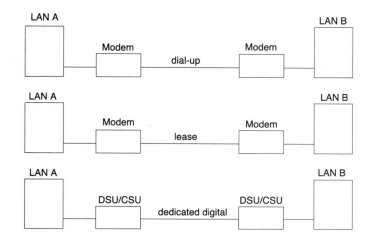

FIGURE 23.2 Frame relay can be transmitted by various methods, dial-up telephone lines, leased lines, dedicated digital lines over DSU/CSU, and ISDN. Frame relay can be transmitted via ATM networks.

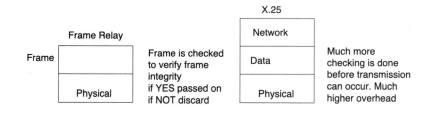

FIGURE 23.3 Checking frame integrity.

Once inside the WAN cloud the signal can take many paths. (See the discussion on routers in Chapter 24.) When your signal leaves your network it has the starting network and destination network addresses attached to the signals by the router.

Inside the WAN cloud it can take one of many paths (see Figure 23.5). Because the circuits are virtual and packet-switched, only one line is needed from each LAN to the network (see Figure 23.6). To hard-wire the circuit and have the same interconnectivity would require many lines.

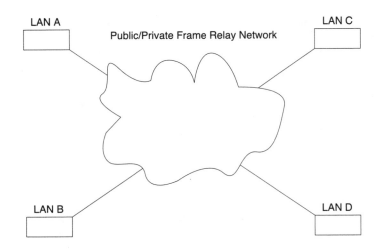

FIGURE 23.4 LANs attached to the frame relay network. Inside the frame relay network, the carrier selects the methods of transmission and then the frames.

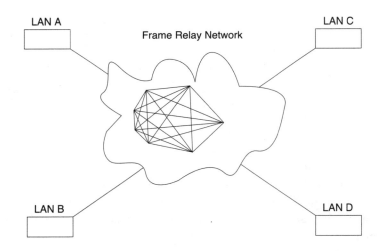

FIGURE 23.5 Routers, or switches, are used extensively to route or forward the frame relay packets from source to destination. They are interconnected to establish many paths, or circuits, the frame can take to avoid down lines or traffic overloads.

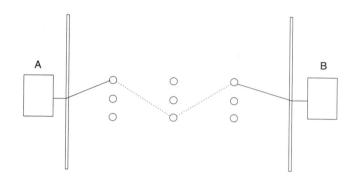

FIGURE 23.6 There is always a hard-wired connection between points A and B. However, the circuit is always changed. It is created when a call is initiated from A to B or B to A. Afterward, the circuit is broken.

Since IPX or NetBios does not go across the frame relay network, the router can assemble and disassemble the frame relay packets (see Figures 23.7 and 23.8). The frame relay may be thought of as similar to IPX. Translation is done in the frame relay architecture to accomplish this. It is not a simple task (see figure 23.9).

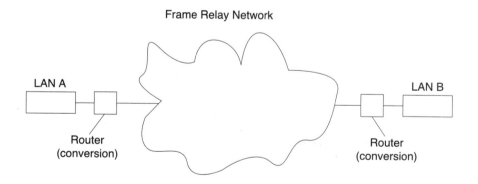

FIGURE 23.7 LAN A converts network transmission into frame relay packets by using a router, also known as a frame relay assembler/disassembler. From the router, the frame is put onto the network.

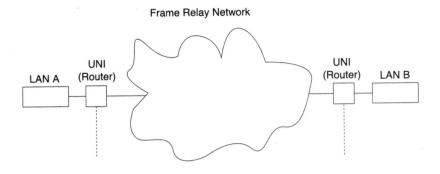

FIGURE 23.8 The User-Network Interface marks the place where the network and business meet. This is where responsibility changes from business to network.

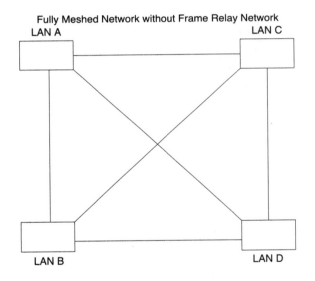

FIGURE 23.9 Just using direct connections requires many more connections and lines than for a frame relay network. Also, this method could be much slower and more expensive.

SECTION V

INTERCONNECTIVITY

CHAPTER 24

INTERCONNECTIVITY

Among the most exciting areas in the field of LANs are interconnectivity and interoperability. New developments in standardization and new products to support communications are common, and these new interoperability products and techniques allow LANs to communicate with mainframe computers and other LANs. They also make it possible for a company to replace a mainframe used for data processing, allowing different departments and their users to take full advantage of the firm's established system of LANs.

Interoperability has brought about pioneering work in software design. New developments allow a LAN node to run software that interacts with software executing on the company's mainframe or that runs concurrently on the LAN and the mainframe. The possibilities are endless. Creating an environment that is both interconnected and interoperable is, however, one of the most demanding disciplines in the sphere of LANs. Anyone who deals with sophisticated interconnectivity must be well-versed in all aspects of LAN technology, communication technology, and software.

This chapter offers a simple introduction to interconnectivity and interoperability. It demonstrates how a LAN can be connected to one or more other LANs and even to a mainframe or minicomputer host. The discussion of wide-area networks, where one LAN can communicate with another LAN across the country, is mentioned in Chapter 23.

While discussions on interconnectivity, interoperability, and internetworking can become very detailed and technical, most of the information presented here is fairly succinct. The goal of this chapter is simply to introduce some of the components associated with interconnectivity—specifically, the repeater, bridge, router, gateway, and backbone. Learning more about these components will give you a basis for understanding how interconnectivity works and the important role each component plays.

The Repeater

As mentioned in the descriptions of Ethernet, Token Ring, and ARCnet LANs, the repeater functions at the lowest level of the OSI model: the physical layer, making it the simplest component used in LAN interconnectivity (see Figure 24.1). While a repeater is not used to interconnect different networks, it does connect segments of the same network to form an extended network. Its purpose is to receive a signal and regenerate or strengthen that signal, extending the cabling-distance limits placed on a network by its architecture.

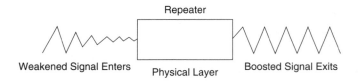

FIGURE 24.1 The repeater operates at the Physical layer to extend cabling distances.

When a repeater is used, it must connect to networks of the same architecture. type, using the same protocols, media-access scheme, and transmission technique. Given that, a repeater can connect segments of an Ethernet LAN or hubs of a Token Ring network, but it cannot connect an Ethernet trunk segment with a Token Ring hub. Nor can it connect a segment of an Ethernet baseband LAN with a segment of an Ethernet broadband LAN.

Ethernet Repeaters

Using repeaters is fairly easy in an Ethernet network because they connect the trunk segments to form one large network. The repeater counts as one node on each trunk segment it connects. Because the repeater doesn't terminate an end of a trunk segment, the end of the cable must be terminated independently.

Token Ring Repeaters

A Token Ring network involves three kinds of repeaters: Token Ring, lobe, and connecting. The *Token Ring repeater* is used when the network has more than one wiring center. It extends the distance between MAUs, enabling the Token Ring network to reach distant nodes. This repeater can be used to regenerate both the main ring path and the backup ring path. Token Ring repeaters allow a distance of approximately 1000 to 1200 feet between MAUs.

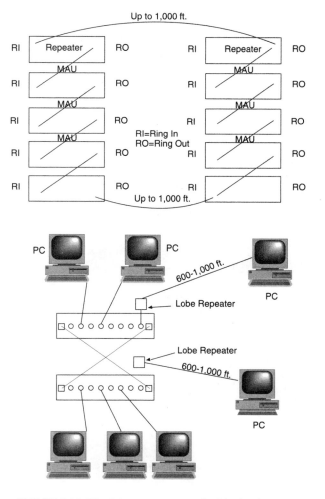

FIGURE 24.2 The lobe repeater can double the distance between a workstation and the MAU.

The *lobe repeater* boosts the signal for only one lobe attached to a MAU, not for the entire network. Of the eight nodes that may attach to the MAU, one, two, or all eight may use a lobe repeater (see Figure 24.2). This repeater usually doubles the distance a lobe may run so that a distant node can be attached to the MAU and in turn be attached to the Token Ring network without IBM Type 1 and Type 2 cables.

Connecting repeaters boosts the signal between hubs, usually doubling the distance between hubs. Two methods are used to install Token Ring repeaters: the main ring path and the backup path.

To understand the main ring path, let's assume we have two hubs, each with three MAUs (see Figure 24.3). Let's also assume that the distance from one hub to the other is 1000 feet. This is more than the limitations of Token Ring allow, so we must use a repeater. The main path's signal is boosted by a set of repeaters, so we need two repeaters (one for each hub). The Ring Out from the third MAU of the first hub connects to the Ring In of the repeater in the first hub; the Ring Out of the repeater in the first hub connects to the Ring In of the third MAU in the second hub; the Ring Out of the first MAU in the second hub connects to the Ring In of the repeater in the second hub; and the Ring Out of the repeater in the second hub connects to the Ring In of the first MAU in the first hub.

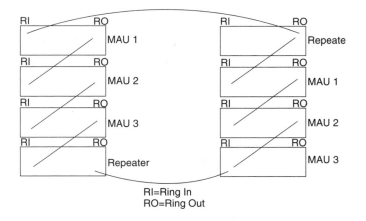

RI=Ring In
RO=Ring Out

FIGURE 24.3 A Token Ring network with two hubs (three MAUs per hub) uses repeaters to boost the signal for the main path.

Although the signal has just been boosted., it is only boosted on the main ring path. If something should happen to the signal on this main ring path, it would not be boosted on the backup ring path, in essence, breaking the ring. To compensate for this, the backup path is also boosted by repeaters.

When the backup path is boosted, it is automatically assumed that the main path is also boosted. Let's reconsider the previous example with the main path boosted. A repeater is placed in front of the first MAU of the first hub; the Ring Out from this repeater connects to the Ring In of the first MAU. Everything else remains the same in the first hub. Another repeater is placed in front of the third MAU in the second hub. The Ring Out of the newly placed repeater in the second hub connects to the Ring In of the third MAU of the second hub. The Ring Out of this repeater connects to the Ring In of the first repeater in the first hub. Thus, the ring is still maintained. No matter what occurs in either hub, the signal between hubs is boosted. Therefore, both the main and backup paths are boosted. To do this, we need four repeaters (see Figure 24.4).

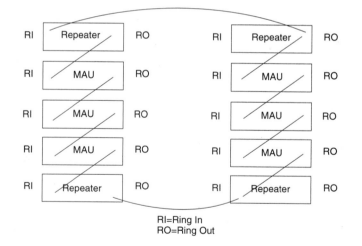

RI=Ring In
RO=Ring Out

FIGURE 24.4 A Token Ring network with two hubs (three MAUs per hub) uses repeaters to boost the main and backup paths.

Using Repeaters with ARCnet

Pseudo-repeaters are used in an ARCnet network because the active hub also serves as a repeater.

The Bridge

The second component used to join LANs is the bridge. Unlike a repeater, a bridge connects disparate networks. It functions as a device on its own but also belongs to the networks it joins (see Figure 24.5).

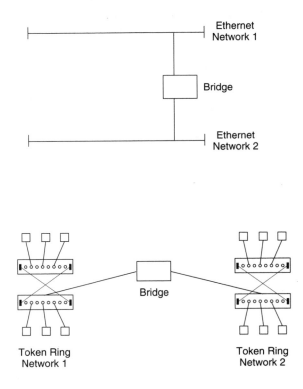

FIGURE 24.5 A bridge is used to connect two distinct Ethernet or Token Ring networks.

The bridge functions at the data link layer of the OSI model, one layer higher than the repeater. It can be either local or remote.

Local Bridges

A local bridge connects two similar networks in the same geographical area. It takes packets from one network and places them on another network, then takes packets from the second network and places them on the first network. Each time the bridge swaps packets between networks, it also functions as a repeater regenerating the signal.

Of course, the bridge does more than just regenerate a signal between disparate networks. It can examine a packet header and decide on which of the two networks that packet belongs. This process is known as *filtering*. Basically, a bridge receives all packets on the networks it is connected to and look at the source and destination addresses of each packet.

Say LAN 1 is connected to LAN 2 via a bridge. LAN 1 issues a message intended for node X on LAN 2. The bridge looks at the packet, realizes that node X is on LAN 2, and forwards the packet to LAN 2. If LAN 1 issues a message for node C on LAN 1, the bridge receives the packet, reads the destination address, and determines that this message doesn't need to cross over to LAN 2. Therefore, the bridge doesn't allow the packet to move to LAN 2. By preventing the packet from moving to LAN 2, the bridge decreases the excess traffic on that LAN (see Figure 24-6).

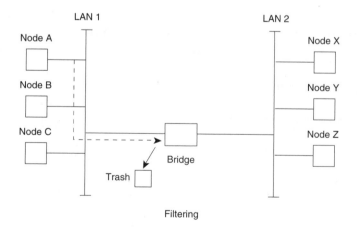

Filtering

FIGURE 24.6 With filtering, if node C wants to communicate with node A, the packet is broadcast and the bridge, recognizing that the packet is destined for the local network, prevents it from generating unnecessary traffic on LAN 2.

As packets pass through the bridge, it stores the addresses of nodes communicating through it, determining which addresses are on LAN 1 and which are on LAN 2. Through this learning process, the bridge builds a table containing the addresses of all the nodes on the networks. Each time the bridge filters a packet, it checks the address table against the node address of the packet. If they don't match, the bridge stores the address and forwards the packet. This process is known as *storing and forwarding* (see Figure 24.7).

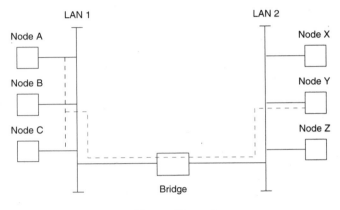

Store and Forward

FIGURE 24.7 With storing and forwarding, the bridge receives a new packet from node A on LAN 1 destined for node X on LAN 2. If it doesn't recognize the packet address, the bridge stores the destination address in its address table and then forwards the packet.

When some bridges, known as *learning bridges*, are attached to an Ethernet network, they immediately send broadcasts asking all the stations on the local network segment to respond. As the stations return the broadcast, the bridge builds a table of local addresses. As nodes are added to the network, it continues to gather node addresses (see Figure 24.8). Bridges that require someone to enter all the node addresses into the bridge are known as *static bridges*.

Multiple bridges can be used, but in such cases the bridge must know all the stations it can reach, not just the stations on the networks to which it is directly connected. For example, if node A on LAN 1 wants to send a message to node H on LAN 3, the bridge between LAN 1 and LAN 2 must know to forward any messages for LAN 3 to LAN 2. The bridge between LAN 2 and LAN 3 then forwards the message to LAN 3 (see Figure 24.9). When multiple bridges are used, only one path can connect any two networks. If more than one path exists, duplicate messages may be created or messages could arrive out of sequence.

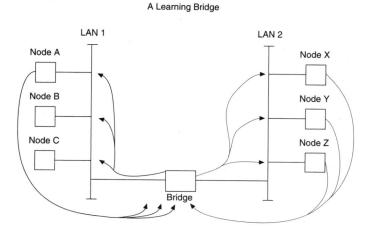

FIGURE 24.8 When a learning bridge is installed, it broadcasts a request for address information and stores the node responses in its address table.

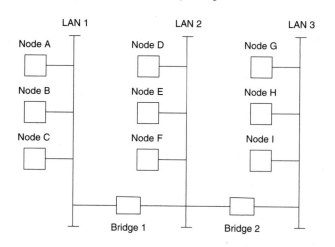

FIGURE 24.9 When multiple bridges are used, address information must be supplied for all the available nodes. Therefore, if node A wants to communicate with node H, bridge 1 must know to forward the packet to bridge 2.

Ethernet networks are an exception to the rule that requires a single connection path between bridged networks when using a spanning tree bridge. Instead, they use a procedure taken from the IEEE 802.1 standards. On an Ethernet the primary bridge fail, the backup bridge takes over to ensure a continuous connection. This is the only time the backup or secondary bridge is used—otherwise, it remains idle.

In the context of bridging, the term *routing* refers to the path the packet will travel—this term has no connection with the interconnectivity device called a router. The type of routing used by the bridges in the preceding examples is called *transparent routing*—not only are the bridges unaware of the route the packet will take, the packet itself doesn't know the route it will travel.

Source routing is another type of routing used by bridges, primarily in IBM Token Ring networks. With source routing, the packet itself contains routing information specifying the networks and bridges through which it will travel to its destination. The sending node is responsible for putting this information onto the packet. It determines the various routes available through the process of *route discovery*. This process is somewhat complicated; all you need to know is that each node on the network has a map of the entire network and all associated networks and bridges.

Source routing does add some overhead to the network, but its benefits more than make up for it. Another of those benefits is that it can aid in network communication management. Since each node specifies the route, its packet will follow, it can always choose the most efficient path at the time of transmission. Source-routing bridges can also be faster than transparent-routing bridges because they have to read only the destination information rather than each packet in its entirety.

One final point regarding bridges:—they are protocol-independent. In other words, the bridge doesn't care what protocol is used on either LAN, it treats TCP/IP, SPX/IPX, and other communication protocols equally. The bridge receives the packets and either transmits them or ignores them without concern for protocols. The bridge does not translate the packet—LANs must do that themselves—but they may be implemented to facilitate the connection of different media types (see Figure 24.10).

Bridging with Mixed Media

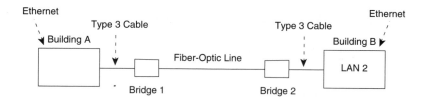

FIGURE 24.10 Bridges can be used to link different media types. LAN 1 is connected to bridge 1 using Type 3 cable; bridge 1 is then connected to bridge 2 using a fiber-optic link. The signal is connected to LAN 2 using Type 3 cable.

Remote Bridges

Remote bridges connect two LANs that aren't in the same geographical area. Usually, some type of telecommunication link—a telephone line or a satellite transmission—is needed to connect remote LANs. A bridge at one end of the telecommunication link puts packets destined for the other LAN out onto the link. A bridge at the other end of the link receives these packets and passes them on to its LAN. This process works in both directions. All the other facets of bridges remain the same for remote bridges: the only real difference is the use of telecommunications link (see Figure 24.11).

The Router

The third component of network interconnectivity is the router. The *router* operates at the network layer of the OSI model, one layer higher than the bridge. Remember that the IEEE 802 specifications only relate to the first two layers—the physical and the data link layers. Since the router is functioning at the Network layer, the communication protocols on both sides of the router must be the same and must be compatible at higher network layers. The first two OSI layers may differ without affecting routing.

The router is used to pass a message through intermediate nodes. This approach doesn't work well with a single LAN because a transmitted message is sent to all the nodes on that network and receiving node determines from the destination address whether or not it should accept the message and process it. However, when a LAN is connected with other LANs or on a wide-area network, the issue of routing becomes more important.

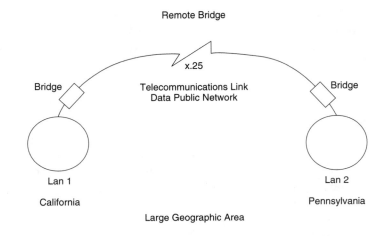

FIGURE 24.11 Remote bridges connect distant LANs using a telecommunications link.

With other types of networks, particularly the wide-area network, a message is ordinarily sent from one node to another specific node on the network rather than to every node. However, it may pass through a series of intermediate nodes before arriving at its destination. A message usually also has more than one path or route available to it, thus, there are various paths to choose from when one node sends a message to another.

When a message is routed through intermediate nodes, it must contain two addresses: the destination address, which remains constant, and the address of the next node along the route. The latter address changes as new nodes are encountered, until the message finally arrives at the destination node.

A router is itself an intermediate system or node. To demonstrate, let's consider one router that connects two LANs. Station A on LAN 1 wants to send a message to station C on LAN 2. The message is first sent to station B (the router), the router processes the information embedded in the packet's network layer, and based on that information, station B sends the message to LAN 2 (see Figure 24.12).

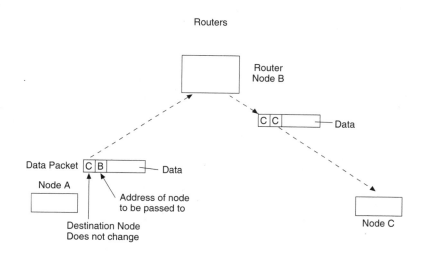

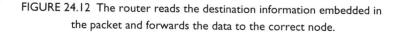

FIGURE 24.12 The router reads the destination information embedded in the packet and forwards the data to the correct node.

Multiple routers can also be used. They can be connected in a manner that allows for multiple paths or routes between any two networks. Since messages are sent to a specific router node, the existence of multiple paths will not cause the message to be duplicated (see Figure 24.13).

The function of a router is to determine the next node to receive the message. Two methods are used to do this. Routing information can be defined when the network is designed, then stored in routing tables that are placed manually within the routers, or source routing,—the technique used for bridges—can be used. Whichever approach is used, a network map is developed for the routers.

The Gateway

The *gateway* is the final component needed for interconnectivity. It is also the most complex. It functions on any layers of the OSI model above the network layer, so different protocols may be used at any or all of the layers.

Gateways are used to connect networks that may have entirely different architectures. For example, a gateway would be used to connect a LAN to an IBM mainframe using IBM's SNA and SAA because it provides translation and conversion. Most mainframe gateways consist of a personal computer, a 3270 board, and the gateway software (see Figure 24.14).

Multiple Routers

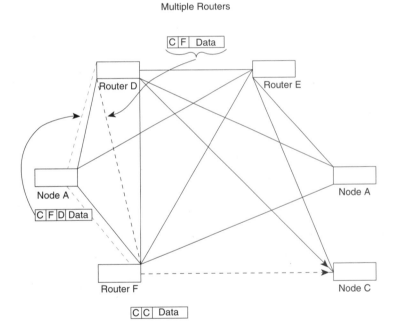

FIGURE 24.13 With multiple routers, all possible paths between node A and node F have been mapped out and the routers send the packet along one of the designated routes.

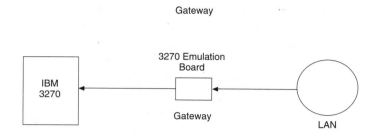

Gateway

FIGURE 24.14 In this configuration, the gateway has a 3270 emulation board and software to provide a central connection to an IBM mainframe. This is much more efficient than equipping individual workstations with 3270 emulation.

Gateways offer the greatest degree of flexibility in network interconnectivity, but for the developers who must create the conversion software, they are complex (see Figure 24.15).

9.15

FIGURE 24.15 Another gateway approach is to provide a small emulation software program on each workstation. The workstations are then connected to an MAU, which provides access to a gateway. With this configuration, individual emulation boards are not required for each workstation.

The Backbone

Another method used to interconnect different networks involves a *backbone network*, a central network attached to other networks. Users are not directly connected to the backbone network, but instead have their own LAN. The network on which the users are connected is called the *access network* (see Figure 24.16).

Using a backbone to connect several smaller access networks has its advantages over using one large network: Each LAN can continue to operate should one of the other access networks fail. Individual LANs are easier to administer than one large LAN. Because the backbone can do the filtering, only traffic that is meant for other networks needs to pass over the backbone.

A backbone network requires a large bandwidth and should be able to transmit over long distances. Because fiber optics are usually used for these networks, the backbone is often designed as an FDDI network. FDDI networks have a transfer speed of 100 Mbits/sec and are very reliable and secure.

Access networks may require a bridge, router, or gateway to attach to the backbone, depending on the architectures of the various access LANs and the backbone itself.

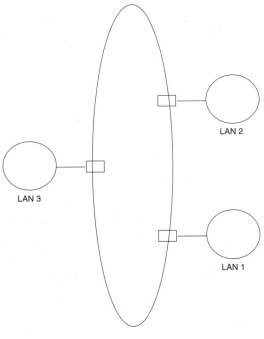

FIGURE 24.16 Access networks 1, 2, and 3 can communicate with each other via a common backbone.

One final note: An interconnected network may use any or all of the components mentioned. Networks may be connected using repeaters, bridges, routers, gateways, and backbones to form one large network, and as with other aspects of networking, interconnectivity can be very complex, requiring experience and study to be used properly.

SECTION VI

IMPLEMENTING THE LAN

CHAPTER 25

THE STUDY PHASE

Organizations are increasingly recognizing that information is a key resource. Today's corporations are relying more and more on computer-based information systems to manage this burgeoning data resource. However, these systems can involve a wide range of hardware and software. They can be as small as a single personal computer or as large as multiple mainframe computers.

The fastest-growing computer-based information system being implemented to meet today's business needs is the LAN. To be effective, a LAN should be implemented according to a planned, systematic series of steps and procedures. These steps and procedures are divided into four phases (see Figure 25.1) that together form the life cycle of a computer-based information system:

- Study
- Selection and design
- Implementation
- Operation

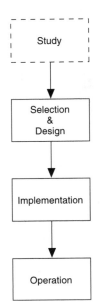

FIGURE 25.1 Steps in developing a LAN.

This chapter discusses the study phase of the system development cycle; the next three chapters will discuss the remaining phases.

The purpose of the study phase is to ascertain the need and/or justification for implementing a LAN as an organization's computer-based information system. The study phase consists of two subphases: investigation and analysis and a feasibility study.

Investigation and Analysis

The investigation and analysis portion of the study phase consists of information gathering followed by preparation of a documented report. The necessary facts and information are obtained by:

1. Collecting background information
2. Defining the problem
3. Assessing information on user requirements

4. Identifying resources and constraints

5. Preparing a report on the information collected

Step 1: Collecting Background Information

Information about the organization must be gathered before any analysis can be performed. This information should include the organization's history, current status and projected growth, operating policies, management styles, office environment, unique components, and office systems and procedures, as well as the attitudes and viewpoints of the people who will be affected by the LAN. This last element—assessing the views of the users—is very important and should not be overlooked or taken lightly; the cooperation or noncooperation of the people involved can make or break a system.

An understanding of the company's politics is also very useful in helping the analyst anticipate problems and needs when implementing a LAN. For example, a key executive in the company may have come from an organization that used a minicomputer exclusively. This person may be opposed to the installation of personal computers throughout the company. At the same time, other employees may like using personal computers; to these people, the idea of being connected to a LAN may mean a loss of independence. In this situation, cooperation for the LAN installation may not be forthcoming.

Step 2: Defining the Problem

As discussed later in this chapter, a study to examine the feasibility of installing a LAN should not be initiated on a whim. The problems in the organization's information processes are most likely of sufficient magnitude to warrant systems analysis. Using the background information that has been collected may make it easier to identify and define these problems, which aren't always apparent.

Step 3: Assessing User Requirements

A computer-based information system that doesn't supply prompt and accurate information is of little use. What's more, the information it produces may not be valuable to the people who need it.

Painstaking care must be taken to ensure that the information requirements of the organization and its workers are met. This requires detailed analysis.

For example, the volume of information processed by the computer-based information system must also be known. What departments need what type of application programs? What departments need what reports and in what formats? The tasks that will be executed on the LAN and those that will be handled locally on a personal computer must also be assessed. Finally, the expansion of the organization must be considered. What information needs will exist in three months, six months, one year, two years, five years? Such needs must be projected and documented.

To be a viable solution, a LAN must meet the overall long-term requirements of the people and the organization. If it doesn't meet those requirements, even the most sophisticated LAN is useless.

Step 4: Identifying Resources and Constraints

During the investigation and analysis phase, the organization's resources must be identified and documented, and the organizational constraints and limitations must also be documented. Organizational resources that will have an impact on implementing a new computer system fall into two categories: computer hardware and software resources and human resources.

The first items to examine are the computer hardware and software the organization already has. Does each person have his or her own personal computer? Does the organization have a minicomputer or a mainframe computer? Are the users connected? If so, are they connected by PC terminal emulation or by dumb terminals? The organization's software applications must also be inventoried. Full knowledge of what the organization does and doesn't have is very important in assessing its needs accurately. It will also help estimate costs.

The people who will be affected by implementation of a LAN must also be identified. Their level of skill and their attitudes toward computers and computer applications should be identified; this will help determine the amount of training required, the people who will support the LAN, and whether additional programmers will be needed. It will also help ensure a smooth implementation.

Organizational constraints and limitations can take many forms, including financial resources (which are too often the primary constraint). During the investigation phase, a budget for the LAN must be established. Another major constraint is the lack of personnel available to maintain and manage the LAN.

When other constraints are encountered, such as conditions that are unsuitable for running cable, they must also be documented.

Step 5: Writing the Report

After the initial investigations are completed, a quantity of information and facts will have been compiled. This information must now be organized and thoroughly documented. This documentation can then be used in the next phase: the feasibility study.

Feasibility Study

The information collected during investigation and analysis can now be applied to ascertain the practicality and feasibility of installing a LAN. Will the LAN fulfill the requirements identified by the investigation and analysis? The feasibility study should answer that question.

Costs and Benefits

The feasibility study must estimate the actual costs of implementing a LAN. It should also show, in dollars, the benefits to be gained from the LAN to justify the costs. It might be useful to use timetables, including amortization schedules, showing how costs are to be recouped.

Study-Phase Report

The feasibility report is drafted next. Using the information gathered during the investigative process, this report should define the details uncovered during that investigation and the results of the feasibility study. All this information is used to assess the capabilities needed for and possibilities offered by a LAN. If any information specific to a LAN has not been gathered during this feasibility study, the analyst must now obtain it.

Finally, the report should offer a recommendation. Of course, a host of unanticipated factors and issues may need to be addressed during the study phase to determine the feasibility of installing a LAN. More investigation and analysis may be needed than originally anticipated. Not only must the needs and problems of the organization be identified, but the analyst must know how LANs operate and if one can be of benefit.

More than one analyst may be involved in the study phase. One analyst may determine or identify all the problems, existing procedures, constraints, limitations, and resources; a second analyst conversant with LAN technology and applications would then write the recommendation using the information obtained by the first analyst.

To write a recommendation, you must know what a LAN can and cannot do. This is very important to the success of a LAN feasibility study or any subsequent phase of LAN development. Without sufficient knowledge and experience, you simply cannot make authoritative recommendations and help others guide the LAN through its life cycle.

Be careful when selecting someone to perform the feasibility study. If a vendor performs this study, the information may become slanted in favor of a LAN.

The study-phase report is usually presented at a meeting so that those connected with the LAN project can review the report and discuss its findings. Three actions may result from this meeting:

- The project is postponed or rejected. If this is the case, all investigation and analysis stops.

- It is decided that more information is needed before a final decision can be made. This results in additional investigation and analysis.

- The review committee endorses the recommendation, in which case we proceed to the next phase of the network life cycle.

To Install or Not to Install?

In most cases, specific reasons prompt an organization to investigate the feasibility of installing a LAN. It is unusual for a LAN to be implemented without a significant reason (though it has happened; someone may decide the company needs a LAN, just to be in vogue). Pay attention to the underlying reasons that prompted the initial investigation and analysis.

The entire information-processing structure should be brought down to a very basic level. First, identify existing problems and needs that are not being met and future needs that will need to be addressed as the company grows. Second, consider whether or not a LAN would fulfill current needs and be able to grow to accommodate future needs.

Using this basic premise, you can easily identify some reasons to initiate a feasibility study: improved efficiency, control, productivity, and services and cost savings.

By understanding why the system study was initiated, you'll be better able to define the need for the investigation and analysis. Knowing this need makes it easier to focus on items that might otherwise be overlooked and whose absence would affect the feasibility study. Should the study overlook some items, additional problems may arise as the system is developed. Oversights could also cause the project to be canceled needlessly.

Improved Efficiency

A desire to create a more efficient operation is one reason to perform a system study. The analyst must look at almost every aspect of the organization to improve its efficiency, and in doing so must perform substantial investigation and analysis. All systems currently in place, all procedures being used, and all plans for expansion must be examined.

One catalyst that creates inefficiency and substantiates the need for a LAN is growth of an organization. What started out as a small endeavor can in a short time grow into a sizable enterprise. Implementing a LAN may be one way to use outmoded equipment. The organization probably has some microcomputers and peripherals that could be incorporated into a network.

When a department in a larger organization expanded, moving to a centralized mainframe or minicomputer once appeared to be the only solution. Unfortunately, a centralized mainframe couldn't always give users timely precise information. Today, LANs are considered a viable option.

Improved Control

Increasingly, individual departments are taking control of the information processing for their groups. Managers often prefer this to having everything stored on a centralized computer-based information system; localizing information-processing capabilities provides managers with more security and control over their departments.

Sophisticated personal computers with more processing power have taken the place of departmental minicomputers as an alternative to a centralized system. This is especially true when the data is provided via a LAN.

Improved Productivity

Increased staff productivity is something most managers aspire to. One tool that has proven its ability to improve efficiency is the computer. Even in today's business environment, however, a centralized computer cannot always provide data in the desired form when it is needed.

Again, whether the work group is large or small, managers are turning to departmental processing. Installing a LAN is one way to increase departmental productivity.

Cost Savings

A LAN may be warranted on the basis of cost savings alone. Implementing a LAN is usually less expensive than installing a minicomputer or small mainframe.

Microcomputers have greatly reduced the cost of information processing. No longer do small companies have to rely on expensive MIS hardware or outside data-processing companies; they can now do the same data processing in-house using microcomputers. Under the correct conditions, a company can use its existing microcomputers to form a LAN that increases data-processing power. Thus, the existing equipment can be recycled into a LAN.

Improved Service

Many companies, and even departments within large organizations, rely on a customer database for their existence. In service businesses, for example, a company must increase the type and quality of service in order to be competitive. Computerized data processing is often the key.

LANs can provide the information processing a company needs to improve its service to customers. In a busy doctor's office, for example, patient information may be accessed from various terminals by several nurses, thus decreasing the time a patient must wait.

LANs are not the only solution to information-processing problems, of course, but they do offer a timely and appropriate solution in many, if not most, cases. Whether a LAN is the appropriate solution for your environment depends on what you uncover during the study phase of the system life cycle.

CHAPTER 26

THE SELECTION AND DESIGN PHASE

If you're beginning the LAN design phase, the recommendations put forward in the feasibility study were approved (see Figure 26.1) and the LAN's benefits are expected to justify the costs.

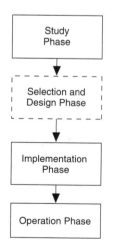

FIGURE 26.1 The second step in the LAN installation cycle
is the selection and design phase.

The design phase begins the process of creating a detailed blueprint of the system. Information collected during the study phase can be used in this phase, but greater detail will be required. First and foremost, the system must be designed so that it falls within budgetary constraints. The system must also satisfy those requirements identified in the study phase.

The following are some of the important issues that must be addressed during the design phase (see Figure 26.2):

- Determine the degree of system security required.
- Determine the proper system management.
- Consult the users.
- Design procedures.
- Develop a chart showing information flow.
- Select the best topology.
- Select the appropriate transmission media.
- Evaluate the available software.
- Evaluate the available hardware.
- Create the most appropriate LAN.
- Prepare a design phase report.

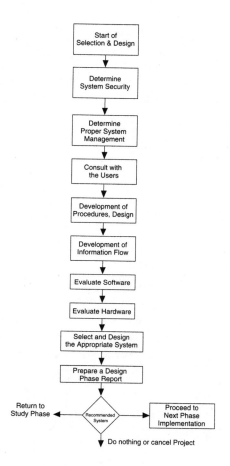

FIGURE 26.2 Issues to be addressed during the design phase.

Determining System Security

Developers of computer-based information systems that consist solely of PCs often don't take security seriously. The common belief that PCs aren't serious data-processing equipment can lead to the opinion that security is not important, yet data on a PC may be just as confidential as data found on a mainframe computer. Once PCs are interconnected, the issue of security looms even larger.

The choice of system components and system design should reflect the degree of security required. After all, an organization's fate, to some extent, may be determined by information security. The system must be monitored carefully to avoid making data available to those who shouldn't have access to it.

A LAN's security needs are similar to those of a minicomputer or a mainframe. The LAN may store data that is confidential, and therefore requires protection. As in mainframes and minicomputers, the degree of accessibility given to each LAN user must be determined.

A security issue unique to LANs is the accessibility of the LAN hardware itself. Is the file server secure? Could someone tamper with or remove it? Could someone tap into the cabling? Providing access to hardware compromises security.

The question of security also involves the safety of data and applications. Is the LAN vulnerable to a virus or other program that might harm the data and applications stored on it? If data is accidentally erased, can it be re-created? Is a disaster recovery plan in place? The file server's storage may be backed up on tape or some other medium, but a backup is useless if the building burns down. A copy of the data should be kept off-site in a secure place.

A study should be undertaken to define the level of security required for the network. Once defined, this information must be incorporated into the design of the system.

Determining Proper System Management

System management falls into two categories: policies and procedures and maintenance.

Policies and Procedures

We have discussed several LAN managerial policies and procedures as they relate to security, such as making sure servers and other hardware are inaccessible, preventing viruses, creating file backups, and having a plan for disaster recovery. Other procedures must be established to ensure smooth, efficient operation. The following list contains procedural strategies you might consider, though this is by no means a complete list.

- **Password schemes.** User password schemes are an important aspect of security. A procedure needs to be developed whereby unique user passwords are created and stored in a secure place. Procedures should also be developed to change passwords at regular intervals and to remove passwords for users who no longer have authorized access to the LAN.

- **Data archiving.** Data backups are a crucial part of LAN maintenance. A procedure needs to be established defining when backups are performed (usually at night, when users have logged off the system), how often they are performed, and how backup tapes or disks should be rotated and stored.

- **User training.** A procedure for training new users should be established. Such training can be performed by the network administrators, department managers, or designated staff members. User training manuals explaining how the LAN environment functions could prevent frantic phone calls from users.

- **Policies for application programming.** A procedure is needed to create batch files and establish support for new users. In addition, access rights for LAN databases must be considered. This is particularly important when LAN-based data, such as payroll records, should be kept confidential.

- **Policies for assigning rights to applications.** These could include assigning read-and-write access to some managers while giving read- or write-only access to other users. Depending on the network environment, other applications-oriented policies may also need to be considered.

- **Connections to other systems.** Interconnecting departmental work groups or connecting one LAN to another, to wide-area networks, or to mainframes requires its own unique policies and procedures.

- **Network logs and journals.** All the information about the LAN installation should be recorded, even if there is only one LAN administrator; that individual cannot possibly remember every configuration option.

  A master notebook or file of network information can be invaluable when it comes to maintenance. This log should detail the LAN hardware and software configuration and the types of equipment and connections used. Records should also be kept of various part numbers and warranties in case equipment or software needs to be replaced or upgraded.

- **Assigning new users.** Procedures must be developed for adding users to the system. These include giving users access to files and applications, assigning an electronic mailbox, and training.

- **Deleting old users.** When users are removed from the system, a procedure should be used to delete their passwords, remove their mailboxes, and archive their files.

- **Installing software.** When new software is added to the network, it must be installed on a hard disk to be accessible to the users who need it most. Does the hard disk have the capacity to handle another application and its associated data? Are the appropriate devices available to support the application, such as a laser printer for a new word processing package? In addition, users must be notified of the new software and trained in using it.

- **Planning for network growth.** In designing the network, identify areas of growth and configure the LAN accordingly. For example, if the organization's sales staff is expected to double within the next year and each new employee will require a workstation, procedures should be established to accommodate that growth on an ongoing basis. After all, you can't string new cable and install new users overnight.

- **Network printing.** When setting up the network, place printers strategically to accommodate those users who need printing services the most. Departments that generate large amounts of correspondence should share a laser printer. Users who need only occasional access to a printer may not need one of their own, but would share with someone else.

- **Network monitoring.** A procedure for monitoring network performance on an ongoing basis can spot trouble before it starts. Performance can be monitored using sophisticated network management hardware (such as a protocol analyzer), using LAN management software, or by running periodic performance tests at various points on the network.

Maintenance

Policies and procedures must be established for overall maintenance and day-to-day management of the LAN. (Maintenance is also discussed in Chapter 24.) These functions can be grouped into two categories: hardware maintenance and software maintenance.

System Hardware Maintenance.

Once the hardware is installed, procedures are needed to make sure it continues to run properly. The hardware should be tested periodically to make certain it is running at or near specification. Diagnostic software is available that provides a benchmark for performance.

If the hardware fails, it will need to be repaired or replaced. Again, diagnostic software and troubleshooting devices can be used to isolate the problem and determine which component failed.

Upgrades should also be considered part of the hardware maintenance process. For example, if the network data has grown to fill the server's disk capacity, a larger disk is needed. Or, if so much data is stored on the network that it cannot be backed up quickly, it might be time to upgrade to a faster backup system.

It's important to keep a written record of all hardware repairs and upgrades (including serial numbers and diagrams of hardware configurations), regardless of the kind of hardware maintenance required.

System Software Maintenance.

Once the application software has been installed, it will require little, if any, maintenance. However, the software may need to be upgraded as new versions become available. This means keeping a record of all the software packages installed on the network, including application version numbers and serial numbers. Upgrades for certain application packages are provided free, or at a discount, to qualified users, so it's important to keep receipts to verify purchase dates and other information.

Part of software maintenance is providing applications to the users who need them. This may entail configuring the system, writing batch files, and modifying access programs to accommodate a variety of needs. It may also mean changing the configuration to accommodate new users. Be careful when modifying software configurations; modifying a program to suit the needs of one user or department may affect the other 50 users on the network.

One aspect of software maintenance that is often overlooked is keeping archived copies of the software and the data those applications support. If the server fails or crashes, you'll need to start over from scratch. This will be much easier if all the application software is at hand, including copies of the batch and configuration files.

Again, be sure to keep a written record of all aspects of the software configuration, including directory and file structures and volumes.

Consult the Users

At this point in the design phase, user requirements need to be categorized and prioritized. In the past, networks were traditionally developed without consulting the users. Without such consultation, however, the LAN may be technically excellent but fail to meet the needs of the users. If users' needs aren't met, it doesn't matter how much money and technology went into developing the LAN; it is a failure. Never leave the users out of the system life cycle, and be sure to document information as you accumulate it.

User contact makes it easier to select the right components and create a design that can grow with the needs of the organization. Remember, too, that users may be somewhat suspicious of a LAN. Staying in contact with them can allay their fears and apprehensions, and when they realize that what they say and feel about the system is taken seriously, their attitudes may change. As users become more knowledgeable about a LAN, they will offer more solid information about what they need now and what they might need in the future.

Users' future needs are very important. The network must be designed to go beyond current user and organization requirements; doing so will prevent costly problems down the road.

Consult the users and listen to them. Try to relieve their apprehensions. Often, apprehension surfaces as a negative attitude. Try to instill a genuine feeling that the LAN won't make their jobs obsolete, just easier.

Designing Procedures

When any new system is introduced, the methods the organization has been using may need to be modified or eliminated. Be prepared to modify the procedures used to perform tasks affected by the network. New procedures often need to be developed to allow smooth operation of the network. When you are creating a LAN, it's important to design new methods of operation for the organization and to be able to justify those new methods.

Developing Information Flow

During the study phase, information was collected on the organization on a broad scale. Part of this information involved the organization's background. However, when a LAN is designed, organizational functions and procedures may change. The flow of information will probably also change.

For example, if the warehouse foreman isn't receiving daily reports, it will be harder for him or her to perform his or her tasks. This will be identified as a problem during the study phase. The LAN remedies that particular situation, so the flow of information is now changed.

When the network is designed, the overall flow of information may need to be changed drastically. The network design should accommodate a change in the information flow when it remedies a problem situation. The idea is not to change what is already in place just for the sake of changing it.

Selecting the Best Topology

Selecting a network topology is extremely important and must not be overlooked in the design process. In many cases, selection of the media access method (such as Ethernet or Token Ring) determines the topology, though that isn't always the case.

Linear bus networks—primarily Ethernet, and occasionally ARCnet—work well in laboratory and school environments, where machines are placed side by side. Distributed star topologies—such as those used by the ARCnet and 10BASE-T standards—are an excellent choice because they lend themselves well to troubleshooting and expansion. If a Token Ring network is chosen, the topology can only be a distributed star (this network externally resembles a distributed star, though internally it's a ring).

Selecting the Appropriate Transmission Media

There is a little more flexibility in the choice of transmission medium. Coaxial cable (for Ethernet and ARCnet) has an incredibly large installed base and is still widely used. Twisted-pair wiring is a much more versatile and inexpensive medium and is capable of high transmission rates. For Ethernet and ARCnet networks, twisted-pair is an excellent choice; for Token Ring networks, it's the only choice.

In many cases, the best choice is shielded or unshielded wiring. Shielded wiring accommodates longer cabling distances and makes higher transmission rates easier, although it is more costly.

Fiber-optic cable is another option available for most networks. Users of this expensive medium usually require a higher level of security or need to cover long distances with a high bandwidth. Many networks consist of fiber-optic cable for vertical and long-distance runs and twisted-pair for cable runs from distribution closets to the desktop. In Ethernet networks, thick coaxial may be used for vertical or long-distance runs.

Evaluating Available Software

The LAN developer is responsible for evaluating the various software packages available and selecting those that most closely meet users' requirements, which were determined in the study phase.

Many other considerations must also be kept in mind when evaluating software. Is the software considered easy to use? If security is important, the software must meet the security requirements set forth by the organization (although the LAN design may compensate for a lack of security in the software). What about hardware requirements? Is the LAN hardware powerful enough and appropriate for the software being considered?

Software maintenance and documentation are also crucial. If bugs are found in the software, will the vendor correct them? Is the software too expensive? Are updates too expensive? Does the documentation provide clear, succinct information so it will be easy to learn the software? Is training required to learn the software? If so, how much does it cost? Is the software compatible with the network to be installed?

Evaluating Available Hardware

The hardware making up the LAN must also be evaluated. After all, the hardware has to support the recommended software.

Consider the maintenance contracts for the hardware. Will the supplier or installer supply ongoing hardware support? Does the vendor guarantee the hardware for a period of time? Should a hardware maintenance contract be signed?

The hardware selected should also comply with industry standards. If a piece of hardware is used that is not well-known or accepted in the computer industry, the organization could be in trouble if problems develop.

The documentation should be adequate. If training is needed to operate the hardware, is it readily available from either the vendor or the supplier?

Finally, the price of the hardware shouldn't be overlooked. Organizations are frequently overcharged for hardware. On the other hand, scrimping on the hardware when installing or upgrading a LAN isn't necessarily advisable. Be sure to invest in a hardware platform that is flexible enough to meet the organization's current and future needs.

Creating the Most Appropriate LAN

Creating the most appropriate LAN for the environment requires all the information gathered in the study phase and presented in the feasibility report. Information on the evaluation of hardware and software will also assist in the design process.

The problems identified during the study phase should be restated so that a system can be designed that addresses and corrects each of the problems listed. In addition, the system must meet the requirements resulting from the hardware and software evaluations. It's also important to be able to change the design and consider alternative products or methods.

Preparing a Design Phase Report

Once the system has been designed, a design phase report can be prepared. This report should be reviewed by the committee involved with this project. If the design is acceptable, the next phase—implementation—begins. If the design isn't suitable, another one must be created that addresses the objections raised by the committee.

CHAPTER 27

THE IMPLEMENTATION PHASE

Once the design of the LAN has been approved, the hardware and software can be implemented (see Figure 27.1). During the implementation phase, also known as the development phase, the LAN is actually delivered, installed, tested, and made operational.

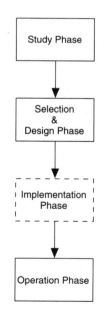

FIGURE 27.1 The implementation phase.

The Implementation phase is when the users finally see the system. The days and weeks of information gathering and analysis are now showing tangible results. The users' everyday routine will also begin to change during system implementation, so the installer—the person responsible for the actual implementation—must be aware of the users and their feelings. The wise system installer takes the time to talk with the users, explain what's happening, and help them develop a positive attitude toward the network.

This is also the stage where the LAN starts to become a reality in the minds of the users. Given the amount of activity and the visibility involved in installing the system and ensuring correct operation, it's important to gain the understanding and cooperation of the users.

You should be aware that the components identified during the design of the LAN may be modified during this phase. This is where considerations that were overlooked in the study and design phases can be corrected. Also note that any major redesign or change in a key piece of hardware or software must be approved by the review committee before being implemented.

The implementation phase, like the first two phases, can be conducted according to a defined set of actions or activities. The major steps in the implementation phase, shown in Figure 27.2, are:

- Implementation plan
- Computer program design
- Review meeting
- Equipment installation
- Computer program development
- System test
- Software test
- Manual development
- Personnel training
- Final review meeting

It's not uncommon for the implementation phase to take substantially more time than the study and design phases. A great deal of work must be accomplished in this phase before it can be considered complete, therefore, more time should be allotted for this phase than for earlier phases.

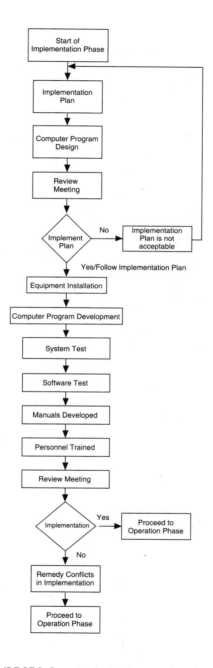

FIGURE 27.2 Steps in the implementation phase.

The timetable for LAN installation may vary. It may take a couple of weeks or it may take longer, depending on the scope of the project. The hardware may be working properly within a month, but the actual application software may take longer to install and integrate.

Implementation Plan

Once the system has been selected and the specifications detailed, the next step is to develop a plan describing how the system is to be installed. The implementation plan outlines the procedures and sequences necessary to get the system up and running.

Installing a LAN is similar to building a house. A couple selects a location and then consults with builders and developers (the study phase). Once the location has been defined, the buyers become more specific about the type of house they want to build. The number of bedrooms is determined, the types of windows is selected, and many more details are worked out. The builder then designs a house and produces blueprints for the couple's approval (the design phase).

After the design of the house has been approved, the builder doesn't go out and start digging foundations, erecting walls, and pouring concrete; the contractor must have a plan for these tasks. By defining and following a series of assigned tasks in a specified sequence, the contractor can build a livable house for a predictable cost.

The same process can be applied to implementing a LAN. A plan must be established and followed if the system is to be developed successfully. Depending on the size of the project, the implementation plan may be quite complex or relatively simple, but at a minimum it must take into consideration all the major steps listed above and have some flexibility.

The developers of the implementation plan should be competent and experienced not only in system development, but also in LAN technology. If a specific vendor is supplying the hardware and packaged software, that vendor may also be contracted to do the installation. Make sure the vendor is competent and experienced. Using a consultant to oversee the installation may be advisable, but one vendor may still provide the hardware and packaged software.

Computer Program Design

The two kinds of computer programs to be considered in this phase are those that need to be customized or developed and commercial programs that were selected during system design.

Customized software may need to be developed. This process can either be handled by an internal network developer or assigned to an independent software development company. A number of programmers and programmer/analysts in the marketplace are qualified to design and implement custom applications. Before hiring one, you should find out whether the person responsible for designing the applications is competent and familiar with the coding implications of a multiuser rather than single-user environment.

Review Meeting

Recall that review meetings were held at the end of the study and design phases. An intermediate review meeting should also be part of the implementation phase. This meeting should include the users, as well as those in the organization who are involved with the LAN project. The purpose of this meeting is to determine whether or not the implementation plan is acceptable.

Two actions may result from the review meeting. First, if the implementation plan isn't found to be acceptable, it must be modified or redesigned. If the plan needs to be changed, it will be reviewed at a second meeting after the modifications have been drafted. Second, if the implementation plan is approved, system installation continues according to the plan.

Equipment Installation

Equipment may be installed by either the equipment vendor or a third party. A number of companies exist solely to install computer systems according to an implementation plan. In either case, the installation should be supervised. That task often falls to the person who developed the implementation plan.

Once the equipment is installed, it must be checked and rechecked. Many systems fail soon after they are installed because the equipment wasn't truly functional.

Computer Program Development

In environments that require customized applications, programming can begin while the equipment is being installed. In fact, because a functioning LAN is not a prerequisite for this step, programming can begin after the review committee gives its approval.

One person should be designated to monitor application program development. This person must be familiar with application design and implementation and with programming methodology and techniques.

System Test

Just as each component must be tested when it's installed, the entire system should be tested to make sure it's functional and that the pieces work together as a whole. These tests are run and rerun using different hardware and software matrices to uncover and correct any bugs in the system.

Software Test

Once the system hardware is up and running, the application programs can be loaded onto the LAN. These applications must undergo close scrutiny to ensure their design integrity. It's better to take some time in the beginning to make sure the programs are correct (if they're customized) or correctly installed (if they're off-the-shelf applications) than to take more time correcting them later. If the applications do have to be changed later, the data will also need to be changed. Using extra care in installing and testing the software will help maintain data integrity. The best-designed LAN is useless if the data is corrupt.

Manual Development

Manuals should be developed to document every facet of the system. The administrator's manual should include the cable layout, specifying such details as the type of cable used and the location of repeaters, bridges, and gateways. The structure of the file server, including the hard disk, should also be documented in the manuals. In fact, as documentation for the system, the manuals should cover anything that has an impact on the design of the network.

With proper documentation, a third party will be able to enter the scene at a later time and understand the system. The manuals also will provide a record to jog the installer's memory when the system needs to be modified or repaired and can help when a new system administrator is hired.

Personnel Training

The LAN may be sophisticated enough to require training. Such training should be accounted for in the implementation plan and may involve the network administrator and users.

One or more individuals must take responsibility for the LAN. The network cannot run itself day in and day out after its initial setup; various duties and monitoring are necessary to ensure smooth operation. Those responsible for operation of the LAN must be trained on the hardware used throughout the network.

It's also good practice to train LAN users. Users should know the basic principles behind LANs to help ease fear of the network. They should also be trained in certain operations of the network operating system so they can do their jobs effectively without continually asking questions of the network administrator.

Final Review Meeting

After the training plans are established, a final review meeting should be held. This meeting typically goes in one of two directions. If everything has gone according to plan, the implementation is satisfactory and the operation phase should begin soon. If the implementation isn't satisfactory, the areas of contention need to be defined and discussed.

Should the implementation be at fault, the developer is responsible for making any corrections. Other difficulties may also arise; for example, once the implementation is complete, the organization may want items included in the system that weren't part of the initial study. The implementer needs to address these items, while the developer should note that those items weren't part of the original design and determine whether the changes can be accommodated. Some modifications may require that the system outlive its usefulness before they can be made. If at all possible, however, they should be made before the system changes over to ongoing operation.

The review meeting usually allows the project to go on to the last phase: operation. New ideas or system enhancements are often requested once the LAN is fully functional and users begin to see its power.

CHAPTER 28

THE OPERATION PHASE

We enter the last phase of the computer system life cycle—the operation phase—only after successfully developing and implementing the LAN. This phase involves:

- Changeover
- Routine operation
- System performance evaluation
- System change

The operation phase is considered the longest part of the LAN's life cycle, because when the system is in operation, at least one of the categories listed above is in effect.

Changeover

During the changeover to a new system, it is critical that the developer remain involved throughout the transition period. This is the most critical phase in the life cycle of the computer-based information system; it is usually a one-way process, and it must result in a system that is operationally acceptable.

Regardless of how well the changeover is planned, unforeseen incidents and problems may develop. This can be an anxiety-ridden time for all involved, and workers may encounter a great deal of inconvenience during the changeover.

Three of the most common approaches to system changeover are:

- cold conversion
- parallel conversion
- phased conversion

Cold Conversion

With cold conversion, the old system simply stops and the new one begins. Because this method has the most severe impact on users, it is best to apply it when the workload is light or halted (such as on a weekend or holiday).

Cold conversion is the simplest and least expensive changeover method; it is also the riskiest. The biggest risk is that the new system may not operate as expected. Therefore, this technique isn't suitable for organizations that rely heavily on mission-critical applications.

If this changeover method is selected, a contingency plan should be in place in the event the new system doesn't function properly or fails altogether.

Parallel Conversion

The parallel-conversion approach allows some overlap between the old system and the new one. The new system is placed into operation while the old one is still functioning, so both systems are in operation for a specified amount of time.

During this period, the systems can be compared, to isolating errors that may occur with the new system. If errors should occur, the organization has the comfort of knowing that the old system is still functioning. Another advantage of this approach is that the new system can be fine-tuned and made as bug-free as possible.

Parallel conversion is almost risk-free; the only major drawback is that significant resources are needed to keep two systems operating simultaneously.

Phased Conversion

With the phased-conversion method, conversion is done in steps. The old system is converted to the new system in a series of preplanned phases with specific time frames. When one phase is completed successfully, the next phase begins.

One advantage is that if you encounter many problems or errors in one phase, you can adjust the timetable for implementing the subsequent phases. Another advantage is that correcting errors in an earlier phase can help smooth the transition to subsequent phases. Phased conversion is also less expensive than parallel conversion.

Routine Operation

When the changeover is complete, the LAN is considered operational. Unfortunately, once an organization has spent considerable time and money to install a LAN, it may devote little consideration or resources to ongoing maintenance. Without proper care, the system may develop problems that negate the benefits and savings of a LAN.

A computer-based information system should have maintenance routines in the areas of hardware, software, and programming to run at optimal efficiency.

Hardware Maintenance

Clear precise measures and procedures should be in place to keep the hardware in good operating condition. The action to be taken when certain problems arise should be outlined.

For example, not all hardware repairs require the attention of a trained technician. If a printer malfunctions, simply checking for a paper jam or seeing if it ran out of paper may be sufficient. If the device continues to malfunction after routine inspections and checks, a trained technician should be called.

This brings up another issue regarding hardware maintenance: Each piece of hardware on the LAN should have a designated service agent. Finding names and numbers of vendors or dealers who support the hardware shouldn't be difficult.

Preventive maintenance should also be incorporated. This involves dusting and cleaning equipment, running the proper diagnostics, and checking the cables to make sure a good connection is maintained.

Software Maintenance

Because software and data are stored on secondary media, these devices must be maintained. Loss of programs or data can cause major problems for the organization.

Backup procedures fall under the category of software maintenance, as does the maintenance of floppy disks. Be sure to install and maintain the software using the procedures outlined by the distributor.

Software maintenance is as important as hardware maintenance. A personal computer can be replaced, but can you replace six months' worth of data?

Programming Maintenance

For those systems that require customized applications, the software that was designed and created for the LAN must be maintained. Programming maintenance requires the same measures followed for software maintenance. In addition, custom-designed software will probably have to be modified periodically to keep abreast of the changes in the organization; such modifications should be monitored very closely.

System Performance Evaluation

After the new computer-based information system has been functioning for a reasonable period of time, it should be evaluated. The results of this evaluation are presented in the form of an evaluation report that allows the organization to see if its LAN is providing the expected results. This is when the system's strengths and weaknesses are brought to the attention of organization executives. This is also when any problems can be corrected.

The following items should be addressed when the system is evaluated:

- Cost analysis
- Ease of information retrieval

- Data integrity
- Personnel in contact with the system
- Amount of data processed
- Security
- Maintenance

System Change

All organizations are dynamic. This fact must be realized when any computer-based information system is implemented. As an organization evolves, changes in the network may become necessary. Requests for change should be drafted for review. Such requests may trigger responses ranging from brief analysis to extensive investigation. An investigation may require a return to an earlier point in the life cycle and perhaps a complete redesign; it could even mean a return to the study phase. A simple request for a modification may yield a greatly modified system.

Just as an organization is dynamic and ever-changing, so is a computer-based information system or a LAN. Many systems analysts say that a system is always 90 percent complete but never completed. Systems are constantly being updated and modified, and system administrators must have procedures in place to allow for such changes.

SECTION VII

CASE STUDIES

CHAPTER 29

ETHERNET AND ETHERNET WITH REPEATERS

The following case studies serve as guidelines demonstrating basic LAN concepts. While they don't attempt to cover every situation, they should provide some insight.

Case Study One

Delaware Ice & Coal is a small refrigeration and heating company. The office automation consists of four PCs, a laser printer, and two dot-matrix printers. All the printers operate as local printers. Two users have a dot-matrix printer attached to their PC, and one user has the laser printer attached to his PC. One PC doesn't have a printer attached, so that user must copy everything to disk and use another PC to print (see Figure 29.1).

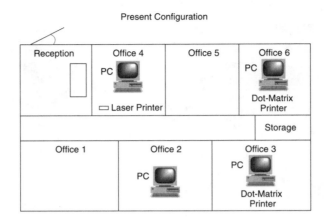

FIGURE 29.1 The layout at Delaware Ice & Coal.

The business has advanced to the point where it needs more data processing power, but the owners don't know how to do it. In fact, the owners don't know what to do. A meeting was called and they decided to contract the services of a data processing consultant.

The consultant did a study of the business and gathered the following facts to help identify the problems causing the loss of revenue to the company.

- The firm has difficulty meeting delivery dates.

- Messages are not being forwarded.

- There is no sharing of resources (such as printers or files).

- Communication among personnel is poor. Because information is not communicated, leads are not being followed up and existing accounts are suffering due to a lack of customer service.

- The customer order system is inefficient.

The consultant gave the following basic recommendations for Delaware Ice & Coal.

- Install a LAN.

- Develop a more efficient order-entry system to execute on the LAN.
- Use E-mail on the LAN.
- Add more workstations.

The consultant justified these recommendations by deducing that the company would benefit from a LAN in the following ways:

- Used appropriately, E-mail enhances communications within the office. With the enhanced communication, messages can easily be forwarded. The improved communication would help the sales department with following lead, and improve customer service.
- Each person would have access to the information and benefits the LAN has to offer, including printer and file sharing.
- Development of a more comprehensive order-entry system that supports multiple users would allow more than one person to work with the orders.

The consultant designed an Ethernet LAN for the company (see Figure 29.2).

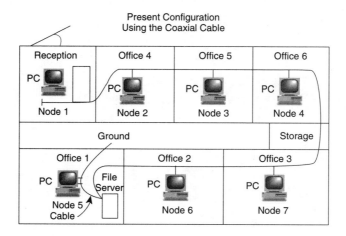

FIGURE 29.2 The proposed network configuration using coaxial cable.

The following additional equipment is required for the Delaware Ice & Coal LAN:

- A high-end PC that functions as the file server. It should have a a minimum of a 500-MB hard disk and at least 8 MB of memory.

- Additional PCs for the other system users.

- NICs for each node and one for the file server.

- The appropriate length of thin coaxial cable.

- The associated thin coaxial connectors (BNC T-connectors and 50-ohm terminating connectors).

- A LAN operating system.

- The existing peripherals must be used, so the laser printer should be made a network printer enabling letter-quality printing capabilities for all the network users. One dot-matrix printer should be made into a network printer that can be used for draft-quality printouts when letter quality isn't necessary. Both printers are attached to the file server. The third printer should be attached to the node that originally had the laser printer (see Figure 29.3).

- The appropriate application software, including E-mail and order-entry programs.

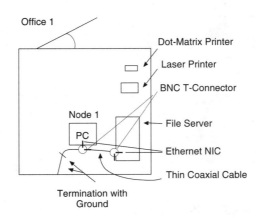

FIGURE 29.3 The proposed server configuration using existing equipment.

After reviewing the consultant's plan, the company agreed to implement a LAN. The managers didn't want to add any additional nodes initially, but they knew that more nodes could be implemented later (see Figure 29.4).

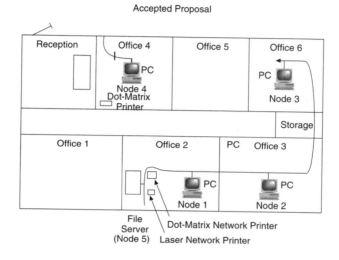

FIGURE 29.4 The accepted LAN proposal.

LAN Installation

It was determined that the network installation should use thin coaxial cable and one trunk segment. An implementation plan was developed, the highlights of which follow:

Step 1

Install the cable. Using the layout or blueprint of the building, it can be determined how the cable must be laid to attach each segment. Once the cable layout is approved, the actual cable installation can begin. This is probably the most inconvenient period for the workers.

Step 2

Install the NICs in each PC and the file server.

Step 3

Install the network operating system on the file server. The network operating system is usually received in a generic (nonconfigured) form, so it must be configured to suit the needs of this particular network.

Step 4

Place the BNC T-connectors in the coaxial cabling so that each of the nodes can attach to the cable.

Step 5

Install the shell, redirector, or requestor on each of the nodes. This software is generated from the network operating system.

Step 6

At this point, the LAN should be functional. Security and operating procedures need to be designed and implemented, and personnel need to be trained.

Step 7

Install the E-mail system on the LAN.

Step 8

Arrange for the programming of a multiuser order-entry system.

Step 9

Provide for additional training that may be needed for company personnel and provide training for the person who is going to administer the network.

Case Study Two

The conditions in Case Study One exist in this example as well, with one exception: the distance between the file server and the four nodes exceeds the limits placed on thin coaxial cabling. In this case, thick coaxial cable was recommended because one trunk segment of thicknet would be sufficient for the installation (see Figure 29.5).

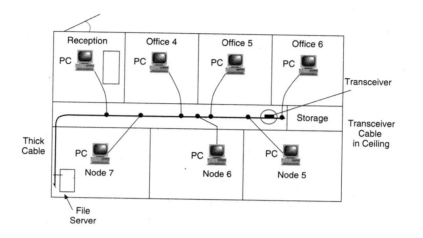

FIGURE 29.5 The same environment wired using thick coaxial cable.

Everything is similar to Case Study One, but thick cable is installed somewhat differently because it's difficult to twist and turn throughout the installation. This problem can be alleviated by using transceiver cabling (transceivers for each node attached to the thick coaxial cable), which is installed from the transceiver and laid back to the node (see Figure 29.6).

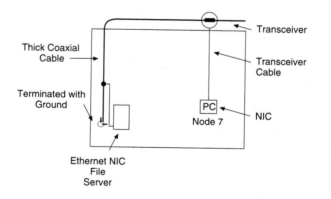

FIGURE 29.6 To connect to the thick coaxial trunk, we use transceiver cables.

Case Study Three

The setting for Case Study Three is similar to that in Case Study Two. Now, however, the distance is too great for even a thicknet cable trunk segment. It is therefore recommended that two trunk segment cables of thin coaxial and a repeater be used to form the Ethernet network. After studying the floor plan, it is determined how and where the first trunk segment is to be installed, then how and where to install the second trunk segment. The design must include two trunk segments connected by a repeater (see Figure 29.7).

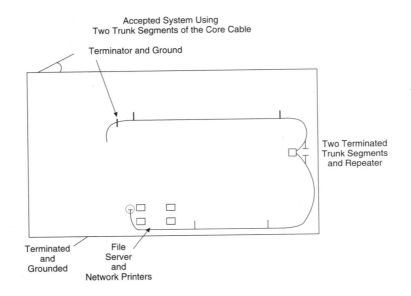

FIGURE 29.7 Another installation variation using two thinnet segments connected by a repeater.

Case Study Four

Using the setting from Case Study One, the cable must run a considerable distance to attach all the nodes. It's too far for one thick coaxial cable or two trunk segments of thin coaxial cable.

There are two options: use either three trunk segments of thin coaxial cable or two segments of thick coaxial cable. The second option is determined to be the better solution, and two segments of thick coaxial cable are installed. The design also includes a repeater to connect the cables.

Case Study Five

Using the environment described in Case Study One, nodes have to be added in a warehouse that's about 1000 feet from the office. The office area uses thin coaxial cable, but the distance to the warehouse is too great for a second segment of that cable. Adding another repeater to reach the warehouse using two Ethernet trunk segments of thin coaxial is not feasible.

The most efficient way to wire the warehouse is to mix thin and thick coaxial cable with a repeater connecting the two trunk segments (see Figure 29.8).

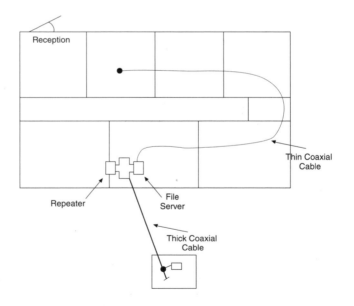

FIGURE 29.8 Two segments are used: a thinnet segment to connect the office environment and a thicknet segment to connect a single workstation in the warehouse.

Now let's expand on the warehouse network. Instead of connecting one node in the warehouse, six workstations there need to be connected. This may call for another trunk segment cable. The first thin coaxial trunk segment is installed in the office, the second links the office to the warehouse, and the third connects the nodes in the warehouse. The second trunk segment doesn't have a node attached to it, but it resembles a backbone (see Figure 29.9).

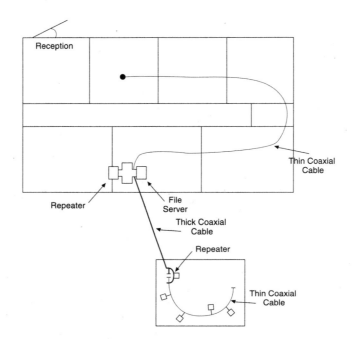

FIGURE 29.9 By adding a third segment, we can connect additional workstations in the warehouse to the network.

Case Study Six

The environment in this example is the same as in Case Study One, with one exception: the building was prewired with UTP (see Figure 29.10). This common practice makes data networks (or the more sophisticated voice systems) easier and more economical to install.

Because the building is wired with UTP and Ethernet is the chosen architecture, 10BASE-T will be used.

Figure 29.11 shows the wiring design of the building. The network will fall into this wiring scheme.

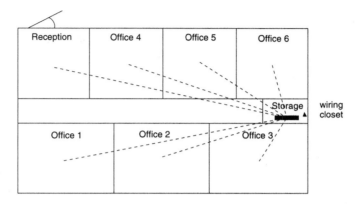

FIGURE 29.10 Each office was prewired with UTP cable.

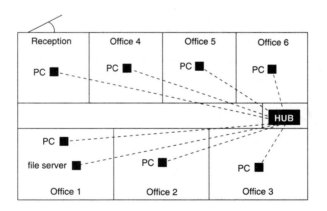

FIGURE 29.11 The network follows the existing wiring, creating a distributed star topology.

When 10BASE-T is installed, a hub (or wiring concentrator for larger networks) must be used. The hub is located in the storage closet and is the central point of the building's wiring (see Figure 29.12).

From the hub, a UTP cable goes to each workstation on the LAN.

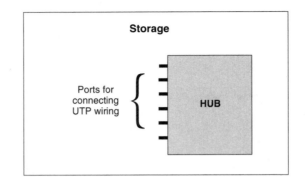

FIGURE 29.12 Placement of hub for 10BASE-T.

Case Study Seven

This environment is the same as Case Study Five, except that the warehouse is within 100 meters of the offices—specifically, in the storage closet.

Again, the office and warehouse were prewired with UTP cabling and the network is 10BASE-T. A line runs from the hub or wiring concentrator in the storage area of the office to a concentrator in the warehouse. From the concentrator, UTP cabling runs to each workstation on the network.

Other Considerations

For applications other than wiring longer distances, thick coaxial cable can be used in place of thin coaxial cable.

Another concern arises when nodes must be added to a network, since thin cable only supports up to 30 nodes. The number of nodes per trunk segment must then be monitored.

In this case, two options are available. The first is to add another trunk segment of thin coaxial cable to the network, allowing 60 nodes to be networked. The second option must be considered when planning for potential growth of the LAN. Thick coaxial cable could have been used for the installation, since one trunk segment can have 100 nodes attached to it. Using thick coaxial cable allows for greater flexibility in network expansion.

CHAPTER 30

TOKEN RING AND TOKEN RING WITH REPEATERS

Creating a Token Ring environment can be somewhat complicated. These case studies should help clarify their installation.

Case Study One

Lancaster Ltd. is a moderate-size corporation specializing in mail-order shipping. Most of the company's business comes from customers calling Lancaster Ltd. with orders. The corporation is using an IBM AS/400 minicomputer to handle its data-processing needs, but the volume of telephone calls received is growing considerably. The minicomputer is adequate to handle the company's batch-processing tasks, such as payroll and monthly reports, but the on-line ordering system—which is also on the AS/400—isn't keeping pace with business growth. Orders are being lost because workers in the telephone order department can't process the information fast enough.

The facts gathered during the study phase are fairly evident. The company is outgrowing the AS/400 that currently processes all the corporation's data, and there are already numerous databases on the minicomputer that workers need to access. After the feasibility study was conducted, it was recommended that a LAN be implemented for the telephone ordering department's data processing. If necessary, the LAN can be enlarged later (see Figure 30.1).

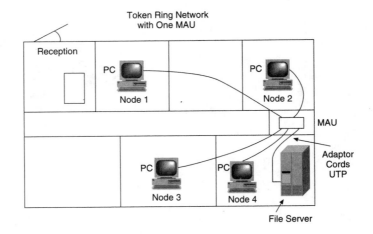

FIGURE 30.1 The Lancaster Ltd. Token Ring network with one MAU.

An IBM Token Ring network is recommended based on one major and one minor rationale. The primary reason is that interconnectivity with IBM mini-computers and mainframes is much easier, more reliable, and more efficient with a Token Ring network architecture, which will enable the company to connect the LAN and the minicomputer at a later date. The minor reason for installing a Token Ring network is that the telephone ordering system generates extensive database use, placing a constant medium-to-heavy load on the network. An Ethernet network would be less efficient in network environments with such loads because it functions optimally under sporadic periods of heavy network activity.

To install a Token Ring network at Lancaster Ltd., the following additional equipment is required:

- A high-end PC for the file server that has a minimum of a 500-MB hard disk and at least 8 MB of memory
- PC workstations for the employees in the telephone order department
- NICs for each node and one for the file server
- Two MAUs to serve as hubs—two are required because each can attach only eight nodes
- The appropriate length of UTP cable

- The associated connectors
- A LAN operating system
- The required peripherals, such as printers.—with 10 employees in the telephone order department, two network laser printers should be enough

Lancaster Ltd. agreed that implementing a Token Ring LAN would meet its needs; the next step is to install the LAN using UTP cable and one hub. An implementation plan was developed, the highlights of which are as follows.

Step 1

Draw up a blueprint of the building before installing the cable. From this blueprint, plans can be drawn to determine how the cable should be laid and how each node is to be attached. Once the cable layout is approved, the actual cable installation can begin. This will probably be the greatest source of inconvenience to workers during the LAN installation.

Step 2

Install the NICs in each PC and file server.

Step 3

Install the network operating system on the file server. The network operating system is usually received in a generic (nonconfigured) form, so it must be configured to meet the specific needs of network users. This is done during installation.

Step 4

Establish the hub using the two MAUs.

Step 5

Install the shell, redirector, or requestor on each network node. This software is generated from the network operating system.

By the point the LAN should be up and running. This is the stage when security and operating procedures should be designed and implemented. It's also the appropriate time to train personnel.

Case Study Two

Let's consider a variation of Case Study One. The difference is that the distance to connect one of the nodes to the MAU exceeds the limit. It was suggested that a repeater be used for this node; a better solution would be to boost the signal for one lobe rather than for the entire network. A lobe repeater is placed on the line where the lobe connects the node to the port of the MAU, boosting the signal for that node. Everything else remains essentially the same (see Figure 30.2).

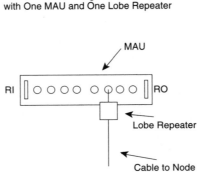

FIGURE 30.2 When a single-lobe repeater is used, a node that exceeds the maximum allowable cable length can be installed.

The network could have been implemented using shielded twisted-pair wire, which delivers greater cable lengths, but in this case the network was designed around UTP cabling.

Case Study Three

Lancaster Ltd. continues to grow, and the minicomputer can no longer provide all the services the company needs. The five employees in the accounting department are concerned with the minicomputer's response time. In addition, the accounting employees would like to have PCs so they can execute spreadsheets and other accounting programs.

Since the LAN has solved the problems of the telephone ordering department and is not being used to capacity, it is decided to attach the five accounting employees to the LAN. Doing this helps avoid an upgrade to a larger midrange system, which would be too costly, but because the accounting department occupies a separate part of the building, two separate work areas exist. This means two hubs are needed, so the accounting employees can have their own hub with one MAU. The design must be structured so that the two hubs are connected and the central ring is maintained.

To accommodate the expansion, a study of the floor plan determines how and where the second hub is to be installed. The two hubs are then established, and the nodes are attached to the lobe ports of the MAU in the appropriate hub (see Figure 30.3).

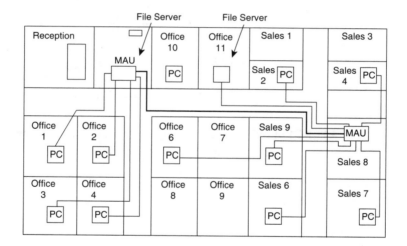

FIGURE 30.3 The Token Ring network can be expanded to support a separate hub.

The accounting department workgroup has five nodes attached to the MAU in the second hub and the original workgroup has 10 nodes plus the file server attached to the two MAUs in the first wiring center. The Ring Out of the second MAU of the first hub is connected to the Ring In of the MAU in the second hub, while the Ring Out of the MAU in the second hub is connected to the Ring In of the first MAU, maintaining the ring.

Case Study Four

This setting is similar to that of Case Study Three. This time, however, the cable must cover a considerable distance between the two hubs. This distance is sufficient to require the use of repeaters to connect the hubs.

To allow for fault tolerance in the system, it is decided that the signals of both the main path and the backup path must be boosted. After studying the floor plan, the design is configured so that the two hubs maintain a ring even though repeaters are used (see Figure 30.4).

Token Ring—Two Wiring Centers with Repeater

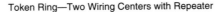
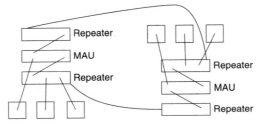

FIGURE 30.4 When a second wiring center is added at an extensive cabling distance, repeaters must be used.

CHAPTER 31

ARCNET

The following case studies will give you a better understanding of ARCnet design.

Case Study One

Dauphin Arts is a small retail art studio. The owners of the studio are not concerned with how fast or how much the company grows, but with the quality of the art it creates and sells; therefore, budget is a major consideration. The owners agree that the company will probably stay small for some time, but they realize that it will eventually grow as its reputation spreads. They also realize that they need a computerized system to operate efficiently.

A LAN seems to be the ideal solution. It would allow resources to be shared, which would, in turn, cut costs. Data files must also be shared, a need the LAN could accommodate quite well.

An ARCnet LAN was recommended for several reasons. It's both inexpensive and highly reliable; the network load will be light, so a higher-speed LAN isn't necessary; and it has sufficient network load capacity to support the studio as it grows. ARCnet also can be easily reconfigured to meet any physical changes to the building, as Dauphin Arts is constantly rearranging its offices and studios.

The LAN is designed to the owners' needs. These include:

1. A high-speed PC with a 350-MB hard disk and 6 to 8 MB of memory
2. Three diskless PCs to serve as nodes on the network
3. One IBM-compatible PC with floppy and hard-disk drives
4. Five low-impedance ARCnet NICs
5. RG-62 coaxial cable
6. The appropriate BNC connectors
7. An eight-port active hub
8. A laser printer
9. A color plotter

The network was designed as illustrated in Figure 31.1.

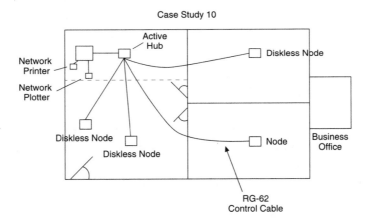

FIGURE 31.1 The ARCnet system designed for Dauphin Arts.

Case Study Two

The art studio profiled in Case Study One needs another node. This requires that the following equipment be added:

- An additional diskless PC
- A passive hub
- The appropriate BNC connectors and terminators
- RG-62 coaxial cable.

The new node is placed in the business office, making it the second node in that office. Rather than running a new line of cable from the active hub to the new node, a passive hub is used.

The cable that was attached to the original node in the business office now attaches to the passive hub. From the passive hub, two cables are attached—one for each of the nodes—and the fourth port on the passive hub is terminated (see Figure 31.2).

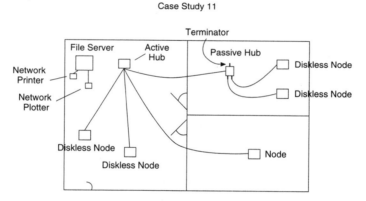

Case Study 11

FIGURE 31.2 To add another node in one office, the original cable is connected to a passive hub, and two nodes are connected to the hub.

Case Study Three

Dauphin Arts has acquired and renovated the adjacent building and three additional nodes in this building need to be connected to the network. It is possible to run three separate lines from the active hub to the new building, but a wiser approach is to run one line from the original active hub to a new active hub in the new building. From the active hub in the new building, one line is run directly to one node and another line is run to a passive hub that attaches to the other two nodes. Figure 31.3 illustrates the new configuration of the network.

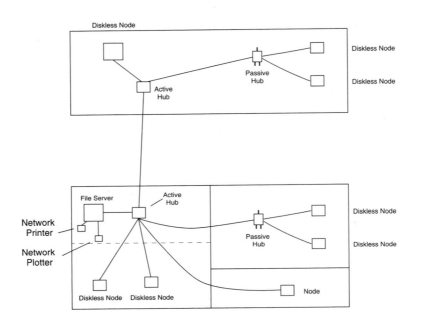

FIGURE 31.3 As Dauphin Arts expands to an adjacent building, three nodes are added to the network.

With ARCnet, the network can continue to grow with additional active and passive hubs.

CHAPTER 32

NETWORKING WITH BRIDGES, ROUTERS, GATEWAYS, AND BACKBONES

The examples in this chapter demonstrate how bridges, routers, gateways, and backbones may be used to connect multiple LANs.

Case Study One

Marine Atlantic, a moderate-size boat dealership, decided to implement LANs to meet its information-processing needs. Two major workgroups, sales and accounting, require individual LANs. Each workgroup decided to implement and administer its own LAN—in this case, Token Ring networks. This configuration met the initial informational and networking needs of the company, but as the company expanded and more information needed to be shared, problems developed.

The biggest problem was that the employees in sales needed access to information stored on accounting department's LAN. At the same time, the employees in accounting needed information stored on the sales department's file server. Since the two networks weren't connected, the employees were spending a lot of time walking back and forth between the departments seeking assistance and complaining that they couldn't use E-mail between the departments.

What is needed is for the two major workgroups to communicate with each other and access each others' information. This is not occurring because each workgroup has its own LAN, and the two networks are not connected.

To remedy this situation it is determined that the two networks need to be bridged. A design is developed that consists of placing a bridge in the wiring closet of the sales group. This enables the two networks to communicate with each other.

Questions asked of this solution include: Why a bridge? Couldn't the two networks be consolidated into one LAN with one file server? The answer is, they could be consolidated, but one large LAN could cause a host of performance problems. As nodes are added to the network, performance would degrade.

The bridge functions as the go-between for the two networks. At Marine Atlantic, the accounting group has its own LAN and the sales group has its own LAN. When sales employees need information from the accounting group, the request is broadcast over the network. The bridge, having the addresses of local and remote nodes stored in its address table, forwards the request to the accounting LAN. The request is processed, and the information is transmitted back to the requesting node via the bridge (see Figure 32.1).

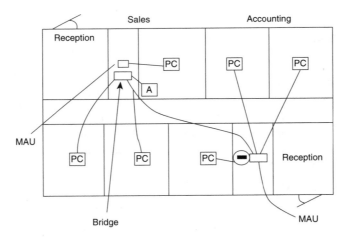

FIGURE 32.1 At Marine Atlantic, the sales department's Token-Ring network is connected to accounting's Token-Ring LAN via a bridge.

Using this approach, the traffic only increases on the accounting department's LAN when the requests broadcast by the sales department's LAN are specific to accounting, meaning the overall network traffic remains the same on both LANs, but there is communication between the two. This allows not only E-mail between the two workgroups, but easier network management and maintenance as well.

Case Study Two

Marine Atlantic decided to computerize its shipping and receiving department, so a LAN has been installed for this workgroup. Now the company has three workgroups, each of which must administer its own LAN. All data processing and networking was performed adequately before the growth, but as the company continued to grow, the problems, described in Case Study One, developed. Three workgroups and three LANs now need to communicate with each other. (For the purposes of this case study, all three LANs are Ethernet networks rather than Token Ring.)

Again, the option of combining the three separate LANs to form one large LAN exists, but this may not be the best solution because of the performance problems that would arise (as in Case Study One). Instead, two bridges are used to connect the three networks. One bridge is installed between the sales department and the shipping and receiving department, and another bridge is installed between the shipping and receiving department and the accounting department (see Figure 32.2).

The shipping and receiving LAN, which is sandwiched between the other two networks, now has to handle more traffic than the others. This is because it receives traffic when the sales department broadcasts requests to accounting and when the accounting department's LAN broadcasts go to sales.

Another important consideration is that if the cabling fails on the shipping and receiving LAN, the connection between the sales and accounting LANs will be broken. The bridging function won't work between sales and accounting without the shipping and receiving LAN to link the two bridges. This potential problem could be alleviated by using a backup bridge system implementing spanning tree bridges and software, as discussed in Chapter 24. It would increase the cost of the network but would prevent downtime. It must be determined if the cost outweighs the inconvenience.

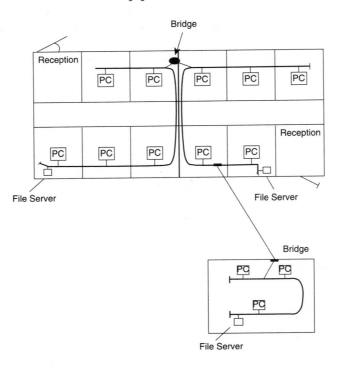

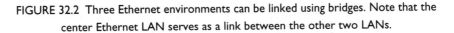

FIGURE 32.2 Three Ethernet environments can be linked using bridges. Note that the center Ethernet LAN serves as a link between the other two LANs.

Case Study Three

With three networks in place, Marine Atlantic decided to put its advertising department on a LAN. There are now four major workgroups with four autonomous LANs. All are Ethernet networks using the same communication protocol. The problem remains communication between networks. The bridging and large-LAN options are not considered, because a third option is now available: placing routers, or intermediate nodes, strategically so that all four networks can communicate with each other and provide adequate links.

Three routers can connect all four networks. To simplify this case study, let's assume that the workgroups' LANS are LAN 1, LAN 2, LAN 3, and LAN

4. Router A is placed between LAN 1, LAN 2, and LAN 3; router B between LAN 3 and LAN 4; and router C between LAN1, LAN 2, and LAN 4. There now exist two paths between any two networks. That way, if one network's cabling fails, it won't halt the interconnection of the LANs (see Figure 32.3).

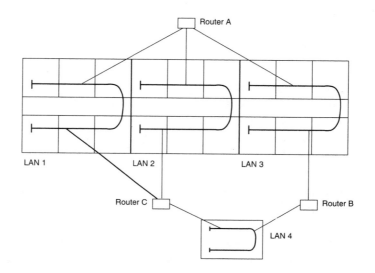
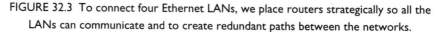

FIGURE 32.3 To connect four Ethernet LANs, we place routers strategically so all the LANs can communicate and to create redundant paths between the networks.

Let's take this example a step further and assume that we have a request on the longest route possible between the four LANs—between a node on LAN 1 and a node on LAN 4. The broadcast starts on a node on LAN 1 and is sent to router A. At this point, the message can be forwarded to router B or C. Router A decides to pass the message to router B; thus, the request goes through LAN 3 to router B. Router B then forwards the request to LAN 4. If there had been a problem along that route, the message could have been passed to router C; in that case, the request would go through LAN 2 to router C, which would then forward the request to LAN 4 for receipt by the appropriate node.

Routers are extremely useful when many pathways exist through the various networks. The path the message takes between routers is usually determined by internetwork traffic. If the traffic is extremely busy on one path, the router uses another path and when one LAN fails, the router can send messages around the failed LAN.

Case Study Four

Marine Atlantic has a small mainframe to handle its data-processing needs. As the company grows, its various departments begin to voice concern regarding their information services. The Information Services department can't meet all the requests coming from the various departments, whose managers want the company data available to their departments so that they can manage their own information needs. After much debate, LANs are determined to be the most logical solution.

Each department has PCs for its employees, but with all the PCs connected to the company's host mainframe using 3270 emulation, it doesn't make sense to use an intelligent device as a dumb terminal—which is exactly what 3270 emulation does to a PC. With the addition of a LAN, the thinking in the company now is that the mainframe can handle the large batch-processing jobs that are essential to the company's existence.

The mainframe serves as the repository of all the company's data, but that data is of little use if programs aren't available that give the departments the information they need. If the departments implement LANs, they can download data from the host mainframe to the LAN and create programs that use that data. This solution makes the programs and data available to multiple users and satisfies the needs of the various departments. The PCs can still perform 3270 emulation to maintain the use of programs on the host mainframe, which satisfies the central Information Services department.

A key component in this scenario is the gateway, the device that allows the LAN to communicate with the host mainframe. Depending on the size of the LAN, a single gateway may support the entire network. If the LAN is large, more than one gateway may be needed because the gateway can only establish a certain number of sessions between the LAN and the host mainframe. (Sessions are the actual node connections on a LAN to the host mainframe.) As new LANs are implemented, each usually requires its own gateway (see Figure 32.4).

One gateway feature in particular should be mentioned. The LAN architecture may depend on the manufacturer of the host mainframe, largely because of the different communications protocols used by the host systems. For example, when an IBM host mainframe is used, the desired network architecture is Token Ring; the IBM mainframe has certain capabilities that make access easier with that architecture. When a Digital Equipment Corp. host is accessed using a LAN, the preferred architecture is Ethernet.

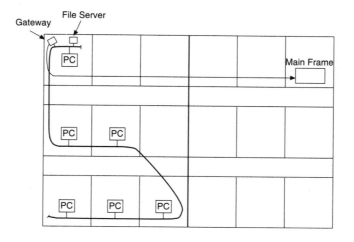

FIGURE 32.4 The LAN is connected to the mainframe via a gateway.
This approach makes it practical to do batch processing on the mainframe
and local processing on the network at the same time.

Case Study Five

Let's return to Marine Atlantic once again, but this time we'll go back to four major workgroups that support four separate LANs.

Another way to interconnect these four LANs is through a backbone. This is a viable approach if the LANs to be interconnected are neither large nor sophisticated. The four department networks function as access LANs and are connected to the central backbone network. The backbone can then filter traffic and forward only those messages destined for a different LAN.

The use of a backbone network removes the problem of communication failure when more than two LANs are bridged. None of the access networks acts as an intermediate LAN, as presented in Case Study Two, but the backbone must be reliable because the LAN interconnection relies on it. The advantage of using a backbone is that it appears to be one large LAN, when in fact it comprises four LANs operating in parallel.

GLOSSARY

802.3 Ethernet—The IEEE 802.3 official standard. A popular LAN architecture that uses a bus topology and CSMA/CD at 10 Mbps. Although 802.3 is technically not Ethernet, the name is commonly used because of the roots of 802.3. *See* **CSMA/CD**.

10BASE-T—IEEE 802.3 standard for a twisted-pair Ethernet network. 10 Mbps transmission rate over baseband using unshielded, twisted-pair cable.

10BASE 2—IEEE 802.3 standard for a thin coaxial (RG-58) Ethernet network. 10 Mbps transmission rate over baseband up to 185 meters.

10BASE 5—IEEE 802.3 standard for a thick coaxial Ethernet network. 10 Mbps transmission rate over baseband up to 500 meters.

active hub—A device used to amplify transmission signals in ARCnet LANs. An active hub can be used either to add additional workstations to a network or to lengthen the cabling distance between LAN stations. *See* **passive hub**.

Advanced Program-to-Program Communications (APPC)—A component of IBM's System Network Architecture. APPC is designed to allow communications between programs running on different systems on a more or less peer-to-peer basis.

American National Standards Institute (ANSI)—ANSI develops and publishes technical standards.

American Standard Code for Information Interchange (ASCII)—A standard for encoding characters (including the upper- and lowercase alphabet, numerals, punctuation, and control characters) using seven bits. The standard is 128 characters; IBM expanded the set to 256 by adding an eighth bit to each existing character. The expanded set provides graphic, Greek, scientific, financial, and foreign language characters.

AppleTalk—Apple's network layer protocol for Macintosh networks.

AppleTalk Filing Protocol (AFP)—The protocol in AppleTalk used for remote access to data.

application—A software program that allows a user to perform a specific job, such as accounting or word processing.

application layer—The layer of the OSI model concerned with application programs such as electronic mail, database managers, and file server software.

application program interface (API)—A method of allowing an application to directly interact with certain functions of an operating system or another application.

architecture—A system's architecture typically describes the type of components, interfaces, and protocols it uses and how they fit together.

archive—A backup made to preserve information for long-term storage.

ARCnet—A widely used LAN architecture developed by Datapoint Corporation that uses a logical token-passing access method at 2.5 Mbps.

ARPANET—A wide-area network developed by the Defense Advanced Research Projects Agency that primarily connects universities and government agencies; it has merged into the Internet. *See* **Internet**.

Asynchronous Communications Server—A device on a LAN that provides the capability for network workstations to access ASCII applications via switched communication lines.

asynchronous transmission—A transmission method that allows characters to be sent at irregular intervals by adding start and stop bits to identify the beginning and end of each character. Asynchronous communications have a 20 percent overhead (the two stop/start bits) added to each 8-bit byte. *See* **synchronous transmission**.

ATM—Asynchronous Transfer Mode.

AppleTalk Print Services (ATPS)—The software utility within the AppleTalk Network Operating System that contains Macintosh computer printer on an Apple Network.

Attached Unit Interface Cable (AUI Cable)—A four-twisted-pair cable that connects an Ethernet device to an Ethernet external transceiver.

backbone network—A network that interconnects other networks.

backup—A copy of a file, directory, or volume on another storage device for the purpose of retrieval in case the original is accidentally erased, damaged, or destroyed.

bad block table—A list of blocks on a disk that are unusable.

baseband—A transmission system in which the signals are broadcast one at a time at their original frequency (not modulated).

batch file—An ASCII text file with a .BAT extension where DOS commands are listed. Each command will execute in sequence as if it were typed from a DOS prompt.

baud rate—The rate at which data is transferred over a serial interface.

binary digit (bit)—Must be either a zero (on) or a one (off).

bottleneck—A factor that restricts the flow of data through a system.

bridge—A device used to connect LANs by forwarding packets across connections at the Media Access Control sublayer of the data link layer of the OSI model. Routers that operate at the network layer of the OSI model are sometimes incorrectly called bridges.

broadband—A transmission system in which signals are encoded and modulated into different frequencies and then transmitted simultaneously with other signals.

broadcast—A LAN data transmission scheme in which data packets are received by all stations on the network.

buffer—A temporary storage area for data. Buffers are used to store data being transferred from two systems that process the information at different rates. Communication buffers and printer buffers are examples.

bus—A common connection. Networks that broadcast signals to all stations, such as Ethernet or ARCnet, are considered bus networks.

bus (PC)—The connectors on a PC motherboard that expansion boards plug into.

byte—Usually the eight bits that represent a character.

cache—To read data into a memory buffer so the information is available the next time it is needed and does not have to be read from the disk again.

cache buffer—An area in RAM used for caching. *See* **cache**.

Carrier Sense Multiple Access with Collision Detection (CSMA/CD)—Ethernet's cable access method.

client—A computer that accesses the resources of a server. *See* **client/server**.

client/server—A network system design in which a processor or computer designated as a server (such as a file server or database server) provides services to other client processors or computers.

coaxial cable—A commonly used cable type that is relatively insensitive to noise interference, consisting of one or two insulating layers and two conductors. A central conductor wire is surrounded by the first layer of insulation and an outer shielding conductor is laid over the first layer of insulation. It is usually covered with a second layer of insulation.

collision detection—The detection of simultaneous transmissions on the communication medium. *See* **CSMA/CD**.

Consultative Committee on International Telegraphy and Telephony (CCITT)—An international communications standards-setting body.

COM1, COM2—*See* **serial port**.

concentrator—A 10BASE-T hub. A multiport repeater for Ethernet/802.3 over unshielded twisted-pair cable. *See* **10BASE-T**.

controller board—A device that enables a computer to communicate with a particular device (such as a disk or tape drive). A controller board manages input/output and regulates the operation of its associated device.

data-link layer—The OSI level that performs the assembly and transmission of data packets, including error control.

database server—The back-end processor that manages the database and fulfills database requests in a client/server database system.

dedicated file server—A file server that cannot be operated as a user's server workstation. *See* **file server.**

de facto standard—A standard based on broad usage and support.

default—A value or option that is automatically chosen when no other value is specified.

digital audio tape (DAT)—Popular tape backup format.

disk channel—All components that connect a disk drive or disk drives to a file server, including the disk(s). This includes the host adapter or disk controller and cables.

disk controller—A hardware device associated with a disk drive that controls how data is written to and retrieved from the disk.

disk duplexing—A method of safeguarding data in which the data is copied simultaneously to two hard disks on separate channels. If one channel fails, the data on the other channel remains unharmed. When data is duplexed, read requests are sent to whichever disk in the pair can respond faster, increasing the file server's efficiency.

disk mirroring—A method of safeguarding data in which the same data is copied to two hard disks on the same channel. If one of the disks fails, the data on the other disk is safe. Because the two disks are on the same channel, mirroring provides only limited data protection—a failure anywhere along the channel could shut down both disks and data would be lost. *See* **disk duplexing**.

disk subsystem—An external unit that contains hard disk drives and attaches to a computer.

electronic mail (E-mail)—A network service that enables users to send and receive messages via computer.

Extended Industry Standard Architecture (EISA)—PC expansion bus architecture that extends the 16-bit PC AT expansion bus to 32 bits, while maintaining compatibility with existing 16-bit cards.

fault tolerance—Resistance to system failure or data loss.

fax server—A network device or service that provides a LAN workstation access to incoming or outgoing faxes across the LAN.

Fiber Distributed Data Interface (FDDI)—A high-speed networking standard. The underlying medium is fiber optics, and the topology is a dual-attached counter-rotating token ring.

file allocation table (FAT)—A table on a disk that records the disk location of all file parts.

file server—A computer that provides network stations with controlled access to sharable resources. The network operating system is loaded on the file server and most sharable devices including disk subsystems and printers, are attached to it. The file server controls system security and monitors station-to-station communications. A dedicated file server can be used only as a file server while it is on the network. A nondedicated file server can be used simultaneously as a file server and a workstation.

file sharing—The ability for multiple users to share files. Concurrent file sharing is controlled by application software, workstation operating system, and/or the file server/database server operating system.

File Transfer, Access, and Management (FTAM)—The OSI remote file service and protocol.

File Transfer Protocol (FTP)—Transfer protocol of TCP/IP.

Frame Relay—A packet switching protocol, similar to X.25.

gateway—A device that provides routing and protocol conversion among physically dissimilar networks and/or computers (for example, LAN-to-host, LAN-to-LAN, X.25, or SNA gateways).

gigabyte (GB, Gbyte) —A unit of measure for memory or disk storage capacity— 2^{30} (1,073,741,824) bytes.

GOSIP—Government OSI Profile. A- U.S. Government procurement specification for OSI protocols.

handshaking—NEEDS DEFINITION.

High Performance File System (HPFS)—Extended file system specification for OS/2.

host—1. A time-sharing computer accessed via terminals or terminal emulation. 2. A computer to which an expansion device attaches. When a LAN card is installed in a PC, that PC is the host to that adapter.

host adapter—An adapter card to attach a device to a computer's expansion bus.

hub—1. A device used on certain network topologies that splits or amplifies signals, allowing the network to be lengthened or expanded with additional workstations. The hub is the central device in a star topology. 2. A computer that receives messages from other computers, stores them, and routes them to other computer destinations. *See* **active hub, passive hub.**

IBM Token Ring—IBM's version of the 802.5 token-passing ring network.

Input/Output (I/O)—The process of moving data, as in the transmission of data from memory to disk.

Institute of Electrical and Electronics Engineers (IEEE)—A group that develops and publishes many of the official LAN-related standards, including 802.3 Ethernet and 802.5 Token Ring.

Integrated Services Digital Network (ISDN)—A CCITT model for the eventual integration of voice and data and a universal interface for networks.

International Standard Organization (ISO)—ISO developed the milestone Open Systems Interconnection (OSI) model.

Internet—The largest network in the world. Successor to ARPANET, the Internet includes other large internetworks. The Internet uses the TCP/IP protocol suite and connects universities, government agencies, and individuals around the world. *See* **ARPANET, internetwork**.

internetwork—Two or more networks connected by bridges and/or routers, a network of networks.

Internetwork Packet Exchange (IPX)—The NetWare protocol for the exchange of message packets on an internetwork. IPX passes application requests for network services to the network drives and then to other workstations, servers, or devices on the internetwork.

Internet Protocol (IP)—The Internet standard protocol that defines the Internet datagram as the unit of information passed across the Internet. Provides the basis for the Internet connectionless best-effort packet delivery service. The Internet protocol suite is often referred to as TCP/IP because IP is one of the two fundamental protocols.

Industry Standard Architecture (ISA)—The IBM AT expansion bus.

ISDN—Integrated Digital Network.

Kilobyte (KB, Kbyte)—A unit of measure for memory or disk storage capacity—2^{10} (1,024) bytes.

LAN Manager—Microsoft's file server operating system based on OS/2.

LAN Server—IBM's file server operating system based on Microsoft's LAN Manager.

linear bus topology—A cabling topology in which devices link to different points along a single length of cable.

local area network (LAN)—*See* **network.**

LocalTalk—The network hardware built into Macintosh computers.

logical units (LU)—These represent end users, application programs, or other devices. Communication under SNA is among LUs.

LU 6.2—A protocol that makes it possible to have peer-to-peer communications under SNA.

MAU—1. media access unit. Ethernet transceiver. 2. multi-station access unit—Token Ring device used to connect several stations to the ring.

mainframe—A large computer, generally with high-level processing power and the capacity to support many users at once.

media access control (MAC)—The bottom half of the ISO data link layer.

Megabits per second (Mbps)—One million bits per second.

Megabyte (MB, Mbyte)—A unit of measure for memory or disk storage capacity—2^{20} (1,048,576) bytes.

Megahertz (MHz)—One million cycles per second.

Message Handling Service (MHS)—Novell's electronic mail platform protocol for LAN messagehandling and routing. *See* **X.400**.

Micro-Channel Architecture (MCA)—IBM's expansion bus for the PS/2.

minicomputer—A multiuser computer, generally with more power than a personal computer but not as large as a mainframe.

modem—Abbreviation of modulator/demodulator multiplexing; A device used to convert computer data into a form that can travel over telephone lines. Transmits signals from multiple sources through a single medium.

NetBIOS—The low-level station-to-station communications protocol developed by IBM for its PC LAN systems. Most network operating system vendors supply software to emulate this protocol to support applications that require it.

network address—A unique number that identifies a physical network.

Network File System (NFS)—A networking protocol suite developed by Sun Microsystems and used widely in the UNIX world.

network interface card (NIC)—A circuit board installed in each network station to allow communication with other stations.

network layer—The layer of the OSI model that establishes protocols for packets, message priorities, and network traffic control.

node—Any network station.

node address—A unique number that identifies a device on a network.

nondedicated file server—A file server that also functions as a workstation. *See* **file server.**

Operating System/2 (OS/2)—Operating system created by IBM and Microsoft. No longer supported by Microsoft, but IBM continues development and support.

Open System Interconnection (OSI)—An international standardization program to facilitate communication among computers from different manufacturers. *See* **ISO.**

packet—A basic message unit for communication across a network. A packet usually includes routing information, data, and (sometimes) error detection information.

parallel port—A printer interface that allows data to be transmitted one byte at a time, with eight bits moving in parallel.

passive hub—A device used in ARCnet networks to split a transmission signal, allowing workstations to be added. A passive hub cannot amplify the signal, so it must connect directly to a workstation or active hub. *See* **active hub.**

peer-to-peer network—A network design in which each computer shares and uses devices on an equal basis.

peripheral—A physical device (such as a printer or disk subsystem) that is externally attached to a workstation or directly attached to the network.

Physical layer—The layer of the OSI model that establishes protocols for voltage, data transmission timing, and rules for "handshaking." *see* **handshaking.**

port—A hardware connecting component that lets a microprocessor communicate with a compatible peripheral.

presentation layer—The layer of the OSI model concerned with protocols for network security, file transfers, and format functions.

print server—A device and/or program that manages shared printers. Print service is often provided by the file server but can be provided from a separate LAN PC or device.

protected mode—The native operating mode of the 80286, 80386, and 80486 microprocessors, where full capacities of these microprocessors can be used. MS-DOS operates these processors in the real mode that emulates an 8086 microprocessor. In the protected mode, each process running in RAM can be protected from other processes. This is not true of the real mode.

protocol—Rules for communicating, particularly for the format and transmission of data.

repeater—A device used to extend cabling distances by regenerating signals.

record locking—A data-protection scheme that prevents different users from performing simultaneous writes to the same record in a shared file, thus preventing overlapping disk writes and ensuring data integrity.

ring topology—A closed-loop topology in which data passes in one direction from station to station on the LAN. Each workstation on the ring acts as a repeater, passing data to the next workstation on the ring.

router—Hardware and software that route data between similar or dissimilar networks at the network layer of the OSI model.

session layer—The layer of the OSI model concerned with network management functions including passwords, network monitoring, and reporting.

serial port—A port that allows data to be transmitted one bit at a time. On PC-compatible computers, COM1 and COM2 are serial ports.

server—A network device that provides services to client stations. Servers include file servers, disk servers, and print servers.

Sequenced Packet Exchange (SPX)—A NetWare protocol by which two workstations or applications communicate across the network. SPX uses IPX to deliver the messages, but SPX guarantees delivery of the messages and maintains the order of messages on the packet stream. *See* **IPX.**

shielded twisted-pair cable—Twisted-pair wire surrounded by a foil or mesh shield to reduce susceptibility to outside interference and noise.

Simple Mail Transfer Protocol (SMTP)—The TCP/IP electronic mail protocol.

Simple Network Management Protocol (SNMP)—The network management protocol of choice for TCP/IP-based internets. Widely implemented with 10BASE-T Ethernet.

site licensing—Procedure in which software is licensed to be used only at a particular location.

star topology—A LAN topology in which each workstation connects to a central device.

star-wired topology—A ring network (such as a token-passing ring) cabled through centralized hubs or connection devices to create a physical-star topology.

StreetTalk—The distributive database serving as a network-naming service for the VINES local-area network.

Structured Query Language (SQL)—An international standard language for defining and accessing relational databases.

Synchronous Data Link Control (SDLC)—An IBM communications protocol, commonly used in an SNA environment.

Systems Network Architecture (SNA)—IBM's proprietary network architecture.

terabyte (TB, Tbyte)—A unit of measure for memory or disk storage capacity— 2^{40} (1,099,511,627,776) bytes.

terminal—A keyboard and display screen through which users can access a host computer.

terminal emulation—Software that enables a personal computer to communicate with a host computer by transmitting in the form used by the host's terminals.

token bus—A network that uses a logical token-passing access method. Unlike a token-passing ring, permission to transmit is usually based on node address rather than position in the network. A token bus network uses a common cable set with all signals broadcast across the entire LAN.

token passing—A unique combination of bits transmitted on a token-passing network. A device can only transmit data on the network if it is in possession of the token

token-passing ring—A LAN design in which each station is connected to an upstream station and a downstream station. An electronic signal, called the token, is passed from station to station around the ring. A station may not send a transmission to another station unless it has possession of a free token or a token that is not currently in use. Since only one token is allowed on the network, only one station may broadcast at a time. *See* **star-wired ring**.

topology—The physical layout of network cabling.

Transmission Control Protocol/Internet Protocol (TCP/IP)—A communications protocol suite for internetwork routing and reliable message delivery, originally endorsed by the U.S. Department of Defense and implemented on ARPANET. TCP/IP is the basis of the Internet and is widely used in local-area networks.

transport layer—The layer of the OSI model concerned with protocols for error recognition and recovery, as well as with regulation of information flow.

twisted-pair wire—Two wires that are wrapped around each other to reduce induction between them. Commonly used for telephone and LAN wiring.

uninterruptible power supply (UPS)—A backup power unit that provides continuous power when the normal power supply is interrupted. UPS systems can be standby (only supplying power when the regular supply is interrupted) or full-time (relying on regular power and/or batteries to supply it while it supplies power to the protected device).

unshielded twisted-pair wire (UTP)—*See* **twisted-pair wire**.

wide area network (WAN)—A network linking computers, terminals, and other equipment over a large geographic area.

workstation—A desktop computer that performs local processing and accesses LAN services.

X.25—A CCITT standard protocol for communication over wide-area networks.

X.400—A CCITT standard for message exchange in electronic mail.

X.500—A CCITT standard for governing worldwide directories for electronic mail.

Xerox Network System (XNS)—The term used to refer collectively to the suite of Internet protocols developed by researchers at Xerox Corporation.

INDEX